Essays in Honor of Elias Canetti

Essays
in Honor of
Elias Canetti

Translated from the German

by MICHAEL HULSE

Farrar, Straus and Giroux

New York

English translation copyright © 1987
by Farrar, Straus and Giroux, Inc.
Originally published in German as
Festschrift © 1985 by Carl Hanser Verlag
All rights reserved
First edition, 1987
Printed in the United States of America
Published simultaneously in Canada by
Collins Publishers, Toronto

Library of Congress Cataloging-in-Publication Data
Essays in honor of Elias Canetti.
Includes bibliographies.
1. Canetti, Elias.—Criticism and
interpretation.   I. Canetti, Elias.
II. Hulse, Michael.
PT2605.A58Z68   1968   833'.912   86-12399
ISBN 0-374-22350-5
ISBN 0-374-51950-1 (pbk.)

FRONTISPIECE
Photograph of Elias Canetti
courtesy of Jerry Bauer

Elias Canetti at Eighty

This festschrift, appearing together with the third volume of his autobiography, honors Elias Canetti, the "keeper of metamorphosis," on his eightieth birthday on July 25, 1985. The whole world over, his novel *Auto-da-Fé,* his plays, his philosophical study *Crowds and Power,* his essays and notebooks, and his monumental autobiography have been read as the unique expression of a lifelong attempt to understand and record the character of our era as shaped by two world wars. If we bear in mind the conditions under which this oeuvre came into being, the resistance it had to overcome, and the sacrifices which accompanied its creation, the successful result of his life's work appears in a still happier light. For Elias Canetti, throughout his entire life, has been a "freelance" writer in the full sense of the word, and has preserved the aura and dignity of that title—a dignity it has so often lost in our culture industry, and indeed lost deliberately. Canetti's profound abhorrence of all ideologies, and his radical rejection of the overhasty conclusions that systems or doctrines may lead us to jump to, have made him one of the most acute critics of power—and one of the most resolute advocates of the powerless. This stance, which for Elias Canetti is a sine qua non which must be taken for granted in the writer, arouses our admiration all the more in the present day, when, in the light of experience, it can hardly be taken for granted at all: the history of literature and of thought in our century reads for long stretches like a voluntary or extorted compromise with power.

This house, which for years has published Elias Canetti's

work with pleasure, a sense of involvement, and total commitment, would like to join the authors who here examine that work in thanking the "keeper of metamorphosis" for his steadfastness, his friendship, and his bearing.

Carl Hanser Verlag
Munich, March 1985
(From the preface
to the German edition)

Translator's Note

In giving English renderings of passages quoted from Elias Canetti's works I have felt it best, for the convenience of the reader used to reading Canetti in English, to give the translations available in existing standard versions, and have taken these passages from the following:

Auto-da-Fé (translated by C. V. Wedgwood), London, 1946 et seq.

Crowds and Power (translated by Carol Stewart), London, 1962.

The Voices of Marrakesh (translated by J. A. Underwood), London, 1978.

The Conscience of Words (translated by Joachim Neugroschel), New York, 1979.

The Tongue Set Free (translated by Joachim Neugroschel), New York, 1979 and 1983.

The Torch in My Ear (translated by Joachim Neugroschel), New York, 1982.

The Numbered (translated by Carol Stewart), London, 1984.

I have amended the English versions of quoted passages only in cases of striking inaccuracy in the translation. Other works by Elias Canetti are untranslated or the translations were unavailable to me: in these cases, as with other quoted German authors, the versions given here are the present translator's.

When the first publication date of a work by Canetti is given, it is the date of the first German-language edition.

M.H.

Contents

One

Werner Hofmann

All Smooth

The most striking natural instrument of power in man and in many animals is the teeth.

The teeth are the armed guardians of the mouth and the mouth is indeed a strait place, the prototype of all prisons. When the gaping maws of dragons had been virtually extirpated, man found a symbolic substitute for them in prisons.[1]

It is violence that confronts us in these sentences from *Crowds and Power,* from the chapter that deals with the entrails of power. If we read them over and over, we can no longer distinguish architecture from this metaphor of menace.

A building, defined as a physical containment of space, has two effects: it protects and it imprisons. What both functions have in common is that they isolate. This links them to the claims of power, and equips them to illustrate the dual character of power. Power isolates, and isolates itself.

The smoothness which Canetti relates to strict order and which he locates in the undecorated walls of today's buildings has its modest origin in crenellation, that crowning toothlike notching of city walls, castles, and fortifications. At a time when secular architecture on our continent did not yet demand regularity in the arrangement of walls and façades, crenellation was the only section of a building that was subject to the law of repetition. This is shown in paintings by Mantegna and other Quattrocento artists. Windows and doors can be placed anywhere—only in the crenellation do we see a repetitive scheme dominant. I suspect that in crenellation we have the basic figuration or prototype of the regularity (that is, the additive lining-up) that makes our housing estates, business premises, and office blocks both aggressive and defensive, in equal measure. From this lining-up there at length evolved the coordinate system of vertically and horizontally aligned zones of windows and, as a final result, the grid of curtain walls which dispels the external distinction between wall and window. The formal convention is impenetrable from without, and within its coordinates tolerates no contradiction or departure from the pattern: everything is "all smooth."[2] Meanwhile the crenellation itself degenerated into a crenellated frieze, that is to say, merely superficial decoration, with teeth that do no one any harm.

Thinking about this process and its prefigurement in the defensive *rows* of teeth (Canetti does not speak of the whole set!), I was reminded of the sketches with which Goethe illustrated the path of architectural development from the simply gigantic to the strict structure of the right angle. These are attached to a plan, written in 1795, for a morphology of architecture, which was found among Goethe's papers after his death. Goethe sees in additive regularity the triumph of art over its materials and their merely random assembly: "as long as stones, whatever shape or size they come in, are fitted together according to *any* patterns and methods, not even chance can lead the craftsman to symmetry; only when he has been laying rectangular stones horizontally on top of each other for a while will it occur to him that he ought to sort them out, join like with like, place them symmetrically, or indeed even cut them all to a uniform size." The path leads from the *opus incertum* to the clear formal conceptualization of the *opus isodomum,* from plurality of form to uniformity (Figs. 1 and 2). Crenellation will be one of the results of this rationalization process, or a by-product, so to speak, since it can be defined as the result of subtraction. If we remove every other stone from the topmost row in the *opus isodomum,* we are left with a crenellated row. The re-

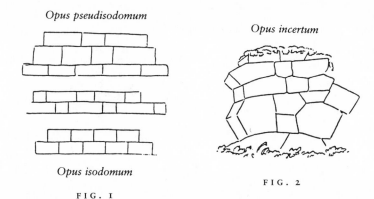

Opus pseudisodomum

Opus incertum

Opus isodomum

FIG. 1

FIG. 2

maining blocks and the spaces between are equal and complementary.

I hesitate to call the crenellated cubes "bodies." Even a flawless row of teeth does not constitute a bodily form, for which reason Canetti has assigned them to an intermediate zone: "By their very nature they occupied a position midway between an actual part of the body and a tool. The fact that they could fall out, or be knocked out, made them even more like a tool."[3] Similarly with crenellations: they are not integral to the construction of a building, and thus dispensable. As a means of defense they have both a real and a symbolic function: as long as their regularity is intact, they are deterrent. If a piece is broken off, the attacker senses victory. In the last analysis, what is figured forth in crenellation is a pattern, the two-dimensional crenellated frieze.

By contrast, in the *opus incertum* we confront physicality. In this assemblage of found or hewn stones we see a construct with body and limbs, whose cumbersome syntax can easily be read in the archaic human figure created about the middle of our century by the sculptor Fritz Wotruba (Fig. 3). Some thirty years ago Canetti dedicated to his Viennese friend, who at that time was at the height of his creative powers, an essay which

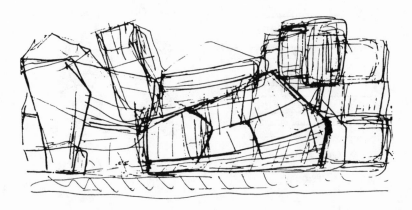

FIG. 3

it is particularly worth recalling because it is not Canetti's most accessible publication.[4] The text deals with the tectonics of imprisonment, for Canetti sees the body as the "first and foremost prison" of Man. This innate prison is enclosed within a second, which tames the human creature, rendering him a societal being. For Canetti, Wotruba is "a black panther driven in among humankind. He has found his place among them, true, but he remains true to his panther's nature. He senses the bars of the prisons where human beings keep him—and themselves—locked up."

In Wotruba's "confrontation of this imprisonment" Canetti perceives "the second, crucial substance of his work." (What is the first—his panther's nature?) For this reason stone is his "most important medium." Wotruba leads people into petrifaction, into a prison from which there is no escape: "Stone, for the man who sculpts it as much as for his work, is the surest and most permanent prison." This is a new interpretation of that violence whose compulsion has dominated a particular form of modern creativity since Romanticism:

Je suis la plaie et le couteau
Et la victime et le bourreau! *

Canetti says of a "squatting man" that he "has made himself a prison in his cowering. Those who dare can enter, but he who is himself the prison will not be freed." At the same time, however, the heightened significance of this dungeon is conceded: the body of the squatting man is the "entrance to an archaic temple precinct." The prisoner is creating a sacramental area for himself.

What Canetti is invoking here goes back to mythic experiences. To him, Man is the unredeemed creature, Sisyphus, and what he does is labor performed in vain. Man's temples, where he erects monuments to this futility, are themselves marked by vanity. Insofar as the shaping act is accompanied by knowledge of this futility, an artist like Wotruba can overcome this *condition humanine* by submitting to it and deriving his formal law from it. His petrified bodies confirm a mute endurance in captivity. They are shaped by myth, like the *opus incertum,* which Goethe locates in the prehistory of architecture. And indeed, in Wotruba's sketches the crude contours of a cave mouth can in fact be discerned: the *opus incertum* bears the same relation to the cave, that primitive shelter which precedes actual buildings, as the positive to the negative.

Considering his own times, Goethe finds fault with the final phase of the tectonic and two-dimensional regularity which begins with the *opus isodomum* on account of its relinquishment of the imagination, and he expresses a caution that our own century has once again made relevant: "The doctrine of the imagination, of its intellectual laws, is necessary to combat certain purists who, in architecture, would dearly love to render

---

* These are the first and fourth lines of the sixth of the seven quatrains of Baudelaire's poem "L'Héautontimorouménos," from *Les Fleurs de Mal.* They can be rendered (in Joanna Richardson's translation) as: "I am the dagger and the wound! / The torturer, the victim bound!" —*Trans.*

everything ploddingly prosaic." What does this warning refer to? Plainly to the beginnings of that relinquishment of the decorative which paved the way for the puritan smoothness Canetti alludes to.

The correspondences make sense. Canetti identifies two kinds of prison: one, the monumental, mythic likenesses; the other, smooth constructs. In the ages-old metaphor of petrifaction, artists of the caliber of Wotruba can today still succeed in fitting man out as an entity with the power of endurance, in giving him concentrated power as an emblem of himself, while the bite of "actual prisons" aims at mental and physical amputation, if not destruction: "The smoothness of teeth has conquered the world; the walls of cells are all smooth and even the window opening is small. For the prisoner, freedom is the space beyond the clenched teeth, and these are now represented by the bare walls of his cell."[5]

Two kinds of prison. Something of this polarity can be sensed in *Fidelio*. The ordinary prisoners are kept in cells, while Florestan vegetates in a lightless dungeon that is more a cave than a jail. Isolated and, as it were, buried alive, he is spared the regulation collective punishments of his fellow prisoners, the walks in the prison courtyard that are part of the ritual of mass imprisonment. The others are numbers, forced into line; he is a maltreated sign of warning, where physical imprisonment hardens into moral protest.

At that time, in 1798, when the French prototype of *Fidelio*, targeted on the arbitrary wielding of power, was performed in Paris, Blake, in his "Newton" (1795, Tate Gallery, London), ridiculed the intellect wholly absorbed within the span of its compasses, and Goethe in Weimar outlined the above-mentioned morphology of architecture, in which the practice of oppression sounds through merely as a loss of poetry. At the same time, at the other end of Europe, Goya was working on his "Caprichos." The cycle appeared in the final year of the *dix-huitième* and (so to speak) as a full stop to an epoch which, in the last analysis, had summoned up all the passions of thought and action only to question itself.

Goya is our witness, because he breaks with the baroque, sprawling theatricality of Piranesi and, in close scrutiny, interprets the prison not as a bravura architecture but as a coldly functional place, and nonetheless as the location of vile, atavistic rituals. Yet perhaps there is neither a tension nor a contradiction here, but far more the discovery that the coldness and the smoothness of functionality are the genuine central signs of modern, thoroughly rationalized power. (Modern relates to the period since the turning point of 1789.)

It was not the principles of clarity and utility that triumphed in the architecture of right angles and mirroring façades in the middle of our century, but, as Canetti was perhaps the first to see, the steel-and-glass pathos-formulae of anonymous power. Smoothness, and "the prestigee of the power it conceals,"[6] can already be found in the characteristics of architectural language "around 1800"—not only in that of built and imagined prisons but also in the purist utopias of communality in which private and public life are regulated in every respect. I am thinking of the architectural fantasies of Ledoux and Boullée, which have one common formal denominator: they resemble fortifications, whether they are places for manufacturing, for dwelling, or for cult purposes. Their functions are concealed behind smooth façades, and are as interchangeable as the façades. It we substitute the word "prisoners" for "the dead" in Ledoux's descriptive commentary on his design for a cemetery, the equivalence of these megalomaniac dungeons becomes apparent: "A gloomy labyrinth of passageways where the dead rest in niches surrounds a massive, cavelike dome, through the vertex of which a shaft of daylight penetrates. From outside only the upper part of this sphere is visible: a mighty cupola. Fearful, one shrinks back from this terrible dome. . . . The image of nothingness should offer the eye no point at which it can rest: neither wood nor meadow, neither valley nor river, and certainly not the life-giving gift of sun." (We think of Dr. Kien's library.) In these mausoleums we see the beginnings of that pathos of denial which is being practiced today in a far, far subtler manner, when windows that can be opened are done away with in office blocks, the outside world is colored with tinted glass, and air conditioning fends off "the life-giving gift of sun."

Alongside the right angle, Ledoux and Boullée also use the circle and its derivatives: rounded arches, spheres, and domes. Their geometrism pays homage to the round form as the locus of a planetary sensibility that aims to ascribe the wealth of visual phenomena to one rationally visualizable primary form. Not only Blake's "Newton" is compassed within the circle; Runge too gathers up the totality of colors into a "color sphere."

Goya exposes what this naïve geometrism conceals or suppresses. Its advocates are questing after one integrated formal unity that excludes fragments. A partial piece would contradict the claim to totality of form.

Goya breaks up the circles and curves that the compasses construct and makes of their fragmentary nature a metaphor for cutting injury. Capricho 34 is entitled "Las rinde el sueño," where "sueño" is no doubt to be translated as sleep. "Sleep overcomes them." Four muffled female figures are squatting and lying together, forming a pyramid; the point where it narrows is a woman with her legs spread, and this woman is drawn into the dark, while the gross physicality of the other three figures is bathed in a glaring light. We cannot make out where this light is coming from. It stiffens the bodily bundles of the three hooded women into a rigor of death. "Do not wake them, perhaps sleep is the sole happiness of the unhappy," the anonymous author of the so-called Ayala commentary has noted on this leaf. It would be still more comforting if they could sleep in the darkness, for the light is doing them hurt. That is what has become of the light of the Enlightenment: an instrument of torture.

In the background Goya indicates with yet greater clarity
the evil part played by the brightness. Light and geometry are
made accomplices. The women have made themselves comfortable on a rise in the ground which we might think indicated an open space, were it not that in the background a black
surface whose material we cannot distinguish—"all smooth"—
is apparent, and in it a barred, arched gateway. This gate defines the black smoothness as a confining wall. Yet this wall
lacks material substance. It is the frontier of the space, but also
the intangible nothing which waits beyond the experience of
space.

The right angle is given its negative symbolic force in the
bars, but a more stark and aggressive effect is made by the
bright arc of light, like a crescent moon, which Goya, by means
of an area of shadow, cuts out of the gateway opening. The
grille and the rounded arch are similarly fragmented, and the
result is a sickle the point of whose blade is aimed at the re-
clining women. The cutting weapon threatens not only the
prisoners; viewed as a fragment, it shows the prison as the
locus of fragmented human experience.

An etching of a woman which was not included in the cycle
of "Caprichos" belongs here. Again the vaulting of a jail, made
of square stone blocks, without decoration. Two steep curves
of wall create at their intersection an asymmetrical pointed arch
which resembles the blade of a knife, or a huge vampire's tooth.
Conversely: if one extended the two inclined edges of the walls
toward each other, they would intersect the body of the cowering woman. But Goya does not abandon the prisoner; he
emphasizes the vital strength that is still in her body. The right
arm is propped as if to resist some pressure, or to raise the
upper part of the body. The artist's greatest attention, though,
is given to the legs. Pressed together, they are in chains and
exposed up to the thighs. The skirt, pushed up, forms a round
arch beneath which is the rounding of the posterior: a whole,
organic curve which seems challengingly to oppose the knife
blade of the fragmented vaulting curves.

Maybe Goya is challenging himself too. Research has noted that at that time, 1797–98, the theme of women in prison as yet lacked a political motivation in Spain. Be that as it may: this prisoner is not only a victim of justice, her defenselessness makes her desirable to the artist Goya. Why should he not have gratified for himself, in the draftsman's license, that wish which at the same time lay behind the Marquis de Sade's founding of a new literary genre? (The ten-volume illustrated edition of the *Nouvelle Justine* appeared in 1797, two years before the "Caprichos.")

Similar experiences of lust are registered by Goya later, in the "Desastres" ("The Disasters of War"), with even greater formal mastery, in the French soldiers doing violence to Spanish women. Once again the vaulted architecture is not merely a stage set or background but—smoothed out and well-nigh unphysical, shadowy—a servering agent which, in sharp bends, visually echoes the knives and rapiers of the occupiers. There are bright areas that, like the blades of circular saws, cut up the darkness. Goya denies the rounded form any of that statuary repose to which Goethe, in his Weimar park, was raising a memorial when he had a sphere placed on a cube and dedicated the combination to Agatha Tyche.

In No. 64 of the "Desastres," "Cartloads for the Cemetery," Goya shows corpses being dragged down off a cart as if they were slaughtered animals. The fragmented wheel has the injurious sharpness of an instrument of martyrdom. It corresponds to the sunken rounded arch in the background to the right, which swallows up the corpses. These two symbols of a cyclical mechanism geared to kill combine with the verticals and horizontals of a building we cannot exactly identify to encode a smooth, cold brutality legitimized by the compasses. This is a production line. But Goya the observer sees what those dragging off the corpses are blind to: the exposed legs of the dead woman. Again, as before in the "Caprichos," the voyeur is seduced into a necrophiliac eroticism.

To the best of my knowledge, Goya is not mentioned in Canetti's texts and notebooks. Yet he is constantly present. Thus the section "The Figure and the Mask" (in *Crowds and Power*) deals with that mummery Goya chooses in order to question the foregrounded grimace; and what Canetti has to say a little later about the physical positions of the human species, about standing, sitting, squatting, kneeling, and lying, immediately recalls Goya's postures. "Anyone who lies down disarms himself so completely that it is impossible to understand how men have managed to survive sleep."[7] A statement such as this is speaking of that proximity of death which envelops Goya's sleepers.

In Goya we for the first time encounter mankind in a condition of madness that is not clinically explicable. This is the distinguishing feature of Man's existence. One moment he is distraught in the dismal prison of his body, which binds him in and often wraps him up to the point of resembling a puppet; the next he is surrounded by smoothness in open spaces, by the undecorated backdrops of power which represent the second, "actual" prison, for it is here that madness is regulated and held in check. It becomes a social institution.

Two kinds of prison. In the second volume of Canetti's autobiography they are both present. We find the prototypes of the madness which imagination creates: the Man of Truth, the Phantast, the Religious Fanatic, the Collector, the Spendthrift, the Enemy of Death, the Actor, the Book Man. They embody the pitilessness of life. Everyone passes everyone else by without contact. "It was obvious not only that no one understood anyone else, but also that no one *wanted* to understand anyone else."[8] This is precisely the basic no-escape situation Goya's people are trapped in.

The second prison appears like a vision in the background of these figures of horror. It is—*nomen est omen*—Steinhof, "the town of madmen,"[9] the many pavilions of which, crowned by the domed church of Otto Wagner, look from a distance like villas in the Vienna woods. But the geometric, Secession-like smoothness of this town is in line with the austere utopias of Ledoux. Canetti's fancy is occupied with the inhabitants of this "ideal city," and from his window he would like to look into their rooms and make out, behind the barred windows, heads that would give him some sign. We do not discover whether he ever visited Steinhof. But neither do we know whether Goya painted and drew his "locos" *after* visiting mental asylums.

I ask myself this one question: why Goya was omitted, why the witness of his work was not appealed to. Goya is an epigrammatic inventor; his configurations are at once harsh and mysterious. In the end, his hermetic pictorial inventions, even when they are accompanied by titles, insist on their ambiguity. Canetti the man of words has ultimately made over his thinking, which is no less visual, to the omnipotence of the Word. The Word elucidates the image. Goya opposes this total appropriation. To his resistance the Word, with its claim to be the highest interpretative authority, can respond only with silent respect. Perhaps this silence is Canetti's reply to my question.

NOTES

1. Elias Canetti, *Crowds and Power* (translated by Carol Stewart), London, 1962, pp. 207 and 209.
2. Ibid., p. 209.
3. Ibid., p. 208.
4. Elias Canetti, *Fritz Wotruba*, foreword by Klaus Demus, Vienna, 1955.
5. *Crowds and Power*, p. 209.
6. Ibid., p. 208.
7. Ibid., p. 390.
8. Elias Canetti, *The Torch in My Ear* (translated by Joachim Neugroschel), New York, 1982, pp. 322–23.
9. Ibid., p. 232.

Manfred Schneider

The Cripples and Their Symbolic Bodies

I

Auto-da-Fé is the epic province of cripples: the reader is presented scarcely a single character that is not conspicuous through some striking disfigurement. The physical images of the central characters populate the novel like some museum of the grotesque: lanky Kien, gradually wasting away to a skeleton; Therese with her head askew, her odd-sized ears, and her awe-inspiring skirt; hunchbacked Fischerle with his immense nose, who enjoys the incomprehensible adoration of the similarly hunchbacked Fishwife; Fischerle's wife or girlfriend, an unnamed whore, earns their joint income with a body as fat as it is insensitive. In the second part of the novel, the monstrous dwarf Fischerle acts as the boss of a con racket, and his employees have been recruited to the last man from the world of the crippled and stigmatized: an insomniac hawker, an invalid simulating blindness, a drunkard sewer man with a face like a "gleaming cow-pat." Like some malevolent virus, grotesqueness has infected and deformed their bodies. The police station chief wears his trauma in the middle of his face, in the shape of a nose that has turned out too small. The sadistic, greedy, gargantuan caretaker Benedikt Pfaff finds the traces of his anomaly—red hair—spread across his whole body. And his name, with its twofold religious ring, is a misleading label for a bestial creature—indeed, even his own family call him "Ginger the Cat."

This cast of the crippled, the stigmatized, and the half-human is rounded off by the appearance of the psychiatrist George Kien, brother of the sinologist Peter. He is shown in a brighter light not only on account of his lack of physical deformities; he is even heralded as a "savior" of his patients. George Kien's sympathy, his empathic sensitivity, his ability at least to listen to the voice of insanity, reveal traits well-nigh angelic in a world of monomaniac egocentrics. But in spite of his store of knowledge, as gynecologist and psychiatrist, George cannot penetrate the mad world of his brother: psychology, psychiatry, and psychoanalysis have at their disposal no strategy of human conduct that might offer help to a Peter Kien—he and all the other inmates of this pandemonium of freaks can scarcely see and hear themselves any longer, they lack the gift of self-analysis, they are at the mercy of their desires and deliria, without volition. In a word, they have no souls. For the search for a unity or coherence in the characters offers the reader only intenseness and obsession. Their crippled bodies are organized units of desires and uninhibited cravings for power. A Faustian pact seems to have cast them into the world, a pact which, from the very beginning, has made over their souls to obsession's unpredictable power game. True, one group of characters constitutes an exception: the women. George proves himself an expert in his field when at the close he succeeds in impressing Therese and removing her from his brother's vicinity. Therese and the other women in the novel still have what might be called a soul, or, to put it in power-political terms, the correlative of psychology. To that extent it is apparent that, in the pathology of *Auto-da-Fé,* gynecology and psychiatry are the same thing.

If we read Canetti as he requires to be read, we see that the lack of therapeutic success of psychiatrist George Kien, otherwise so successful, is of great significance. In the last analysis, George can neither understand nor help his brother. And this inability exactly characterizes the pitfalls of any reading that would penetrate Canetti's novel by way of other knowledge, or would discover in it the truths of our era. There is no knowledge that can turn this novel into its correlative (as George Kien's psychiatry finds its correlative in women). There is no knowledge that might lighten the darkness of this text, no hermeneutic or philosophical or psychological knowledge—in this fact lies the "madness" of the novel. *Auto-da-Fé* seals itself off autistically against all these familiar modes of discourse, and a closer understanding of it can be achieved only if the functional laws of the text are attentively examined, the driving powers of its own obsessive momentum.

To give a term to the general features of this inner mechanism, let us tentatively speak of Canetti's "myth." This concept ought in the first place to be understood in the most neutral of senses, as a wholly personal truth, a story that is this author's and this author's alone. The functional aspect of this myth is its ability to retain its vitality through countless variations and transformations. Perhaps every writer has only *one* story, and telling it is his life's work: this would rightly be called an individual myth. And the variation and transformation of this mythic basic narrative would be the symbolic activity of life, an activity that is more fundamental and thus "truer" than all of psychology.

A unity of this kind, a mythic structure, is present in Canetti's works; it can be extrapolated from a series of variations and metamorphoses, and embraces both the author and many of his characters. The name of this myth, and its relationship to *Auto-da-Fé,* have nothing surprising about them: the Cripple, his Obsession, and his Symbolic Body.

Let us turn first to one of Canetti's most attractive texts, *The Voices of Marrakesh.* The last section of this book bears the title "The Unseen." The traveler encounters this unseen being on the great square in Marrakesh, and its voice is the ultimate and final sound to remain in the ear of the narrator, and also of the reader of this travel journal. To be exact, it is the un-articulated utterance of a human being that cannot even be said with certainty to be in fact human. The unseen being is a creature wrapped up in dirty brown material, a cripple, a beg-ger, who produces as a sole sign of life "a deep, long-drawn-out, buzzing 'e-e-e-e-e-e-e-.' "[1] This encounter, repeatedly sought by the narrator, gradually creates an idea or image of this being, in its dark invisibility, and at length the author sub-scribes to an analysis and synthesis of the incomprehensible sounds: he imagines that maybe the crippled beggar no longer has a *tongue* to articulate the word Allah, the name of God. Only the guttural sound of the vowels, of a single vowel, re-mains; and this "e-e-e-e-e-e-e" heard by the stranger be-comes, through a kind of mythological conjecture, the articu-lated name Allah. Such conjectures—let us note this at the outset—are among the recurring procedures in Canetti's myth.

A second cripple, and thus a further inhabitant of Canetti's myth, appears at the end of the second volume of autobiogra-phy, *The Torch in My Ear*. This cripple, Thomas Marek, par-alyzed by some unknown illness, has (unlike the Marrakesh cripple) an unusually adroit tongue: it is the instrument of his philosophical discourse, and at the same time it serves to re-place his paralyzed hands. With his tongue Thomas, to the boundless amazement of his visitor, leafs quickly and dexter-ously through the pages of the many books he reads. Thomas Marek, cripple and obsessed philosopher, as pathetic as he is fascinating, appears in the mythic radiance of a story that might be a fairy tale. This story, the narrator recalls, seemed to him at the time so beautiful he felt he had "never heard such a lovely story."[2] This is a remarkable statement coming from a young person who has already encountered so many stories, novels, plays, fairy tales, and myths. Thomas Marek's story does indeed follow the pattern of a fairy tale. The role of the good fairy is played by an unknown lady who visits crippled Thomas and promises to pay him a stipend that will free him and his family too from material want. She grants the money in the expectation that Thomas will write a book that will benefit all mankind. This book, or rather the wish to write it, constitutes the work fantasy of the cripple, who has long given up hope of a cure or of God's help. Thomas expressly forbids his family to pray to God.

This, then, is the second mythic tale. In spite of the good fairy working her charitable miracle, our doubts remain as to whether such autobiographical episodes can so readily be raised to the rank of myth. Yet a story that strikes a man as the *loveliest* he has ever heard, a fairy tale like this, is no mere biographical episode, for various reasons.

The histories of the two cripples have a number of similarities, not only the tongue which the beggar in Marrakesh lacks and which is so important an organ for the paralyzed Thomas. There are further elements linked by polarity or contrast: for example, the money which is tossed to the Marrakesh beggar in small coins and which Thomas receives in fabulous abundance. A third element is the name of God, which the traveler supposes he detects in that single sound made by the beggar; in the tale of Thomas Marek, by contrast, we are told that the name of God never passed his lips and that he had forbidden his family to call upon God. Thus from the start the story we have called Canetti's myth includes three core variables: the cripple, money, and the name of God—whose place, in Thomas Marek's case, is taken by work done for mankind. This work, here and in other places, constitutes a fourth element.

But two examples are scant nourishment for that so universal and (as far as interpretations are concerned) greedy concept of myth. The hypothesis of a basic story in Canetti gains a certain workability and a further conceptual dimension only if we recall a third biographical episode. This is a story from *The Tongue Set Free,* the first part of his autobiography (and here we should note that the *tongue* is another variable in Canetti's

myth). The chapter is headed "The Magic Language; The Fire."
In it, the boy Elias witnesses a fire that has broken out in a
neighborhood house. He hears from the maids that the numerous people tirelessly running in and out of the burning building, carrying bundles, are *thieves*. The narrator, the reader is
then told, rediscovered these images of little, obsessed people
busy as ants years later, in the paintings of Pieter Brueghel:
indeed, Brueghel's painted people seemed so familiar to him
that the narrator can no longer tell which was in his mind first,
the gallery of memories or the series of images by Brueghel.
The final sentence concerning Brueghel reads: "I found him
present within me as though, certain that I would have to come
to him, he had been awaiting me for a long time."[3] But the
story is not yet finished: in the second volume of the autobiography we are told more about this encounter with the paintings, and the narrator particularly emphasizes two of Brueghel's works, "The Parable of the Blind" and "The Triumph
of Death," the originals of which hang in Naples and Madrid.
In these two paintings a chamber of horrors of cripples and
skeletons is opened up, at once real and hyper-real—an obsessively detailed panopticon of the branded and beaten. The
thought occurs to us that the painter's vision of Brueghel was
made text in *Auto-da-Fé*. Canetti has often drawn attention to
such relations between paintings and his texts. *Auto-da-Fé* takes
its original German title* from a third painting, Rembrandt's
"The Blinding of Samson," which likewise belongs in the gallery of paintings which, for Canetti, mark the boundary between the real and the symbolic: pictures that seem to contain
some vision, or experiences that have already been preformu-
lated in pictures (this kind of crossing of memory and symbolism unfolds the same mythic power as fairy tales—stories that
seem to be the *loveliest*). We should also note in passing that
in Brueghel's painting "The Triumph of Death" (for instance)
all the elements of Canetti's myth are present: cripples/

* *Die Blendung*, literally *The Blinding*. —Trans.

skeletons, money, and God/obsessive busyness—albeit in a different order.

The fundamental quality of a myth, be it personal or collective, consists in its having neither origins nor truth nor psychology. It simply exists. Naturally clues can be found: there is a biographical archaeology to a myth just as there is a historical one, and the traces of the *Iliad* lie scattered in the archaeology of Troy; but the power of the epic by no means lies in the earth. Canetti tells us of his lifelong trauma of blindness, and of the fear of having his tongue cut out. Indications such as these, however, have nothing to do with the strata and histories of the soul. Canetti's soul, as he himself tells us believably enough, consists of stories and myths, of figures and texts from literature: there is no personal truth beyond this complex. There are only crystallizations, a mysterious interpenetration of life and text, experience and symbol, and this we call myth.

A myth thus marks a boundary line, and not merely the boundary between nature and culture, as Lévi-Strauss has made clear, but other boundaries too: in Canetti's case, the boundary between speech and dumbness. *The Tongue Set Free* testifies to this, as do the throng of obsessed tongue-characters, from Thomas Marek through Frau Weinreb to the "character" of the Namelicker in *Earwitness*. Canetti's myth also marks the boundary between seeing and blindness (*Auto-da-Fé* attests this) and the great throng of cripples. Above all, the myth marks the boundary between life and death, and that between the subjective self and the crowd. These are the twin interrelated themes to which Canetti's whole obsessive authorial and investigative passion is devoted.

II

We have now sufficiently introduced the concept and literary substratum of the personal myth to return to our scrutiny of the text itself—where Canetti's myth has been expressed in its fundamental and most acute form.

Canetti has repeatedly accounted for the genesis of *Auto-da-Fé*.[4] Of the many statements, one has particular importance for our present purposes. As we know, the young author, in the conception of his work as a *"Comédie Humaine* of the insane,"[5] aimed to pick up a great epic tradition. It is true, though, that in *Auto-da-Fé* he quotes this tradition only to repudiate it: in the distant past stands the example of Dante's *Divine Comedy,* the cosmic epic of a world in which God's name and God's Word still exercise their unbroken dominion. The threefold division of the medieval world into Inferno, Purgatorio, and Paradiso can be seen again in the modern, secularized comedy of the world, in Balzac's *Comédie Humaine,* as a class distinction: workers and peasants, the bourgeoisie, and the aristocracy there occupy the three steps of a social cosmos. No universal explorer of the stature of a Dante, no wanderer gradually approaching enlightenment, strides through these Balzacian worlds. In the great novel *Les Illusions Perdues,* for example, Lucien de Rubempré, a careerist driven on by ambition, rises to the heights of fame and fortune. *Auto-da-Fé* too, that novel in which the various obsessions of the *"Comédie Humaine* of the insane" have been compounded into a unity, reveals a tripartite structure; but the trilogy of sections, "A Head without a World," "Headless World," and "The World in the Head," contains neither a cosmic nor a social order, but instead, at most, a triad of madness. The blinding which in Dante's Paradiso still came from the light of Truth, the essence of God, is in Canetti's novel the twofold effect of a world of books which has taken the place of God: the scholar Kien, whose existence is spent among nothing but letters and books, is just as blinded as the madman Kien, who sets these very books on fire and attains the illumination of death. But this does not yet cover the whole of the Canetti/Dante nexus. The cripples in *Auto-da-Fé* have put in place of God's name (the guarantee of worldly coherence in Dante's epic) and in place of their souls (the foundation of social unity in Balzac's human comedy) something else: an obsession which is at the same time a kind of imaginary substitution, symbolically creating anew their deformed bodies. Let us recall once more the four elements of Canetti's personal myth: the crippled body, the utterance or denial of the name of God, money, and the object of obsession, the work. The work of the beggar on the great Marrakesh square is fully done in croaking forth the name of God, minus consonants: in its intention, the beggar's work is wholly equal to Dante's. Thomas Marek, by contrast, places the phantasm of his philosophical work in the position of God's blotted-out name. And Canetti—what is his own place in the myth?

At the period of the genesis of *Auto-da-Fé* there is one man whose discourse replaces God's Word: Karl Kraus. On Kraus we read: "For a year and a half, I had gone to every reading, and I was filled with him as with a Bible. I did not doubt a single word he said. Never, under any circumstances, would I have acted against him. He was my conviction. He was my strength. . . . I heard only his voices. . . . One gesture, and I would have thrown myself into fire for him."[6] That voice of *Die Fackel*, which for many years sounded in the young Canetti's ear like the voice of God, is at once the instrument of obsession. What in Dante's *Purgatorio* was a metaphysical-cosmic institution, Karl Kraus tried to elevate into his life's work as a writer. Kraus himself described *Die Fackel* as a "purifying institution,"[7] and his satire aspired to cleanse the world of the sins and filth that bore so many names: capital, feuilletonism, corruption, lying, war. That God, Karl Kraus, palpably presided over the literary beginnings of Canetti. The severity and relentlessness of the voice of *Die Fackel* entered *Auto-da-Fé* as an artistic discipline and hardness. The repudiation of Viennese feuilleton literature is at once the repudiation of a soulfulness whose lyrical triviality is perpetuated satirically in the female characters in *Auto-da-Fé*. Nonetheless, *Auto-da-Fé* also represents the act—initially unconscious rather than otherwise—of deleting Karl Kraus's divine name: in this novel of cripples and their obsessions, the voice of Deity which sounded forth from *Die Fackel* and the readings of that great judge Karl Kraus gradually grows softer. The place of this God and his laws is taken by the production of the personal myth, which in turn makes this very production a subject: the trinity of crippledom, money, and denial of the Deity is used by the characters in *Auto-da-Fé* for the creation of a second, symbolic body. The epic of this remarkable trinity is Canetti's myth and his decoding of God's name. Canetti's obsession, which in *Auto-da-Fé* spelled out its first mythic variations, lives on in those many years of research for *Crowds and Power,* where the symbolic name of God is still perpetuated.

Tradition indicates that the occidental epic was at one time a hymn of praise of God's work, of the first and greatest Creation. This is a clue to the twofold movement of Canetti's work: writing oneself into a tradition of works and at the same time repudiating that tradition. The repudiation (or dementi) is figured forth in the madness (or dementia) of the characters. In the Inferno of *Auto-da-Fé* they are all subject to one law, which decrees they be disfigured in order obsessively to engender new bodies for themselves, symbolic bodies in which the soul and God at once disappear and are given concrete form. With the exception of George Kien, all the characters in *Auto-da-Fé* are subject to this law, and thus they function as broken delinquents in whom the consequences of a mythic truth are manifested.

The exemplar of the principle of the mythic order is Fischerle, the hunchback, the blustering hero of the bar which bears the name The Stars of Heaven. Like the celestial explorer Dante, the visitor at first notices nothing on entering this remarkable paradise; but it is the "appalling fog" of the bar that strains the eyes. Fischerle consists solely of "a hump, a majestic nose and two black, calm, sad eyes."[8] Fischerle's symbolic

body, though, is the game of chess, a body without monstrosity and one that guarantees power. "The word chess rang in
his mouth like a command, as though it depended on his gra-
cious mercy, whether he would not add the mortal 'check-
mate.' "⁹ In his wide-ranging fantasy of power, Fischerle hallucinates posters on the walls of the world's cafés, on which
the chess matches he has played as world champion are marked
up. "World champion" is in fact a secularized name of God;
but it is not the image of his stigmatized body but the chess
match that is to give the proof of Fischerle and his power. Like
a beggar with his alms, like Thomas Marek with his fairy's
bounty, Fischerle finds the "stipendium" made over by Kien
dropped in his lap. Thus in him we discover all the elements
that characterize Canetti's myth: the crippled state, the denial
of God's name, obsessive work as a symbolic body, and the
money given by a kindly donator. His driving energy, the quite
rudimentary psychology of this cripple, operates between chess
and money. Fischerle is neither wicked nor good, neither com-
passionate nor cruel; he merely generates a second body, the
world champion body. As the wad of gifted and stolen money
stowed under his armpit gradually grows, the bulk of his hump
seems to dwindle. In the end his wish to be delivered from his
crippled state comes true in a way as ironic as it is terrible: a
doppelgänger of the blind invalid Johann Schwer kills Fischerle
by cutting off his hump. Initially this "button man" was one
of Fischerle's employees: he is an invalid beggar who pretends
to be blind and endures the greatest torments when he sees
buttons being tossed him as alms instead of coins. His symbolic body is the fantasy of a gigantic emporium where he keeps
a great crowd of fat women who all have to be at his service.
Led on by Fischerle's fat wife, he will murder his onetime boss
in the end, and take his fortune.

The other epic associates of Kien and Therese are also wholly
subject to the basic rule. Thus we have the hawker, for example, who suffers from insomnia and hunts through God's sym-

bolic body, the church, for drugs; thus too, among the same group, we have the sewer man, who descends to the underworld for his many-headed (though admittedly real) family-body, and regularly drinks away the fourth quarter of his wages in The Stars of Heaven. These four parasitic beings—the thief, the beggar, the hawker, and finally the caretaker Benedikt Pfaff, who regularly receives his gratuity from Kien—personify in *Auto-da-Fé* the prime exemplars of the Canetti myth. They are satellites and variants of Peter Kien, the sinologist and hero of the novel. Peter Kien's symbolic body needs no lengthy analysis: it is his library, the largest private library in the city, we are told. That this mass of books is a gigantic body without organs is already apparent from the fact that for Kien every book, and the bag he carries his books in too, serves as an extension of his own body:

He clasped it tightly to him, in a very particular manner which he had himself thought out, so that the greatest possible area of his body was always in contact with it. Even his ribs could feel its presence through his cheap, thin suit. His upper arm covered the whole side elevation; it fitted exactly.[10]

In the world of things and facts, Kien draws strength from a symbiosis of his real body and the symbolic book-body, just as Fischerle finds support in the money he carries in his armpit, regularly checking with his nose to see (if the synesthesia may be permitted) if it is still there. As symbiotic objects, books take on in the imagination the function of living bodies: for Kien, not only are books a satisfying substitute for women, but in his fantasies they also repeatedly metamorphose into human bodies. In the second part of the novel Kien even attains the status of a savior who saves book-bodies from the fire. This madness is the reflected image of the system the unworldly scholar is caught up in: if in his delirium he is himself the godlike redeemer who with his money saves the bodies of books, in the everyday system of the sinologist Peter Kien books themselves take the place of God and his Word. There is ample textual evidence for this. For example, Kien is planning to subject the gospels to textual criticism and above all to write a new version of St. John, which, as we know, Goethe's Faust had already attempted. Every era in European thought has redefined the *logos* of St. John, and what lay beyond was always madness. St. John introduced the Word of God into European culture, as the alpha and omega of the world. Kien's new version is to eliminate that, and create the rule of his own book-delirium. In his nightmares, however, Kien is time and again haunted by the voice of God: this voice alternately denies and confirms his visions, visions that show him the whole world as a book, or that show all mankind in purgatory, as books. At one point he hears the voice of God: "There are no books here." And not long after, the mocking contradiction follows, again from the mouth of God: "Now come the books!" [11]

At the end of the first part of the novel Kien pays homage to his new god, "the (masculine) Past." * This name of God fulfills a dual denial, of the female gender and of the biblical God. Kien likes to define women and God as illiterates,[12] and this is in fact the most contemptuous word in his vocabulary. "Past," on the other hand, gives us the key concept in Kien's intellectual activity. It consists of a vast store of knowledge, and also of his work as a sinologist. The past as contained in written records enters the massive archive of Kien's memory; and writings that have been lost to the past—destroyed, incomplete, illegible—are reconstructed by Kien. Memory and the restoration of what is past offer resistance to Time, God's eternal power. Thus the past is robbed of its ability to sym-

---

* The German word for the past, *Vergangenheit,* is grammatically of feminine gender, i.e., *die Vergangenheit,* but Kien pays homage to *den Vergangenheit,* where *den* is the accusative form of the masculine definite article. The words quoted are the solution offered in C. V. Wedgwood's translation. —*Trans.*

bolize Time. Kien is going about the business of taking from God the power of texts:

Countless texts owed their restoration to him. When he came to misreadings or imperfections in ancient Chinese, Indian or Japanese manuscripts, as many alternative readings suggested themselves for his selection as he could wish. Other textual critics envied him; he for his part had to guard against a superfluity of ideas. Meticulously cautious, he weighed up the alternatives month after month, was slow to the point of exasperation; applying his severest standards to his own conclusions, he took no decision, on a single letter, a word or an entire sentence, until he was convinced that it was unassailable. . . . A sentence once set down by him was decisive and binding. In controversial questions he was the ultimate appeal, the leading authority even in related branches of knowledge.[13]

Kien sees himself as a kind of pope before the absolute text which is yet to be created: the whole is merely a brain process, however, and of course the brain stores an entire library, a crowd of books that are trying to take the place of Creation and of Man. What Kien interpolates into defective texts is *conjecture*. As one who conjectures, his activity too belongs in the symbolic operational area of Canetti's myth. Another emender of corrupt texts was the visitor to the great square who heard the voices of Marrakesh. Confronted with the croaking brown-clad beggar, he offered a twofold conjecture: he saw in this unseen creature a human being, and he detected in the sequence of sounds an articulation of the name of God. Canetti's Kien does the opposite: his conjectures offer resistance to the name of God, and produce a symbolic body in place of a real one. Kien, who "eager yet cool . . . pick[s] his way from phrase to phrase"[14] in his conjectural work on texts, is a hunter. And as a hunter of conjectures he is the total opposite of his wife, the *absolute* opposite. Nonetheless they are linked: Therese too is a hunter, as indeed her name says, in which we find the

Greek word *therao*. And she is also a huntress who avails herself of conjectures.

But what Therese hunts is money. What has dropped in the lap of this obsessed bag of bones Kien by way of inheritance, Therese has to hunt out for herself. It is remarkable, however, that this woman, in her hunt for money, increases the size of her prey: the sum that Kien's will shows to be his estate does not satisfy her, so she emends the corrupt text of her wealth by simply adding two zeros to the sum of 12,650. This is what we call a conjecture. Therese has long been practicing for mathematical conjecture of this order; even as a schoolgirl she was the best in her class at writing zeros, and she consolidates her talent in all-night exercises. While in Kien's philological work "the right characters simply streamed from his pen,"[15] Therese goes in for mass production of zeros. Through conjecturing the figure of his estate she has contrived the reward for her labors. Still, the increase of a fortune by the simple addition of zeros is that same lunatic operation that was ridiculed by one who was (as it were) related to her husband and whose name was rejected: Immanuel Kant. One working title of *Auto-da-Fé* we know to have been *Kant Catches Fire*. So for some years, in the manuscript of *Auto-da-Fé*, Therese the huntress bore this name. In view of Therese's symbolic achievements this was a richly meaningful title; for Peter's and Therese's namesake (at this stage in Canetti's work), the philosopher Immanuel Kant, concluded the first part of his *Critique of Pure Reason* with a refutation of the three classic proofs of the existence of God. For this reason Heinrich Heine called him a deicide. At the end of that section where he subjects the Cartesian ontological proof of the existence of God to withering criticism, Kant declares with veritable scorn:

Thus the famous ontological (Cartesian) proof of the existence of a higher being by conceptual means is a total waste of time and effort, and a man might as little increase his stock on insight through mere ideas as a merchant would increase his fortune by adding a nought or so to his credit column.[16]

In Kantian terms, Therese's writing of zeros amounts to an absurd assertion of the presence of God. Her conjectural hunt is both analogous to (the "stream" of characters) and in contrast with Kien's work. Kien's absolute text, in process of creation inside his head and on paper, wipes out the name, works, and power of God, or, in Kantian terms: interest in speculation makes him replace the God that exists with a dual store of memory and text. The fortune-hunter Therese, on the other hand, creates a real god for herself through her artificial manufacture of numbers, and to this real god she gives the name Mr. Puda—the "superior young man." The name of the furniture salesman she calls Buddha is actually Brute. In this way Therese pulls off a twin christening, for not only is the man she desires hallowed by the nimbus of godliness but, in the echo of the Austrian vulgar term *pudern*,* she is also articulating her sexual desire for the man's body: this is the difference between male and female production in *Auto-da-Fé*. The women quest for the fulfillment of their deformed bodies not through any symbolic body but through a real male body. The same is true of Fischerle's woman, the unnamed whore, and Fischerle's hunchbacked admirer who is called the Fishwife on account of her hopeless passion.

In the natures and obsessions of the characters in *Auto-da-Fé* the structure of Canetti's myth can be very clearly recognized—the crippled real body and the symbolic body in which that substance termed a "soul," once lost, is reorganized and where the name of God is either blotted out or replaced. The obsessions in which symbolic bodies originate are of course parasitic. They are financed by the charity of fellow human beings, by Chance, or by some fairylike appearance, whether Kien squanders a considerable inheritance or Fischerle receives

* Austrian slang for fornicating. —*Trans.*

a stipendium from Kien or the numerous beggars, hawkers, and tip-chasers do their best to jog Chance's elbow. And this structure, this functional rule of the myth, is seen in reverse form among the women, Therese foremost among them. They are women of a kind that bear within them the rudiments of souls, who idolize the real body of a man and literally finance it: in *Auto-da-Fé* they are the last patients of psychology. This is true in a literal sense of Therese, who, as we are told, "perfected her method of speech; everything which came into her head she spoke out at once."[17] This is of course the fundamental rule of psychoanalysis.[18]

III

Let us in closing ask what analytic function such abstract concepts as "myth" or "symbolic body" or "absolute text" have. To begin with, the concept of "myth" has two uses: on the one hand, myth denotes the inner functional unity of a text, which embraces the life of the author as much as the author's production, above all in cases where he appears in an autobiographical text; and, on the other hand, myth is tantamount to negation of anthropological discourses and valid systems of knowledge. The essence of a work or text does not consist in some truth, beyond the text, of a theoretical or philosophical nature, or to do with authorial psychology, but in fact consists in structure, unity, the dynamics of a form of creativity. This ascertainable unity we label "myth" because its symbolic ambience includes the author and what he creates: Canetti's myth is the symbolic ensemble of his own obsession and that of his characters. And obsession is a lack of depth, where depth is seen as a hermeneutic dimension.

This will become clear if we take a last look at the figure of Peter Kien. Throughout the novel the reader is afforded no position or perspective from which he might *understand* the scholar. Kien's reactions lack any pattern and are closed to our empathy, and hence incomprehensible. There is no deep structure to Kien, no psychological unity. This madness (dementia), as a denial (dementi) of the soul and of spiritual coherence, manifests itself in two other ways. First, Kien has bequeathed his brain to an anatomical institute, and plainly he does not consider his genius a spiritual gift of Nature but, far more, he believes that memory and the faculty of reason—intellectual disciplines he holds the records in—have a physiological existence. Where this anatomy of the brain begins, the science of the soul ends. Second, Kien is a man who lives without mirrors. The scholar has blotted out the optical image of himself: in this respect, Canetti's play *Comedy of Vanity* continues one of the blinded Kien's idiosyncratic traits. The "blindness" of the bookworm is a blackness that blots out the image of his own body too. But those who have no mirror image of themselves also lack a soul. Throughout both art and psychology we find this confirmed: for that depth of the self which the people and science agree in calling the soul is the epitome of what the looks and words of those around us create, the image of others. And where this soul is absent, psychology gropes about the empty space. This is demonstrated to the reader when he is given the opportunity to listen in on the psychiatrist George Kien during his inner monologues, in the course of which he is continually making wrong diagnoses of his brother's condition.

Kien's soul is his *work,* his obsessive labors over it, his personal myth. This myth is psychologically and hermeneutically impenetrable. No science of the soul, no procedures for understanding Man, can get a grip on an obsession that eliminates the body and creates a symbolic second. From bizarrerie of this order one might induce a theoretical paradigm: the cripple allegorically represents spiritually wrecked Man in the alienated society of late capitalism (to quote a formula that has gone out of fashion).[19] But in fact this would amount to confirming the truth of a quite different text, such as Georg Lukács's *History and Class Consciousness,* and it would also mean obscuring the uniqueness of Canetti's novel—it would in fact be a blinded reading of *Die Blendung (Auto-da-Fé).* An enlightened reading of the novel, by contrast, registers the presence and effect of the personal myth. This myth, to express it differently, is a dynamic power whose energies are unknown but whose structure remains constant: it is a kind of spending of physical powers in the service of a second, symbolic and complete body, a body that thrusts God's Word aside and which lives on the stipendium of Chance. The crippledom of the characters in *Auto-da-Fé* places its grotesque potential wholly in the realm of incompletion, lack, or defect. Grotesqueness is exhausted in this testimony to the actuality of the created being before the backdrop of the symbolic eternities. At the same time, deformity is the point of origin of all obsessive endeavors to eradicate the defect. The bodies' conjectural handling of money or books, and the conjectural reconstitution of defective texts, are in this respect aspects of the same symbolic activity; for one of the many monologues that echo in the empty inner spaces of Kien's soul maintains that texts too are bodies. Obsession or passion thus has no depth, solely an origin, intensity, and goal: a kind of powerful completeness in a symbolic body. These bodies can, however, also be described as aspects of the crowd: Kien's library is a crowd of books, Fischerle's chess-body finds a tangible form in a crowd of posters, and the beggar Johann Schwer imagines his department store as a crowd of voluptuous women. In that crowd of things that constitute the symbolic body we can already see the adumbration of the theory of *Crowds and Power,* which Canetti had been at work on since 1925. In *Auto-da-Fé,* the author expressed his knowledge as it then stood through the mouth of the psychiatrist George Kien, who in this way makes possible the impossible, his brother's triumphant death by fire. This death must needs be seen as impossible by a science which has *logos* in its name: psychology. And thus Peter Kien's most radical denial of the *logos* does not turn out to be a philological study as he had once thought, but the triumph of his desire and the total expending of his obsessed powers. If we are here put in mind of Georges Bataille's *Théorie de la Dépense*, that is by no means wrong. The denial of the *logos* takes the form of an orgy of waste and the loss of the self in that crowd which Kien had always thought of as a human crowd: the burning books.[20]

To conclude these reflections, one final speculation: in the elements of Canetti's myth—the crippled body, the obsessive work at a symbolic body, and finally its absorption into the crowd, its expending in a crowd of symbolic bodies—in this triad of elements, seen as stages, we see again, in the "*Comédie Humaine* of the insane," the order and dynamics of Dante's *Divine Comedy*. The real world of *Auto-da-Fé* reminds us too directly of Dante's Inferno, with its revue of tormented bodies and its catalogues of punished desires. The symbolic bodies are products of a redemption-fantasy such as the great purification mechanism of the Purgatorio expresses in mythic form. And at the close the Paradiso world of brightness is answered by an echoing glow in the flames of the final pages. Nothing, though, could be more un-Christian, indeed more anti-Scholastic, than Peter Kien's auto-da-fé. It is heathen and wicked, celebrating a triumph of sorts over the Christian mythology of death. Thus, in the resemblances to Dante's mythic epic, we see the full concentrated power of a denial at extremis: what lies beyond the *logos,* or, to put it less philosophically, this side of God's Word, is the *triumph of life.* And it is this that Canetti's myth bears witness to.

NOTES

1. Elias Canetti, *The Voices of Marrakesh* (translated by J. A. Underwood), London, 1978, p. 100.
2. Elias Canetti, *The Torch in My Ear* (translated by Joachim Neugroschel), New York, 1982, p. 345.
3. Elias Canetti, *The Tongue Set Free* (translated by Joachim Neugroschel), New York, 1979 and 1983, p. 25.

4. See Elias Canetti, "Gespräch mit Horst Bienek," in *Die gespaltene Zukunft*, pp. 93–103; "The First Book: *Auto-da-Fé*," in *The Conscience of Words* (translated by Joachim Neugroschel), New York, 1979, pp. 203–13; and most recently *The Torch in My Ear*, pp. 362 ff.

5. *The Conscience of Words*, p. 206, and *The Torch in My Ear*, p. 323.

6. *The Torch in My Ear*, pp. 159–60.

7. Karl Kraus, *Briefe an Sidonie Nâdherný von Borutin 1913–1936*, 2 vols., Munich, 1974, vol. 1, p. 321.

8. Elias Canetti, *Auto-da-Fé* (translated by C. V. Wedgwood), London, 1946 et seq., p. 175.

9. Ibid., p. 177.

10. Ibid., p. 11.

11. Ibid., pp. 40–41.

12. Ibid., pp. 159 and 172.

13. Ibid., pp. 17–18.

14. Ibid., p. 68.

15. Ibid., pp. 130–31.

16. Immanuel Kant, *Kritik der reinen Vernunft*, Hamburg, 1956, p. 575. (Translation by the present translator.)

17. *Auto-da-Fé*, p. 109.

18. Cf. J. Laplanche and J. B. Pontalis (eds.), *Das Vokabular der Psychoanalyse*, 2 vols., Frankfurt. 1973, vol. 1, pp. 172 ff.

19. Cf., for example, Mechthild Curtius, *Das Problem der Verdinglichung in Elias Canettis Roman "Die Blendung,"* Bonn, 1973.

20. Without a doubt fire—the fire the young Canetti would have walked through for Karl Kraus, and which on July 15, 1927, gave him his ending for *Auto-da-Fé* and the substance of *Crowds and Power*—is a further fundamental in Canetti's myth.

Alfred Hrdlicka

A Physiognomic
Portrait

For a sculptor it would doubtless be apt to ask: What access does a visual artist have to Canetti's work, and to what extent is Canetti interested in the visual arts? Everyone can answer the question for himself as far as the visual stimuli offered Canetti's writings are concerned, and Canetti's interest in the visual arts is far too specific for me to venture a judgment—Fritz Wotruba, his friend since youth, would no doubt have had more to say on this. As far as Canetti's interest in myself goes, it is not free of sentimentality: I reminded him in 1968 of the young Wotruba, whom he describes as subject to powerful inner tensions and with something heavily eruptive about him. (To tell the truth, I see myself in a more intellectual way.)

How do I see Canetti? Measured against his and my favorite figure from the Old Testament, Samson, he has turned out on the short side, but as for his leonine head, whenever I looked at him I reflected that perhaps Canetti's strength too lies in his head of hair; I could not conceive of a Canetti shorn of his mane—and indeed he has something of the "just man," including the opinionatedness (*Crowds and Power!*), tolerant as he can be in conversation. Stocky people supposedly have a more developed sense of space and of the body than gangling people: it is no coincidence that Canetti has a penchant for sculpture. His speech and gestures are plastic, seizing hold of space, though this in no way runs counter to his distanced bearing—and distance is highly important to Canetti. Unfortunately, the meeting we had arranged in front of Rembrandt's painting "The Binding of Samson" in Frankfurt's Städel Gallery did not come off. Samson and his tormentors have every man of them the proportions of Canetti, he might have leapt from out of the picture—which neatly illustrates his dualist attitude toward violence. As chance would have it, it was also the director of the Städel, Claus Gallwitz, who in 1966, on the occasion of an exhibition of my work at the Karlsruhe *Kunstverein*, pointed out the common ground between our artistic interests.

"He has the eyes of a cannibal," Elias Canetti said of the Viennese bookseller Wilhelm Herzog at the beginning of the 1970s, and, strangely enough, I thought something similar about Canetti when we first met in London in 1968. In a sense, *Crowds and Power* is a cannibalistic book. Shamans, tyrants, survivors, those who incorporate others and those who destroy themselves, etc. Canetti worked at the book for twenty years and undoubtedly devoured a load of books—seen in terms of its aspirations, the book is in a way boundless, however systematically it is ordered, however much scholarly meticulousness has gone into its composition.

When I observe my cats roaming at liberty outside my studio at the Prater, it strikes me that, even in sleep, their ears rotate like radar disks, always intent to avoid being surprised; as soon as they awaken, they occupy themselves with the most innocuous of business, or lie patiently in wait the moment they have fixed their attention on something in particular, forever out for a catch and at the same time afraid of being caught. The mentality of the predator = the mentality of the cannibal.

Canetti too is forever on guard against being misappropriated and keeps a suspicious watch to see that his works are not misused, although he ought to know that many works of art and literature owe their survival to misinterpretation and misunderstanding. If the powerful had always seen clearly what was being expressed they would have seen to it that a good deal they accepted as mere aestheticism was nipped in the bud. Perhaps, though, it is in Canetti simply the conscious assumption of an Austrian tradition. Whenever Kafka, Kraus, Roth, or Musil are spoken of, it is pointed out how concerned these gentlemen were, in their private as in their literary lives, to be selective, consistent, uncompromising. All of this seems to me to be somewhat overdone—I shall not deny, naturally, that Canetti has on several occasions made apparent his feeling that I am irresponsible. To what extent and why, he has never said exactly, but I still remember well how strict he was in selecting from the etchings I drew in reaction (illustration would not be the right word) to *Crowds and Power:* he rejected two, saying I had arbitrarily introduced the themes and that they had nothing to do with his intentions. Thank God Canetti too is at times lured into inconsistencies; otherwise he would never have written *The Tongue Set Free* and *The Torch in My Ear.*

Canetti, who can tell such vivid tales of his childhood and youth, replied, when my wife, Barbara, asked him why he had never written anything like that, that that was not his business, as if to say that the writing of memoirs was a second-rate occupation, and one had the feeling he was afraid of being taken possession of—after all, the recollections are a part of himself. The mistrust of this brightly alert, sharply observant cannibal once again became apparent.

This root instinct enables him, or indeed impels him, to play the most various roles, and there is no better performance of his play *The Wedding* than his one-man show. *The Wedding* is highly effective in theater terms, yet, on the other hand, the language dominates the action so considerably that everything which is intended to transmit the clarity of the word—the direction, acting, stage set—makes a fussily tautologous impression if one has once heard the way Canetti speaks the text: precise, distanced, slyly reserved, in a voice constantly varied,

disguised, always "staccato," as the young writer Bernhard
Buderath calls Canetti's delivery, only to correct himself: "non
legato."

Disguise and pretense are among Canetti's secret amuse-
ments and no doubt have not been restricted to answering the
telephone using his brother's voice. Whether this is related to
his years as an émigré I do not know; his mummer's skills are
practices on a *l'art pour l'art* basis, for of course he is anything
but one who naturally assimilates, far more what John Berger
called Picasso in connection with the latter's move to Paris: "a
vertical invader."* Whatever he owes to Vienna—*The Wedding, Comedy of Vanity, Auto-da-Fé*—he never succumbs to
that arch-conservative tendency that has marked Austrian literature even since 1945. He writes neither in a hedonistic nor
in a seigneurial nor (least of all) in a larmoyant spirit. He is a
foreign body, an intruder, who cannot share in the bittersweet
pain of the downfall of the monarchy.

I have often wondered what cultural ambit *Crowds and Power*
should be seen as belonging in. Ernst Fischer considered it veritably grotesque that Karl Marx is not mentioned, not with a
single word—come to that, Sigmund Freud is not mentioned
either. I take the motivation for this to be self-assertiveness, a
will to survive, a too high self-esteem. However much he took
from others, Canetti was possessed of the notion of creating a
work without models. A timeless work? Much in it is of burning contemporaneity, for example what Canetti writes of the
pack: there he provides a graphic explanation of the inability
of most revolutionary cells in our times to overcome their isolation. "Characteristic of the pack is the fact that it cannot

---

* The phrase comes from John Berger's *The Success and Failure of Picasso*, Penguin,
Harmondsworth, Middlesex, 1965, but does not in fact originate with Berger, who (p.
40) is quoting from Ortega y Gasset's *Revolt of the Masses*: "The European who is
beginning to predominate . . . must then be, in relation to the complex civilization
into which he has been born, a primitive man, a barbarian appearing on the stage
through the trap-door, a vertical invader." —*Trans.*

grow. It is surrounded by emptiness and there are literally no additional people who could join it. It consists of a group of men in a state of excitement whose fiercest wish is *to be more."*

Doubtless many acts of terror are nothing other than signals of a powerlessness to organize a desired people's movement on a broad basis, and even the PLO, which claims to be the sole representative of an entire people, is ailing with this fragmentation. One war pack hunts the next. Not so long ago the media showed them tragically tearing each other apart in Beirut.

Brilliant as the individual chapters of Canetti's study may be, the real fascination comes from the staggering nature of the undertaking to offer an analysis of power and crowds in our parts by exposing atavistic structures.

In the case of Nobel laureates it is usual, after the name has been given, for the nationality to be established, even before the laureate's achievement has been lauded. Elias Canetti presented difficulties, as "émigré" or "citizen of the world" will scarcely do. Who can claim Canetti as their own?

A Vienna taxi driver, when the news came over his car radio, said to me in a glow of local patriotism: "What do you say to that? Canetti's gone and won the Noble Prize!" But he had not the slightest idea what Canetti had written. Of course Canetti is not concerned with popular, pithy interpretations of the nature of being along the lines of "where do we come from, who are we, where are we going?" such as supposedly (with commercially oriented founders of sects in the fore) are so touching the young and certain Austrian literati at present. Scribbling of this kind is available to excess, in spite of the fact that the question might be answered in a couple of sentences: we all of us come from the womb, life originated in the test tube, the homunculus is still to come; we can readily find out who we are, as data protection laws are not quite up to their job; and as for where we are going, we are going the way of all flesh, or, in the Bible's words: "all flesh is grass."

"Whatever Man eats in this world will eat him in the next."

This gnomic and unsettling statement occurs in the Shatpatha Brahmana, one of the oldest sacrificial tracts of India, Canetti notes.

Or again: "On the psychology of eating. . . . The bond between the eaters is strongest when it is *one* animal they partake of, one body which they knew as a living unit, or one loaf of bread. But the touch of solemnity in their attitude cannot be explained by this alone; their mutual esteem also means that they will not eat, *each other*."

Cannibalism wherever we look. Canetti's obsession with the fleshliness of the flesh, with being devoured and reconstituted, is surely what affected me in *Crowds and Power* from the very start, and the reason I take up the book time and again. Incarnation is the central theme of my artistic activities. It is manifested at its most graphic in stone sculpture, in the transformation of the unhewn block into a human image, a piece of flesh. (Sculptures such as the man on the cross, the thieves, Marsyas, which I have myself interpreted as creations for the halls of the meat market.)

Before I got to know Canetti I was told—as it were, sotto voce, as if it were something scandalous (I have never asked Canetti about it)—that Canetti was convinced he was not mortal—which is not the same thing as immortality. Today Canetti is a Nobel laureate, which is tantamount to a guarantee of immortality. Will he be able to exchange that for nonmortality? I'd wish him that.

Serge Moscovici

Social Collectivities

I. Crowds Everywhere

It was a dangerous era. Groups of people would appear, pour into the broad avenues, and proclaim their demands for freedom and justice. Workers in uniform work clothing carried banners. Officials whose task it was to marshal the crowds and who could be recognized by their armbands tried to channel the flood, and separated the old from the young. At times a peasant would go by, a man in traditional costume, another in cheap overalls, or tight white trousers. Then unexpectedly a stout housekeeper came along the pavement, a basketful of provisions on her arm, plainly on her way home. She was walking as quickly as possible, without looking at anyone. Minute by minute the crowd grew denser, full of young and old, workers and onlookers going their separate ways. Some went ahead with a firm stride, others came along more slowly like the ripples in a river. Across the loudspeakers a speech came to our ears. The passionate voice got carried away by the frenetic cheering it inspired. The pavement was overflowing with people. One of the men turned to a young woman: "Come on, let's go along with the people."

Every one of us has been in a position to experience such scenes dozens of times. They might take place anywhere in the world. A painter who took such a scene as his subject might give his painting the title "Expectant Crowds." But, during the last hundred years, the masses have for the first time been seen in action, loudly shouting out their raw or heroic passions or dreams: it is as if what we saw was the social animal torn loose of its chains. There are many causes for this: a series of revolutions, the dissolution of bonds that had lasted for millennia, the increased speed of communications, the constant mingling of populations, and finally the accelerated and unnerving pace of modern life. Collective bonds are being torn apart and reappearing in the shape of unstable and growing masses. Thus the struggle for control of the masses is changing the nature of power and of the conquest of power. And we are now aware of a deep affinity between crowds and power. This affinity shows us that essentially politics everywhere means a rational form of exploitation of the irrational deep level of the masses: all propaganda methods, all the arts of welding crowds together and influencing their thought by suggestion, draw upon this fact. A game is being played with the emotions of individuals, with the memories of peoples that are to be molded into one uniform collectivity—a process which, as we know, has been crowned with exemplary success in some cases. The phenomenon's limits are unknown, and it is this that constitutes its historical novelty.

But what is newer still is the transformation in the ways of looking at the crowd. Crowds have always been spoken of, from ancient Rome to the Crusades, from religious processions to English risings to gatherings in marketplaces. They have been described as a blind and uncontrollable force, a hydra with a thousand terrible or wonderful heads. The crowd is supposed capable of overcoming all obstacles, moving mountains, or destroying the work of centuries. But it is only in the modern world that crowds have freely and triumphantly come into their own, among institutions, religions, and traditions that are dwindling and disappearing. To govern them from outside by some time-honored means is impossible. Viewed like this, the various masses appear nakedly as a quasi-physical and indeed the only form of collective life: hence the currency of expressions such as "mass society." At the same time, with work manifestly taking on an abstract, general form in thousands of factories, the masses are appearing in an abstract, general form in thousands of cities in Europe, Africa, and Asia. The extraordinary overlapping of numerous kinds of crowds focuses and keeps our attention on one single being: its regularity and its constant structures are of the kind that make a phenomenon the object of fantasy and mediation. It also has something of that aura of mystery in which we feel we have recognized a little of the explanation of human nature. Today we tend to forget or reject it, as if in the age of the masses we were rid of it—but this is a mistake which may cost our generation as dearly as the previous generation, and maybe even more.

II. Finding a Way of Looking

Of writings by authors who have not been satisfied with talking about this mystery but have tried to get to the bottom of it, Canetti's are among the most fascinating.[1] Constantly we find ourselves being drawn back to them, and for a long time to come their magnetic attraction will continue to be felt. It goes without saying that his work occupies a unique position, simply because it is the only one to deal with crowds and ways of looking at crowds. His work illuminates the phenomenon in all its novelty, as a painter or sculptor might do. What in fact Canetti succeeds in—by means of a series of analyses and aphorisms, a construct of examples—is a demonstration of the triumphant presence of the crowd in the life of each one of us. Everything that is put into words in Crowds and Power can doubtless be treated as a theory, but its essence consists in a vision of the forms of collective life, communicated by the seer. It goes far beyond reason, and beyond language too. This is the way artists go to work, churning up the dark bottommost layers and giving a way of seeing to an era. So it is scarcely amazing that he embraces the whole of Western civilization, and that his track can be followed passing through everything that is typical of this civilization, like a musical motif: for everywhere that civilization is to be found, what impresses us is not so much industries, skyscrapers, or television but the genesis of new masses—and the genesis of new power, personified in venerable or charismatic leaders whose calling requires them to unite men around one world view and re-create firm communal bonds.

But let us return to the work which interests us now and consider it more closely. In its vitality and extent, the phenomenon of the masses caught most practicians and scholarly theoreticians unprepared: for some it is a sign of madness or confusion, for others a temporary deviation, an accident on history's production line—all of them basically ignore it. It is seen primarily as a modern means of defending the social order against revolution, under one man's leadership—though, on the other hand, by acting under the leadership of a party the masses can introduce a socialist order and complete the revolutionary process.

For sociologists, the masses are the result of the amalgamation of groups, and in this process of amalgamation the bonds of communality and identity are canceled. Individuals turn up again, atomized and scattered, somewhat among the anonymous masses. Hence the insecurity and anxiety of Man, who feels like the ball in a game played by opposed and unknown powers. From the psychologists' point of view, a new science wholly devoted to this burning issue comes into being, crowd psychology, which goes straight for the jugular. How—in Freud's words—can we "solve the puzzle of the masses"? This puzzle is to be found in the spiritual affinity of people when united, an affinity which transforms them and makes them accept without thinking the opinions of their friends, neighbors, or party. More seriously, the people who constitute a crowd are capable—once the crowd has swallowed them up and immersed them in a shared emotion—of excesses of joy or panic, enthusiasm or cruelty. Deeds are done which the conscious mind condemns and which run counter to personal interests. Everything happens as if a collective soul had subjugated the individual soul by wholly transforming Man and making a different being of him.

In attempting to elucidate this metamorphosis, the majority of thinkers from Le Bon to Freud, from Tarde to Reich, have examined the general aspects of the spiritual life of the masses and what is distinctive about it. Their studies make plain to practicians and politicians the meaning of crowds, and these people then put their newly gained knowledge into practice, as I have shown in detail in a recent study.[2] Here it will suffice to say that, at the time when Canetti was observing the flickering twilight of Vienna, crowd psychology was the third epoch-making theory alongside Marxism and psychoanalysis. That at least is the impression we gain from Musil's *The Man Without Qualities* and his related diary.[3] Of course, each one of these theories has gone its own way since then, and has had its influence, for better or worse; but at that time the die had not yet been cast. People were still at each other's throats in their attempts to explain the nature of the masses—literally so, using weapons and terror, once the masses had been transformed and had attained power. What they were, and what effect they have had, is imprinted on the memory of Man: each of us can test it and find once again the image of reality that haunted Canetti's thinking. But that thinking is of a special order since it proceeds from two basic positions. The first of these is that the "puzzle of how crowds are formed" is totally accepted, without the slightest hesitation or reservation. The second consists in a no less radical rejection of the whole of crowd psychology, as if it had never existed and no one had ever written a word about it. True, I am exaggerating, but this is my genuine conviction: as if he were alone in his confrontation of this puzzle, Canetti opts for a fresh start and takes a new path.

Whatever significance we see in (first) the emotions and (next) the powers of the subconscious, collective life means first and foremost contact. In this I am speaking of physical contact, such as arises from the co-presence of individuals in one place. The avoidance of this contact—as if men were potential enemies and constantly ready for attack or defense—is a fundamental fact. Mixed with fear and terror, this aversion familiarly has not an oblique but a direct and immediate effect on our relationships with our own kind. This fear of touch, which Georges Bataille called heterophobia, is inherent in Man. It represents the first and fundamental fact to which Canetti draws our attention, the power we have to overcome if we are to live with each other. In contrast to Freud's claim, the *primum movens* of our behavior is not love (or identification) but rather the very opposite. This view is by no means exaggerated. But how is this fear to be overcome? How, if we start from that fear, are we to create bonds between individuals which have never before existed? Fear must be overcome through the masses, so to speak, and in the masses. In the crowd we are thrust against each other, in spite of our fear and our inhibitions concerning touch. Above all, the crowd activates those energies which threaten to dwindle away, gathers together scattered bodies, and at length sees to it that the individual develops fully within a group. Canetti writes:

It is only in a crowd that man can become free of this fear of being touched. That is the only situation in which the fear changes into its opposite. The crowd he needs is the dense crowd, in which body is pressed to body; a crowd, too, whose psychical constitution is also dense, or compact, so that he no longer notices who it is that presses against him. As soon as a man has surrendered himself to the crowd, he ceases to fear its touch. Ideally, all are equal there; no distinctions count, not even that of sex. The man pressed against him is the same as himself. He feels him as he feels himself. Suddenly it is as though everything were happening in one and the same body.[4]

This passage alone would be worth extensive commentary. We see the (scarcely psychological) sense in which the crowd is a personification or embodiment of the collective. Where does it derive its strength from? What is the operational principle that liberates the body of each individual or, rather, that succeeds in forcing him into a single, shared body? To find that out, let us investigate what crowds themselves are. They can be defined as gatherings or ensembles, which, like organisms or living matter, have the tendency to increase in size and to assimilate everyone in range. These gatherings or ensembles are by their very nature open and thus by definition have no limits. Growth and openness probably engender an area of attraction and of protection. The distance between the different elements decreases as the whole expands. Indeed, this ability to decrease distances, if not to abolish them totally, is one of the laws of this corporeal state. It is expressed in an occurrence Canetti calls the discharge, where distinctions of sex, age, status, and so forth collapse and are replaced by similarity and equality. Canetti writes:

Only together can men free themselves from their burdens of distance; and this, precisely, is what happens in a crowd. During the discharge distinctions are thrown off and all feel *equal*. In that density, where there is scarcely any space between, and body presses against body, each man is as near the other as he is to himself; and an immense feeling of relief ensues. It is for the sake of this blessed moment, when no-one is greater or better than another, that people become a crowd.[5]

The crowd takes as much interest in this pleasure as the individual does, not only because it profits from individual liberation but also—and above all—because this liberation prolongs as far as possible the crowd's togetherness. So it is important for social collectivities to experience pleasurable enjoyment and that that enjoyment be physical. Later there will be disintegration and separation; distinctions and hierarchies will be reinstated in their old importance. For this to happen a point of termination is needed, and institutions to cause that termination; and the crowd has to scatter abruptly like a storm cloud. And the individuals will fall like raindrops to earth, back to their everyday lives.

We arrive at a conception such as this by abiding as faithfully as possible by observed experience. I stressed at the start that this conception has nothing in common with the hypotheses of the psychology or sociology of the masses. Canetti concentrates on a number of real impulses of energy, and sees them clustered about two polarities. One of these contrasts the individual fear of touching with the crowd enjoyment of contact. The other takes as its poles our individual body and our collective body, the crowd—a crowd where we can again find ourselves both as parts of a whole and as distinct individuals.

III. Collective Matter

Time and again we are assured that the individual is of no significance in society or in the universe. Still, physically he takes up more space than is generally acknowledged. For if our body is the matter that surrounds our instincts and our consciousness, then in fact it includes everything we feel: and for that reason it will go on growing. But this body changes and enlarges, sometimes abruptly, in consequence of being discharged into another or amalgamated with it in order to become the shared body of the crowd. This collective body, immense and central, is at all times present, and, more than merely present, it is active. Through it, and only through it, we give continuity to the forms of the animal world, at the same time as we reach out to the other parts of that great body, the universe. Far from being squashed and ground down by the crowd, as is commonly supposed, the individual thus expands within it and is expanded by it. He goes beyond himself, and then returns within himself, transformed: how else can we explain that he so eagerly seeks out the crowd and derives so much pleasure from it?

These few indications show that we are now crossing the frontiers of crowd psychology. We are being led into a kind of anthropogony, if the word may be allowed. Its model and method are not hard to find—both, if I am not mistaken, may be found in Goethe, and particularly in places where the poet is aiming to show the basic archetype in a mass of living forms. With the same composed patience and with happy inspirations, Canetti draws up an archetype of collectivities. This much will serve to emphasize the essentials of the sketch and Canetti's originality. Starting from this point we can reconstruct an entire universe of the masses, just as the universe of stars and galaxies can be construed: just as a cosmologist analyzes and describes the heavenly bodies, so Canetti describes and analyzes social bodies.

Thus, for example, at one extreme there are these crowd crystals, packs, hordes which consist of only a few individuals. A great deal has already been written about the concept of the horde, which Darwin introduced and which Freud gave his own twist to.[6] But it is only Canetti who shows us the full breadth of possible variations of the phenomenon—Canetti, who has researched the abundance of anthropological material that has piled up in the course of a century. On the one hand there are what might be called the life-packs, which get together for the hunt or for increase. On the other hand there are the death-packs, which gather for war or funeral rites. The feeling that characterizes them is one of the necessity of breaking the resistance of the individual and of Nature, in order to reestablish a normal pattern of existence. This feeling would be one of fear rather than pleasure, were it not that it is poised between the two. Communion makes reconciliation and consolation possible; but it also, together with other ceremonies, permits transfers from one pack to another. The thesis can be argued that religions came into existence to ease these conversions and this transferring of collective matter: they owed their rise to the requirements of the crowd and shaped the mentality of the animal Man: "The dynamics of packs," writes Canetti, "and the particular kind of interplay between them, explain the rise of the world religions."[7]

At the other extreme we find crowds in the true sense of the word. Always double, dead and living mixed, they are now visible, now invisible. Crowds can be distinguished according to their emotional climate: stationary crowds (e.g., prohibition crowds) and crowds in motion (e.g., flight crowds or baiting crowds). But in this way we are defining and classifying crowds according to the way we ourselves want to see them. Their genesis and growth seem subject to no law, unless it be the biblical one: "Go forth and multiply." They can be found in every combination, and the combinations are not random: symbols are used to represent them. It is beyond the scope of this essay to summarize the fine pages Canetti has devoted to them. Let us simply note that they have a sensuous and perceptual character based on the elements of fire, water, air, and stone. It is these that shape the precise contours of the human crowd among the material crowd. In a sense they are traces of the collective microcosm inscribed in the natural macrocosm. We are familiar with the realization of this inscription through the shaping of space—for example, by such architectural means as Hitler used, and which he dreamt up on an ever more grandiose scale. Who better equipped to decipher their meaning than the great German writer? "On huge squares," he writes, "so big that they are hard to fill, the crowd has the possibility of growing, it remains open. Its passion, which [Hitler] is especially aiming at, increases with its growth. . . . For the regular *repetition*, he wanted buildings of a cultic nature. Their model is the cathedral."[8]

In this development from microcosm to macrocosm we recognize one of the fundamental metaphors of the Renaissance and of the thinking of Vitalism. It constitutes the axis of this modern anthropogony. If we get to the bottom of this metaphor and think its logic through, we find it has a trajectory which in the past it lacked. I am not concerned here with its philosophical continuation, or the historical inferences Canetti has drawn from it. Let us merely say—though it should be stressed—that they all follow from this view of social corporeality, a view that is reflected in the choice of images and words relating to our senses (seeing, tasting, feeling pain) or our organic functions (eating, drinking, etc.). But there is something else we should not forget either. Analysis of the morphology of the crowd as one social body among other animal and cosmic bodies revolutionizes and refreshes our way of seeing—and in the last analysis it is this that makes Canetti so incomparable.

IV. A Meditation on Death

Man is the only animal that knows he will die. Other living creatures do not escape this end but, even if they intuit it, none of them has certainty and the knowledge of the inevitable.

"It is with death and the fear of death," wrote the philosopher Franz Rosenzweig, "that all perception of the universe begins. To cast off earthly fear, to take from death its sting and from Hades his pestilential breath—that is what philosophy presumes to do." [9]

I can only see in this exploration of crowds and power a meditation on the terrible fact of our death. I read it as an atempt—yet another, we might say—to take from death its sting.

"Death," writes Canetti, "is the first and oldest, one would even be tempted to say: the only fact. It is of a monstrous age and yet new every hour. . . . So long as death exists, any utterance is an utterance against it. So long as death exists, any light is a will-of-the-wisp, for it leads to it. So long as death exists, no beauty is beautiful, no goodness is good." [10]

I have known only one man who spoke with such hopeless vehemence, my friend and fellow countryman Paul Celan, who kept the inevitable rendezvous all too early.

How could we fail to see that the crowd is on the side of

vitality? For all our persecution mania and imagined suffer-
ings, we feel that through the crowd we are again connected
to the roots of the universe. One jostling shove will free the
individual of his fear of being touched, and one pleasurable
sensation will make him a part of the social collectivity. The
life of the Others is there. This means, conversely, that power
is on the side of death. Doubtless Man can dream of escaping
death, can dream that death is not really predestined for him;
but this dream is not enough to diminish his terror of it. What
Man needs is the experience of immunity, or postponement.
And what experience is more powerful than that of the death
of others, particularly the death we inflict on others? Our first
reaction when confronted with its reality is disbelief: so death
really exists, we can see and touch it. Then horror: if people
die, *I* shall die too. Presentiment and Fate are giving me a sig-
nal. Common sense at length prevails: it is not me that died
but the *other* one. Hence the relief and satisfaction, a profound
Schadenfreude: "what was first terror is now imbued with satisfaction." [11]

If body-to-body contact with a living individual frees us of
our fear of being touched in the crowd, body contact with a
lifeless individual frees us of the fear of death. It returns us to
the loneliness and egoism of the survivor. Frequent repetition
of this experience can induce a sense of invulnerability which
places us above the dead of past and of future. We acquire a
taste for survival. Indeed, we want to produce this unusual
sensation ourselves: and how else are we to produce it than
through multiplication of these lifeless bodies?

For the sense of happiness in concrete survival is an intense pleasure.
Once it is admitted and approved of, it will demand repetition and
quickly mount into an insatiable passion. The man possessed with it
will appropriate the forms of social life around him in such a way as
to make them serve this passion. The passion is that of *power*. It is
so closely attached to the fact of death that it strikes us as natural;
we take it for granted, like death, never questioning it, never even
seriously investigating its ramifications and repercussions. [12]

Here the Other is quite plainly Death. To cause him to vanish in the monotonous and cumulative repetition of a premeditated murder makes an ascension possible—but to what peak? To that vanishing point which shows us the one who has been the downfall of all our fellow men, friends and foes. Above and beyond the crowds, surrounded by vast numbers of people who, as the phrase goes, are all prepared to give their lives—for that one who is only waiting to take them. So their idol is nothing other than their destroyer: "the great man swallows them. They literally enter him and vanish. His effect on them is annihilatory. He attracts and collects them, he reduces and devours them. Everything they once were now benefits his own body."[13]

An antisocial body par excellence. Like antimatter, he thrives on the weakness of matter, to be exact: of human matter. he lives on its dying. I have highlighted the paradox here in another place[14]—at the heart and peak of social life is the most antisocial of beings. Fascinated, the masses pour on toward him. Fascinated by what? By the sign of their own death? Let us not forget that power, confronted by these inexhaustible crowds, is condemned to failure. It withdraws from reality and hallucinates what it cannot attain: survival at the expense of all. This is the first step toward madness—a madness documented and described in detail in the memoirs of *Senatspräsident* Schreber. Madness now has the form of pursual of power by other means. Let us agree on one thing: that meditation on death is by its very nature one of these meditations that are without end. Likewise meditation on power, which surprises us at every step by its ability to defy time and the extremes it touches upon.

V. Broch, Canetti, and the Masses

It is not exactly usual to find the selfsame theme simultaneously in literature, in scholarly work, and *(nota bene!)* in history too. The theme of the masses enjoys this dubious distinction. We could take it as one of the central motifs of modern thought and writing, and it is truly regrettable that historians working in this field have not devoted attention to it and shown us its significance. So I should like to conclude with some observations on this subject. It is easy to show that the great French writers from Balzac to Zola, from Flaubert to Maupassant, were those who took a new look at the masses.[15] They were not content to discover the masses and use them as material in their novels; they also provided the theory. With admirable precision they sketched out the larger outlines of what was to become crowd psychology. Crowd psychology has met with a considerable response, above all in German-speaking countries, in all fields, from the social sciences to history, from politics to literature. To check this we need only recall the writings of Mann and Musil, Freud and Weber, Reich and Adorno, to name but a few.

But two writers gave the subject of the crowd a particular place in their work, and indeed made it a leitmotif: one is of course Canetti, and the other Broch. The perceptions of the French novelists antedate and anticipate those of crowd psychology; those of the German-language writers follow crowd psychology and are shaped by it. It is a paradigmatic case of the exchanges between the social sciences and literature. Without going into this point any further, let us note that both Broch and Canetti devoted a theoretical work to the problem of the masses. From description to description, from analysis to analysis, each stated his original conception more precisely. But in each case the central motif is different. While Broch takes his bearings from crowd psychology,[16] Canetti bases his considerations on anthropology and the history of religions. It is true that in so doing he confronts questions his predecessor did not need to confront. This is one of the first points of distinction in their procedures that explains the difference between their ways of seeing. For Broch, the advent of the age of the masses heralds a total collapse of culture. The masses confirm that rule of psychology over politics and economics which Nietzsche proclaimed. They are the sign of that twilight phase a society always enters when it fails to control them. Thus democracy, for example, has still not found any formula comparable to that applied by other political or religious systems. Who can say whether the totalitarian blunders democracy has fetched up in are not the consequences of its inability to deal with mass hysteria?

But Canetti places the masses in wider time perspectives and is out to investigate their forms and evolution. They are a part of the tragedy of *our* era, but that part is lent meaning by what has happened since the beginnings of time. And if a tragedy occurs, its cause is not to be sought in some twilight phase: it is the affinity to power that must be held responsible. Thus each of the two writers, in approaching the same subject, follows his own path: Broch that of crowd psychology, Canetti that of anthropology and history.

As I have said, this is only a first distinction. In order to perceive the second difference we have to bear in mind the more strictly literary work of the two writers. If I am not mistaken, the masses play a significant part in Broch's novels, while Canetti's diary mentions them only in connection with personal experience. Could we venture that the one always holds on tight to an idea and the other to an experience? The specialists can decide. At any rate there is a difference in their way of seeing. If we read through the hundreds of pages where Broch formulates his, and presents the life of the masses to us, we find the word "daemonic" springing to mind: this word, once Goethe's, defines that side of human nature which is revealed and symbolized by the masses.[17] They appear in the twilight of reason: to be exact, at the moment when the inner and outer powers of Man are crashing down upon him and obscuring his consciousness. Thus they uncover the relentless rule of chaos to which, because of the laws of entropy, everything that exists must tend. Still, for us living beings entropy is only another name for death. And the struggle fought against it thus becomes one with the struggle fought against fear by the crowd and by the individual. This is Broch's poetic rendering:

Was not human activity, however and wherever it went on, invariably revealed as issuing from an animal fear, as the obsessed busyness of fear, from whose gloomy dungeon there is no breaking out or escaping, since it is the fear of a creature lost in the woods? He had become aware of this fear more profoundly than ever before, he understood better than ever the unstillable wish of the lost soul for a conquest of time that would annul death, better than ever he understood the unquenchable hope of the animal masses, he understood what they too, all of them down there, voices upon voices, were desiring in their wild, desperate noise.[18]

These are masses willful in the face of any reality, placing their hopes and their "rabblish fervor" in the leader or caesar who, they believe, can pull them out of the whirlpool of fear.

These are only general observations. Do they, through the contrast, enable us to grasp how Canetti's vision approaches the matter differently and from an alternative angle? At all events it seems to me that the crowd stands for the *cosmic* side of human life. Crowds express the visible side of social animality, through their most earthly and elemental aspect: their bodies. It is not too much to assert that there is something Pre-Socratic in Canetti's way of seeing and in his guiding conception. Psychology has been absorbed into and limited by this morphology of social collectivities, which came into being alongside the doctrines of psychology and evolved beside it; but it has been absorbed within certain basic types, which develop spatially and include time within them. What has flowed into the inmost depths of these collective bodies is a vital current of life which is forever reaching beyond them to win other people too. Crowds on which every one of these types imposes its distinct mark. Crowds into which every individual is accepted for his own sake and on his own merits, with the effect that through and for that individual other people will make their bodies available to communal contact and communal bonds. It is not my intention to make a comparative study of the two writers. Let us simply say that, fascinated by the same human reality, Broch and Canetti have focused our preception of it too: the former by illuminating its daemonic side, the latter by revealing its cosmic side. It may perhaps be claimed that they are the same thing.

NOTES

1. The time he spent on it is a further confirmation of his earnest dedication. In this respect too, Canetti is unique. I assume that his biographers will give full attention to the basic experience of the individual's confrontation of the crowd, which his diary so precisely describes. The impression this made is undoubtedly related to the time span Canetti allotted to studying the problem of the crowd. Furthermore, I believe that those who dealt with this problem before him had perhaps not had a similar experience and may indeed have done their best to avoid it. This no doubt explains the circuitous route by which the great German writer approached the subject, and his originality.

2. Serge Moscovici, *L'Age des Foules,* Paris, 1981. In German translation as *Das Zeitalter der Massen,* Munich and Vienna, 1984.

3. Cf. also the following passage in Jaspers: "Because Marxism, psychoanalysis, and crowd theory have singularly destructive properties. Just as Marxism supposes it can expose all spirituality as merely so much superstructure, psychoanalysis imagines it can explain it away as the sublimation of repressed drives; what then remains to be labeled culture is constructed like a theory of compulsion. Crowd theory leads to a conception of history that is without hope." K. Jaspers, *Die geistige Situation der Zeit,* Berlin and Leipzig, 1933, p. 143.

4. Elias Canetti, *Crowds and Power* (translated by Carol Stewart), London, 1962, pp. 15–16.

5. Ibid., p. 18.

6. Cf. S. Freud. *Crowd Psychology and the Analysis of the Ego.*

7. *Crowds and Power,* p. 128.

8. Elias Canetti, *The Conscience of Words* (translated by Joachim Neugroschel), New York, 1979, p. 147.

9. F. Rosenzweig. *Der Stern der Erlösung,* The Hague, 1976, p. 5.

10. *The Conscience of Words,* pp. 6–7.

11. Ibid., p. 15.

12. Ibid., pp. 19–20.

13. Ibid., p. 27.

14. Serge Moscovici, "Les Foules devant la Foule," *Stanford French Review,* September 1983, pp. 151–74.
15. Ibid.
16. Hermann Broch, *Massenwahntheorie,* Frankfurt, 1979.
17. A. Kiel, "De romans van Hermann Broch en zijn massawaantheorie," *Mens en Kosmos,* 1962 (18), pp. 58–76.
18. Hermann Broch, *Der Tod des Vergil,* Frankfurt, 1976, pp. 86–87.

Franz Schuh

The Writer as Model and Rival

Killing in order to survive is meaningless to such a man, for it is not now that he wants to survive. It is only in a hundred years that he will enter the lists, when he is no longer alive and thus cannot kill. Then it will be a question of work contending against work, with nothing that he himself can do. The true rivalry, the one that matters, begins when the rivals are no longer there. Thus they cannot even watch the fight. But the work must be there, and, if it is to be there, it must contain the greatest and purest measure of life. Not only does he abjure killing, but he takes with him into immortality all who were alive with him here, and it is then that all these, the least as well as the greatest, are most truly alive. . . . Thus the dead offer themselves as food to the living; their immortality profits them. It is a reversal of sacrifice to the dead, which profits both dead and living. There is no more rancour between them and the sting has been taken from survival.[1]

It is difficult to write about a writer one agrees with. One cannot achieve that distance seen from which he becomes simply a subject. It is the very sense of agreement that renders any other understanding problematic. One would like only to quote the writer, and to quote him triumphantly, for quotation is generally the attempt to place oneself on the same level, so as to be seen up there by everyone, by the audience: while in reality one is obsessed with his example, one would like to show how fully one has appropriated it.

The model usually does not much care for this; if model and imitator remain too close, the latter robs the former of his effect, and supposedly it is emulators that drive out originals, for the simple reason that copies can take their bearings from external, popular effects while originals must needs keep a close grip on the intractable raw material.

But if there is already too great a distance between original and imitator, the originator will perceive himself in the imitator not only without envy but even with pity; for the follower embodies the agonized throes of the model, indeed is nothing but that very model, and yet is immobile, frozen, barren, and with no future of his own. Nonetheless, no one has taught us more than Canetti about the impossibility of literature without models.

The technique of working without models—which I take the inflexible, loveless use of models in day-to-day commercial life to be a part of, this art that casts society from the womb onto the market—cannot create any tradition. Yet tradition is not an empty, lip-served continuity over longer periods, but rather is something instituted by the dependent, through their attachment to models. This attachment is the human dimension of tradition, and remains distinct from the propagandist traditionalism of the suprahuman ethic we see in the great communal feeling of packs and crowds, states and nations.

For while these last need an enemy in order to achieve their full potential, models owe their tradition-forming power to a kind of love. Like any kind of love (which for some may never be more than a species of jealousy or competitiveness), this kind too is complicated. Love of a model, if it is truly to develop, already includes infidelity: as I have said, the model is only the mirror in which one would like to see oneself, yet from which one has only just learned to see for oneself. One day, once one has recognized this, one sees in the model the Other and no longer oneself, and then one must be rid of the model, one has to destroy it.

Overdependent love, and that deliberate destruction which proceeds from self-awareness, both generate that kind of intensity which keeps a tradition alive. The cults of the dead in which great empires celebrate their own permanence are as little concerned with life as is the traditionalism of a societal culture worshipped but not loved, a culture which does not even inspire imitation but only a passively uplifting enjoyment. It is that culture too that produces the curious power-figure of the conductor, which Canetti has described in *Earwitness* and in *Crowds and Power:* "Every detail of his public behaviour throws light on the nature of power."[2]

Power, in art too, is founded on death, and we do not know where death really begins or if there are not in fact certain forms of seeming life where death is in fact more insidious than in the simple, irreversible forms of the clinical condition: once art is dead, it can be conducted, and perhaps the conductor kills it, in order to survive, powerfully and visibly, at its grave. As the murderer he states hypocritically that he is serving his victim, and he is believed, by an audience for which art is not a model but which in fact needs the conductor —as actors need a director—in order to be shielded from real life.

In society, others who do things similar to what one does oneself appear as competition if they do not take one as a model. The hatred and the uninspired curses ("aphorism-peddler for the times," "mini-Kant," and "pocket Schopenhauer") which Canetti provoked in a popular artist are curious—even when he has palpably been hit, the artist is unable to go beyond the orbit of his make-believe word-power. The bitcher bitches (and there is nothing more agreeable than defending one's pet writer against a base critic); and the only function of the names he thinks up is to confirm his empty identity as a bitcher.

While, however, one can adopt a simple antithetical position toward one's competitors and enemies in the intellectual marketplace, one's models both demand and make possible a more complex attitude. Evidently they are not preserved in all their vitality if they are done away with the moment one has one's independence. The models need to survive, if tradition is not to perish at that very point where it begins. The writer is not merely someone who writes, he is not simply somebody or other, some director or conductor—he is constantly dependent on his vitality, that is to say, a strength within him which integrates even negation into productivity. This was the point where Canetti turned away from his model Karl Kraus: Kraus (Canetti felt) was no longer capable of harnessing negation productively, and all he could create was a wall of verdicts on either side of which nothing but deserts could exist: "I believe it was an uneasy feeling about the nature of this wall and the bleak view of the desert on either side that gradually made me rebel against Kraus. For the ashlars he built with were judgements, and everything that had lived in the surrounding landscape went into them."[3]

Tradition is that place where the immortality of works is preserved, where survival has lost its sting, and the rancor of rivalry is at an end: tradition is not some temple of the worshipped, but neither is it a wilderness strewn with the tumbled ruins of models. Mere negation of love, which leaves nothing behind but its death and the accusation that it was always deadly, is the wall behind which most people, not only writers, manage to come to terms with their lost idols.

The writer who upholds the vitality of tradition has the power productively to integrate his tumbled idols into his own work. His models are still there for him but they have had to forfeit their tyrannical character. Now they have a free rein without getting in the author's way; and yet, without their doing a thing, they have changed. The author has formed them anew; through his break with them he has become their equal and now, for that very reason, himself embodies tradition, because through his independence he departs from it.

This departure in turn gives back to his models their autonomy—unthinkable, as long as the author is an enthusiastic adherent. At worst adherence ends in its opposite, in rejection, in hostile opposition, in smashing the mirror which, in showing the Other, only reflects the image of one's own discontent—the very thing one does not want to see there.

This dialectic of models, of toppling and reconciliation, may cover some chronological distance in a life story, but in the principle of artistic production it always remains the same. Long before his two essays on Kraus (in which the toppling and reconciliation appear as distance and closeness to the idol), Canetti had played his own game with Kraus's figures. In *The Last Days of Mankind* (which incidentally is the first play to deal with those crowds that are now universal enough to cause a world war, though today—progress!—they would no longer be needed for a war) we meet one of those intellectuals who explain and obfuscate at once, who without much ado declare to a lady, as they stroll across the stage, that they quite accept terrible warlike acts—acts that give the lie to the harmless small-talk tone of their conversation. Theirs is a typical tone, a bastard offshoot of language and tendentiousness, as indeed all public speaking is—in private places it takes on an abridged form, but it is all the more pretentious.

Such an intellectual reappears in the *Comedy of Vanity*. Here he is explaining to a lady the historical importance of the ban on mirrors, and why the ban is necessary in order to oppose the feminization of civilization all the more resolutely. This sophisticated lady certainly perceives male intentions; but as she shares these intentions, or a mirror image of them, she agrees, for reasons of self-love and eroticism, even to a political strategy that does not match her own instincts in any way. She has to share the man's megalomania, and act as mirror for this man who advocates the ban on mirrors: "Really, my fiancé knows everything. . . . My fiancé knows everything."[4]

While Canetti's *Comedy of Vanity* is acted out in the writer's nowhereland, however, the dramaturgy of *The Last Days of Mankind* transcends its own realism by virtue of that very realism: the unbelievable and transcendent come into existence because the people onstage say nothing other than what people say in real life, during a real war—and thus the real war is re-created, and happens once again, in Karl Kraus's theater of war. In Canetti, the characters are immediately seen to be acting in a realm of pure imagination: they represent reality through the very fact that their artificial world blots out the real. It is a matter of phrase and voice, as it is with Kraus too, but Canetti's "acoustic masks" are reductions or distillations of what (with *Die Fackel* in one's ear) one hears in life. While in Kraus the noise of the real crowd can still be heard in the dialectical, pamphletlike scene with the nitpicker and the optimist, and indeed gives that dialogue its meaning, Canetti's voices are, as it were, on their own. This solitariness gives them an uncanny quality and removes them from the conventions of any real or possible action. In fact, it is uncanny that they are speaking at all, albeit that that is the first and most normal thing one expects of voices. The characters in *Comedy of Vanity* have a paradoxical existence, not the existence of ghosts, but (like myth-figures) an existence which, in its contextual parameters, strikes the enlightened mind as impossible. In this cleared space of autonomous imagination, the voices echo and resound; this mirrorlike distance from reality is the sounding board which transforms them into recognizability. It is as if a film were being shown in the making of which it had been forgotten to record an original sound track—and yet the voices have created their own sound track, one that is surprising and has never been heard before.

The "original sound track" lays bare the artificiality of cinema procedures: a conversation has a "natural" effect only on account of the accompanying sounds and noises that in reality one scarcely registers consciously. These have to be fitted to the speaker in the film, usually by methods quite independent of the dialogue itself: the original sound track is grafted onto the film because the voices would otherwise remain lifeless and the conversation would seem to be emerging from nowhere, from an acoustically screened-off, uninhabited void. This curious silence that voices emerge from exists in Canetti's comedy too, but there it cannot be created or edited out by technical means, but rather is the result of the dramatic efforts of people whose speech has been fragmented into commonplaces. "The commonplace," says Kraus, "is a starched shirt worn over a normal set of attitudes that are never changed."[5] And in Canetti's *Comedy of Vanity* one character, who is conceivable as the distillation of Hofrat Schwarz-Gelber in *The Last Days of Mankind,* says, "I am speechless. I don't have a mind to anything."

This is the very essence of normal attitudes, and their apposite expression. Both are harshly illuminated by the constant repetition of the statement: it symbolizes the unchanging of these attitudes, and it is strange that one can observe with so much pleasure the reduction in this way of a character to its stock of commonplaces. This reduction rests on a satirical procedure which mercilessly limits the character's demands of life: the bounds of his stock of commonplaces are now the boundaries of the character's world, the character is imprisoned, and the reader, listener, or audience triumphantly and speechlessly contemplates him from outside.

Commentators, doubtless in order to elevate and praise themselves, have always seen Canetti as a devout humanist and manifest lover of mankind, but the extent of his talent for hatred has been passed over, although he himself does not deny it. There is no doubt that those who do not call human baseness by its name will never get beyond kitsch in art; there are indeed tasks one can perform surpassingly well through knowledge of it. Canetti has the evil eye, no doubt to escape the danger of blinding, but also because it is fun to focus on baseness, and everything one considers base, and satirically do away with it: the doctor who was too familiar with his mother for

Canetti's taste reappears in *The Wedding* as a randy old goat,* seemingly for the sake of revenge on the doctor but also for revenge on his mother, who so willingly and pleasurably put up with so much!

The spiritual dynamics of a satirist rarely derive from those high values in whose name he writes. Canetti's autobiography, whether intentionally or not, also tells the story of a distinctly thorny sensibility. It twists and turns, it loves, even at the age of five it experiences hatred, it struggles, it wounds, it shoves in front, at school it likes putting its hand up, it will draw back the better to get ahead—briefly, it is itself a compound of power, and not a model of sovereign contempt for power.

But if it were otherwise he might find himself barred from his insight into the pedantic inner world of power—pedantic, because power niggles and splits hairs, and creates deformities of detail in its subjects, which in many cases are also its proponents. The characters in *Auto-da-Fé* are miniature versions of this twin aspect of power, regressive and aggressive, but so is Kafka: the Kafka who actually lived is a detailed and doubly effective product of great power, and even as he suffers under it he causes others to feel it. This is an aspect of Kafka to which Canetti could really have devoted closer attention in his study.

"It is very bizarre," says Canetti, "that all thinkers in human history who understand something about de facto power *approve* of it. The thinkers who are *against* power scarcely penetrate its essence."[6] Can we use this against Canetti too? In our culture, understanding always signifies a kind of affirmation, and this is not altered solely by awareness of the process. Even precise knowledge of power is of no assistance in breaking free from it—on the contrary, that knowledge may derive its clarity of vision from the kind of involvement with power

---

* The name of the doctor in the play is in fact Bock, which literally means billy goat but also has popular connotations of randiness. The doctor whose attentions to his mother vexed Canetti appears in *The Tongue Set Free*, p. 84. —*Trans.*

that one might not suppose in an opponent of power, even if he openly acknowledges it.

The peculiar strength of Canetti comes from his having preserved a childlike quality in his relations with matters of the intellect; that is, he does not rob them of their amazing sides, and never gathers them up in comfortable routine groupings, even when analyzing them.

But being childlike has its cruel side too, particularly if it comes from a childhood dominated by jealousy of Mother. Nothing in the world can match love of her, and all the cruelty one receives at her hands can be compensated for by negation, by the rejection of others. Canetti's collection of characters is full of marvels, each one of them impaled like a butterfly by a childlike but clever zoologist's hand; it is magnificent how Canetti listens in on his characters' most intimate use of their pet commonplaces—but it is not unproblematic. He knows this himself: of course he does; he himself wrote, "There is something so despicable about cleverness that one would rather have the wisdom of the fool."[7]

Man is a being subject to metamorphosis. What else is his history, if not one of metamorphosis? Yet this history is paradoxical, for it is a transformation which, insofar as it is a process of civilization, at the same time limits the possibility of transformations. This is the fundamental problem of Man, a problem which, according to Canetti, gives the writer his special identity, as the "keeper of metamorphosis."[8]

The concept of metamorphosis presupposes that of identity; but "identity" is that key point where power takes hold—in the power game of question-and-answer it is identity that clamors for a first definition.[9]

There is good reason to leave identity aside, and this good reason lies in the attempt to elude the grasp of power by oneself becoming a structure that resembles power, a self-canceling bind, everywhere taking hold but difficult to take hold of, indefinite and therefore very difficult to define. What is definable can be grasped, and once you are defined you can also be found—all that is needed is the mere elimination of everything that is not you (and all the places where you are not).

One is caught in this net, and the simplest of admissions is enough to betray one. If one were *indefinite,* constantly another, subject to metamorphosis, the traitor's confession would needs be far more complicated, and indeed he could only practice betrayal with any success if he were an adept at fabricating confessions.

But, on the other hand, merely to elude its grasp, even if this were possible by a voluntary act of will, can achieve nothing of moment against power. Maybe one remains uncaptured in the many shifting shapes of one's metamorphoses; but power itself is still unaffected. One must resist power, but one can do this only if one is visibly its opponent and for that purpose is identifiable: there must be a personification of opposition, one stable human being who is not interchangeable and yet who is forever changing, resisting all definitions, including his own definition of himself as an opponent of power.

Naturally these are "idealistic" notions: in the world we actually live in, everyone collaborates with his own kind of power, even if that means the power of the cultural institutions which have greater experience at masking themselves than those which history has long since unmasked. But the idea of resistance is all too easily deprived of its force by a realism which is familiarly close to kinds of cynicism. The true opportunist, too, is in the last analysis a master of the art of metamorphosis, always eluding the grasp of the powerful in the place they are just launching their offensive because, skillfully anticipating the move, he has already gone over to their side.

Clinging fast to identity, to a resolute, unchanging role of opposition, is not, however, the sign of genuine resistance. This is paralysis, the somatic, absolute identity through which, paradoxically, the crowd gains its power over Kien in *Auto-da-*

Fé: he had set himself against transformations of any kind and persisted in this as long as the world, the woman, indeed the Other, continued to make it possible for him.

But, quite apart from Canetti's ingenious inventions, the weakness of identifiable resistance is clearest at the very moment when it least lacks courage; for power needs opponents in order to be real power. Opponents keep power's hand in and provide its triumphs, and it is through attempts at resistance that one becomes its victim.

Man's cunning consists in hitting upon the balance between identity and metamorphosis appropriate to his historical situation. Granted, the two Kien brothers, one paralyzed in his own identity, the other a virtuoso in the art of metamorphosis, would add up to the "universal" man, taken together. But it would only have been an original synthesis that was universal, not a *post factum* unification of the two.

So perhaps we can say that Canetti's oeuvre constitutes a kind of poetic philosophy of history recording the loss of that balance between identity and metamorphosis in this century. Ours is not a century of the cunning but rather, in its first half, the century of crowds and power; but in spite of that (or in the end *because* of it, perhaps on account of epoch-making invention and spread of photography, among other things) it is the century of vanity. Man, gifted with words, is addicted to identity, and at the same time lusts after power, where power means forbidding mirrors to others. Addiction to identity requires mirrors: only in the mirror do we see ourselves, nothing else so wholly embodies us, we can move in front of the mirror and see what our movements look like, we can talk and hear ourselves in the mirror, only our mirror image gives us pleasure and is truly uplifting. For this reason Man tries to transform everything into his own mirror image, including his neighbor, in whom he sees himself as in a mirror: Barloch collides painfully with Garaus in the street, they look very like each other. But Barloch is poor and ragged, while Garaus, as always, is elegant and well groomed. Garaus is a director, Barloch only a packer. Nonetheless, in the comedy of their vanity they now experience a moment in which social distinctions disappear. In an age when mirrors are banned, this moment is the climax of their craving for identity: they touch each other and recognize themselves. Each considers the other's head and Garaus establishes that they are "identical."

The ban on mirrors makes the Other into a hallucinated mirror image of oneself. Perhaps this too is a way of approaching the unique atmosphere of Canetti's play; in it, as in real life, people are only the mutual projections of each other's desires and needs. The abstract nature of social relations makes us into copied images of realities which, as people with bodies and senses but no material being, we at first master in an agreeably unreal way but then are unable to come to terms with after all. This wrecks the shared identity of Garaus and Barloch. It all comes to naught. Garaus soon realizes that Barloch is one who is "paid off" and who excitably expresses everything to do with this fact, unlike a director, who is not a packer and receives his due as a matter of course. Garaus demands that Barloch return his hat and coat, which he after all gave to himself and not to the Other, who can no longer keep what was promised by Garaus's own need of a mirror image. "I was wrong about you," says Garaus. "It's hard to take. Very painful. I don't know if I shall survive it. But just give me my coat and my hat, will you!"[10]

This is the sweet sentimentality of disillusionment. The world is full of it; it grows apace and consists of thousands of millions of words, and does not appear (as it does in the play) in the glittering costume of its neatest words. Garaus has a total mastery of the dialect of an identity that knows no change. Who can achieve this mastery in reality?

His disillusionment is the quintessential image of all such disappointments as originate in a sudden realization that we have not been mirrored properly. In such cases we always want our hat and coat back. It is our disappointment that now confirms our identity, and to consolidate both our identity and our disappointment we charge with anger our imagined right to have back what we had mistakenly given to the Other and not to ourselves. This anger in turn gives intensity to self-assertion, and, as it is directed against the one we expected our identity of, and as our identity is now derived from our very disappointment, we are bound with a deep intensity to the one we now turn from in disappointment. A relationship of this kind can indeed be deadly: in order to recognize myself once again I have to smash the mirror that does not show me, although I would like to see myself there—and that is dangerous. "I don't know if I shall survive it," says Garaus; but he and Barloch are already living in a world in which emotions have been subdued and dangers are expressed only in hand-me-down phrases that blunt their edges. All the more dangerous if these phrases come up against the reality of death—against war, for example, which can no longer be imagined because of the comfortable muting and quietening of the emotions. But for Barloch and Garaus, who met on the street, it is enough if, after a brief flaring-up of a rage they are basically unfamiliar with, they casually part again.

Since there is a demand for identity it will be supplied. People can place themselves at the disposal of others as mirrors, but this needs organization so that it does not evaporate in a purely private, temporary way. Sociologically speaking, what follows the emphatic destruction of the mirrors is the introduction of hierarchic structures into the possession of forbidden mirrors. This creates a lawless situation which in turn cries out for order, and Frau Fant's mirror-brothel answers the cry: there are luxury cabins, but also third class.

A certain Leda-Föhn-Frisch works in one of the luxury cabins. This name, surely, is the very epitome of psychoanalysis! Psychoanalysis depends on people with such names: Franz Schuh cannot be a psychoanalytical name, and is not even good enough for a patient. Still, there is hope, because the organizations that serve the doctrinal theory are split up among numerous luxury and lower-class cabins. A psychiatrist, who has to put himself into many other lives, needs identity through the one, true organization: in it, one is called Leda-Föhn-Frisch or Leupold-Löwenthal—it is a cult of high-class double-barreled names which lends weight to the doctrine so that no one can assume it is to be taken lightly.

In the *Comedy of Vanity* the doctrine is of course not spelled out by name, but Leda-Föhn-Frisch proceeds in a wholly psychoanalytical way: "You'll see how much I know. Don't hesitate to tell me what's going through your mind, I know everything anyway—whether you say it yourself now or not, all the difference it makes is that we'll get ahead faster." [11]

Analysis is always well aware in advance of the things we plan to confide. It is a transcendental world of experience, with an order of its own that takes precedence over individual worlds, with austerity though also with a touch of blasé boredom. The analyst has no need to listen: from the word go he is already in possession of the necessary information about everything we might be able to tell him. He has already gathered everything beforehand, even including things that will happen to us in the future. He is familiar with the realm of conflicts: he has classified them all and reduced them to the common denominator of the essential, primal conflict: "Just remember, once when you were quite a big boy, you'd done something dreadful, something really terrible, you were afraid of Dad, really you quite often felt full of hatred of Dad, and you went to Mother and laid your head in her lap and told her everything." [12]

In the commercial scheme of things at the mirror-brothel, psychoanalysis is the form of clinical assistance which, as it were, keeps the mental books in order: what is Man?

The answers to this must not take confused forms but must be trim and tidy, so that the widespread demand for an interesting identity may be met with a clear supply. Thus in fact it is to a social skill that neuroses are entrusted, and for that reason this skill is subordinate, in the mirror-brothel, to the rules of the house. The way to Leda-Föhn-Frisch is through the gentlemen's hairdresser—"It's Luxury you'll be wanting"—and she is used as a prop in the sealed-off thought habits of those who look to our wishes and needs in return for money: "Sir is blunt and monosyllabic today, depressed, why not treat yourself to Luxury with Soul? Just try it, see how it goes! A tip-top impeccable lady, elegant, a doctor out of the top drawer, speaks real intellectually. People go in sick and broken and when they come out they're innocent as a newborn babe."[13]

It is easy to tempt Director Garaus with the promise of innocence—Garaus, this figure from out of the old-fashioned showcases of Austrian directors' suites, which after all, for all the domestic power-fuss, are just centers of institutionalized impotence and mummification for characters like Garaus. He killed his wife not long before and is thus in urgent need of therapy. Fortunately, his case coincides very nicely with Leda-Föhn-Frisch's awareness that murderers do not really look like the Garauses of this world, that feelings of being responsible for the death of a spouse occur in a multitude of forms across the spectrum. Garaus, you see, puts up a certain resistance to looking in the mirror, and this shows us his problem right away: the mirror, "archetypal image of all Man's joys,"[14] was broken at some earlier date when his wife was still alive, so that even then he no longer took pleasure in anything, and for that reason he now believes, now that she has really died, that he was to blame for her death: "But it's not like that at all, believe me, everything you're thinking on the subject is wrong—your wife died *first* and *then* the mirror broke."[15] And in a sense this is even true, as Garaus only killed his wife because she dared to bring him his mirror with a crack in it—and doubtless the mirror got smashed along with her.

Since the days of Kraus there has been no more powerful

attack on psychoanalysis. Kraus attacked the elaborate banality of its explicatory system and equally its greedy interventions in matters of art. Any philistine of some education now had a tool at his disposal with which to break open the mysteries of life with ease. What remains is a world brought down to the level of those who interpret it for money, and pyschoanalysis, a procedure which (like liberalism in politics) concedes validity to relationships, human relationships included, only according to the rationalistic criteria of practical business life. At the same time psychoanalysis is a science which provided salon entertainment for the effusive Jewish bourgeoisie Kraus so hated: "Those circles who were at one time under the spell of Heine's poetry have now succumbed to one who knows full well *was soll es bedeuten* * [what it means]." [16]

This is not aimed as much at Freud, though, as at the adherents he attracted. This is true in Canetti's case also. Canetti's Garaus, who undergoes therapy on his hairdresser's advice, makes elegant use of the closed circuit of psychoanalysis: while analysis knows everything about him, it gives him only what he wants from it—his innocence. Behind this there lies not any theatrical trick on Canetti's part, nor even some socio-critical volte-face, but in fact substantial historical experience. When men returned home from war, "they knew what things they had been capable of doing—on orders—and they eagerly grabbed at all the explanations that psychoanalysis offered for homicidal tendencies. . . . It was odd to see how *harmless* everyone became as soon as he got his Oedipus." [17]

Psychoanalysis as a system of excuses—plainly Freud's will to found a science beyond Good and Evil that would be of benefit to mankind is being rendered meaningless in this way. Nevertheless, it may be on account of this one scientific pose and method, still in keeping with the times, that things turn

---

* The phrasing of Kraus's German alludes to the first line of Heine's poem about the Lorelei: *"Ich weiss nicht, was soll es bedeuten."* Heine was, of course, also Jewish. — Trans.

out differently from what we expect: "Myth reaches into a human being, throttling him and rattling him. The 'law of nature,' to which myth is reduced, is nothing more than a little pipe for him to dance to."[18]

Is it understood that *Crowds and Power* is searching for the inner images that seize and shake up human beings so that they can envisage, or be brought to envisage, what it is to break free of civil order? As a theoretical analyst of civilization, Canetti is a rival of Freud: in his *Mass Psychology and the Analysis of the Ego,* Freud did not even acknowledge what was to be Canetti's main thrust, the phenomenon of the crowd as an independent force, an epochal, historical power. As with any rivalry, this one does not lack parallels in the polarities: for example, the Freudian concept of "identification" corresponds inversely to Canetti's "metamorphosis."

But their rivalry is nevertheless one of fundamental principle, and not only because *Crowds and Power* derives its inspiration from that rivalry: "My rejection of Freud came at the start of my work on the book, which I didn't deliver to the public until thirty-five years later, in 1960."[19] Nor does this principle of rejection reside in any chance of refuting Freud's conception of the crowd at first glance: true enough, both church and army are not so much crowds as hierarchies held together by tight structures of command, with the aim of preventing them from leading the dangerous and almost uncontrollable independent life of crowds.

The principle that distinguishes Canetti from Freud resides in a different, opposed understanding of what is known as the "concrete." Admittedly this tends to be overlooked, as Canetti says in "Power and Survival" in *The Conscience of Words;* but this does not necessarily mean that he himself is always sure to see it. Philosophy tells us of the extent to which abstractions (such as money) are thought to be concrete in the world we live in, and it is for this reason that progressive theories, Freud's among them, never appeal to the direct, persuasive powers of what is palpably before us. Rather, they attempt on the one hand to render the concrete systematically abstract, yet on the other hand to free the concrete of its general theoretical trappings. That is to say, the concrete is integrated into the generalized in order to produce a comprehensive theory, but at the same time it is reconstructed out of the general: the concrete is the end product of a complicated procedure which scholars and scientists call a "method."

This does not mean that psychoanalysis fails to perceive the weight of the experiential moment: Freud himself knew that moment on which Canetti based his theory of survival as the innermost core of power. For the analyst too, culture originated "by the corpse of the beloved person"— to be exact, in its most important commandment, "Thou shalt not kill"—and this commandment in turn proceeds from a state of mind that is distinct from but not unlike that of the triumphant survivor in Canetti: "It had been won," wrote Freud, "as a reaction to the sense of satisfied hatred of the beloved deceased which was concealed behind the mourning."[20]

Whatever value novelty may have, Canetti's concept of the survivor is in any case not a new theory. In Hegel's *Phenomenology*, for example, it plays a central part, albeit in different forms—there, the two abstracted forms of self-awareness can only attain concretion if one survives the death of the other. As this, however, would bring the spirit's process of becoming to a standstill, the spirit has recourse to trickery, and has one self-awareness subject itself to the other: in this way, true enough, the bloodbath is at an end, but humanity emerges from the innocence of a natural violence into the social nexus of master and servant.

The writer is the keeper of myths, and thus he will not express himself in philosophical parables or in scholarly systems. *Crowds and Power* is a tale told in images. The images are as clearly pictorial and eloquent as those on tarot cards, and each one can be considered independently, its meaning deepened by mediation. Abstractions are assuredly not null and void, but, since they have been produced by experts and have thus themselves evolved from the painful modern process of separation and alienation, they too are infected with the ailments which they are offered as therapy for. Yet there has to be some form of knowledge where Man expresses himself in concrete and whole terms, a kind of memory geared to the future, one which still narrates and is not merely constructed—experiences that are not science and equally are not its polemically irrational opposite—some knowledge that is at once expressive, poetic, and analytic.

It is not certain that knowledge of this order still exists at all. It may be that even conceiving of it is one of those gestures of escape with which today we so often console ourselves for the fact that in reality everything is quite different—mercilessly so, and without any way out that might be different from the ways we must otherwise go. Canetti's vivid art admittedly includes many of those symbols that have seized and shaken human beings, but the book itself has not taken hold of anyone as an irrefutable myth. That is not the book's fault but the fault of history, which is in part its subject and where, not by chance, poesy and science have been separated. In the age of the Bomb, abstraction, even the highly precise abstraction of mathematics, doubtless contains more of the world than the excited, pseudo-concrete chatter of institutionalized art. But the fact remains that Man does not live in the abstract, and the images he lives by, because they bring the world alive for him, are as much with him still as death, which allows him to survive others until he himself at last falls victim to it. The sin of psychoanalysis was that, like all sciences, it made general what was individual; and for Canetti it may have been particularly bad that this generalization was formulated under one mythic name, that of Oedipus.

However, Canetti's autobiography confirms, in a paradoxically vexatious way, what he normally denies. The strange thing about his life story, where everything is related to a meaning as if there had never been a wasted moment in his life, is that it reveals a curious interweaving. This begins with the strangely intimate circumstances in which Canetti learned the language that has been most important for him, German, the language his parents used to each other. The child Canetti felt excluded, and learning German was his most urgent concern. After his mother returned from a stay at a spa, Canetti's father died, perhaps not of jealousy, though he was certainly jealous. While his father was alive, his mother had meant little to the boy, but after his father's death she became the object of passionate jealousy. Canetti finally learned German in three months: his mother read out sentences and, if he repeated them wrongly, mocked him. Canetti feared nothing more than his mother's derision, and after initial failure by the oral method he suddenly learned the German sentences by writing them. It was writing that first enabled him to match his mother: "the language of our love—and what a love it was!—became German."[21]

So German was Canetti's mother tongue, not in any symbolic sense but quite literally: he tells us of this in a book entitled *The Tongue Set Free*. German was likewise the language in and through which he became a writer. But he could only become a writer after he had broken loose of his mother, for she wanted him to be a chemist, a good bourgeois citizen. So Canetti sought out an ally against his mother—a father, as it were—and of course he had to be a writer; and he hit upon Karl Kraus. In Kraus's lectures he got to know Veza, and again the definition he attaches to their love is linguistic: "Our sentences entwined like hair, the embraces of our words went on for hours and hours."[22]

Is this not indeed a family novel with a classic cast—an oedipal ensemble fit for Leda-Föhn-Frisch—and don't we know for certain that inevitably there will be jealousy of the man at whose lectures Veza sat in the front row? "I was jealous of the god I was possessed of."[23]

It looks as if either a truth is being confirmed here, unnoticed and unintentionally, or the writer, in this veritably pedantic parody of psychoanalysis, is defiantly out to prove that he remains the Other, given to metamorphosis, even if all the doctrinal generalities fit him too.

NOTES

1. Elias Canetti, *Crowds and Power* (translated by Carol Stewart), London, 1962, p. 278.
2. Ibid., p. 394.
3. Elias Canetti, *The Conscience of Words* (translated by Joachim Neugroschel), New York, 1979, p. 36.
4. Elias Canetti, *Dramen*, p. 121.
5. Karl Kraus, *Beim Wort genommen*, p. 224.
6. *The Conscience of Words*, p. 172.
7. Elias Canetti, *Die Provinz des Menschen*, p. 154.
8. *The Conscience of Words*, p. 240.
9. Cf. *Crowds and Power*, pp. 169 ff.
10. *Dramen*, p. 153.
11. Ibid., p. 178.
12. Ibid.
13. Ibid., p. 175.
14. Ibid., p. 180.
15. Ibid.
16. Karl Kraus, *Die Fackel*, 588–94 (March 1922), pp. 41 ff.
17. Elias Canetti, *The Torch in My Ear* (translated by Joachim Neugroschel), New York, 1982, p. 121.
18. Ibid.
19. Ibid., p. 149.
20. Freud, *Studienausgabe*, vol. 9, Frankfurt, 1982, p. 55.
21. Elias Canetti, *The Tongue Set Free* (translated by Joachim Neugroschel), New York, 1979 and 1983, p. 70.
22. *The Torch in My Ear*, p. 187.
23. Ibid., p. 126.

Salman Rushdie

"The Worm of Learning Turns, Swallows Its Tail, and Bites Itself in Half"

I embark on this talk in two minds about whether I'm doing the right thing. For fifteen years Elias Canetti has been a secret pleasure of mine; do I really want to share him with the world, or even with that small but exquisitely formed part of the world that listens to talks on Radio 3? I'm afraid I have always had a penchant for esotericism, and have unworthily rejoiced in the stealthy company of writers of whom most of my friends have never heard: Grimmelshausen, Machado de Assis, and, until recently, Elias Canetti.

So, when I heard that Dr. Canetti had been awarded the Nobel Prize for Literature, I felt much as I had done when, some years ago, the gnomic fictions of Borges—for so long, as it seemed to me, my own private property—became common property virtually overnight. It was almost offensive to hear other people—strangers!—discussing Funes the Memorious, and Red Scharlach, and Martin Fierro, and various other close personal friends of Borges and myself, as though these prized characters were also intimately known to them. Now, I suppose, the same thing is about to happen to Peter Kien, the mad sinologist, and Therese, his housekeeper, she of the terrifying starched skirt, and Benedikt Pfaff, the evil house porter, and Mr. Brute, the seductive furniture salesman who works for the firm of Gross and Mother, and Fischerle, the chess-playing dwarf. The Swedish Academy has, in my opinion, much to answer for.

Elias Canetti is a one-novel writer. This is usually a condescending term, but when that one novel is *Auto-da-Fé* only a fool would dare to condescend. I was just nineteen when I first read it, and already harbored fantasies of being a novelist. At that time, a girl I knew was wandering in the cold labyrinths of the French *nouveau roman,* and I felt obliged to keep her company. So I read Alain Robbe-Grillet, and Nathalie Sarraute, and Marguerite Duras, whose books were so frigid as to convince me that the novel really was dead, and that these were the corpses.

I have now forgotten how it was that I first got hold of *Auto-da-Fé,* but if there is somebody who remembers introducing me to it, I'd like to thank him or her for rescuing me from those arctic experimental wastes. Reading it then, filled with all the ambition and arrogance of my nineteen years, I not only felt that there was life in the old form yet, but that I had learned something about how I wanted to write. I decided that all I had to do was—like Canetti—to combine vast erudition and awesome intricacies of structure with a sort of glittering, beady comic eye and of course, like *Auto-da-Fé,* my books would remain marvelously accessible as well. (To one whose mind had recently been numbed by *Finnegans Wake,* it was a joy to learn that great modern novels could actually be easy to read!) . . . But I was young, which may permit you (not to mention Canetti) to forgive this piece of teenage presumption.

Elias Canetti was born in Bulgaria in 1905, but his mother tongue, exotically enough, was seventeenth-century Castillian Spanish. He grew up to be a polyglot, but has always written in German, the language of Robert Musil, Alfred Döblin, and Thomas Mann, whom I mention because *The Man Without Qualities, Berlin-Alexanderplatz,* and the *Confessions of Felix Krull* are the only books with which I can compare this otherwise incomparable story. What *Auto-da-Fé* shares with these three great novels is an irony that at first seems simply deadpan and ends up being utterly deadly. This quality—which, it now occurs to me, is also present in the stories of Kleist—may be the German language's greatest gift to world literature.

Canetti has also written plays, travel books, literary essays, and a study of group mentality called *Crowds and Power,* which is perhaps best compared to something like James Frazer's *The Golden Bough.* I am aware that this is a slightly two-edged comparison; but *Crowds and Power* displays the same kind of voluminous learning as Frazer's book, and, again like Frazer, Canetti employs methods which now seem somewhat old-fashioned; so I think the analogy is pretty fair.

More recently, he has published two volumes of autobiography. This autobiography was one of the two works singled out for special mention in the Nobel Prize citation. The other was *Auto-da-Fé.*

Canetti has a house in Hampstead. Its doorbell doesn't work. Apparently it once did, but it went wrong in about 1960 and he decided not to bother to have it fixed. This is clearly a man who values his privacy.

Inside this house, I'm told, is to be found a library of staggering proportions; books rising in Himalayan splendor from floor to ceiling, books occupying every available inch of wall space, a babel of books. Canetti has donated both his sense of privacy and his priceless library to the central character of *Auto-da-Fé.* The world-famous sinologist Peter Kien is described as a man who always looks the other way whenever anyone passes him on the stairs. The first part of *Auto-da-Fé* is titled "A Head Without a World" and describes Peter Kien perfectly. Kien, who loves his library, appears to loathe just about the entire human race. His passion for books, Canetti tells us, "is the only one which he had permitted himself during a life of austere and exacting study."

So is Peter Kien really Elias Canetti in disguise? It would be easy to think so. Easy, that is, until you read the book. Then you discover that Kien is a character containing a kind of warning—a warning, in fact, precisely against the solipsistic bookishness which, in the case of Kien, degenerates into insanity. It is a mark of Canetti's objectivity as a writer that he has been able to detach himself so expertly from his bookworm hero.

This detachment is what, to my mind, makes the book work. Without it—if, that is to say, the book had been on Peter Kien's side—it would have been little more than an elitist tract about a man of high intellect and refined sensibilities brought down by the brutish philistinism of the lower orders of society. But in *Auto-da-Fé* no one is spared. Professor and furniture salesman, doctor, housekeeper, and thief all get it in the neck. The remorseless quality of the comedy builds one of the most terrifying literary worlds of the century.

It is also a prophetic world. *Auto-da-Fé*, under its original German title, *Die Blendung*, was completed in the early thirties. Yet its analysis of the wellsprings of Fascism, and its central image of burning books, is all too exact. There are moments in every writer's life when he finds that what he created as fantasy is nó less than the literal truth; and the nightmare of Elias Canetti ended up as the world's bad dream.

The title, of course, refers to the bookburnings carried out by the Spanish Inquisition. And in case anyone thinks that Canetti might be flogging a dead horse, it's worth pointing out that the urge to burn books has by no means vanished from the minds of our masters. Only last month, in Indonesia, the powers-that-be built a bonfire out of no fewer than 10,000 copies of the novels of the country's most renowned living writer, Pramoedya Ananta Toer, who has been spoken of as a possible

Nobel laureate himself. And, nearer home, proving you don't even have to be a government to behave like this, the Moral Majority movement in America has put the works of such intolerable subversives as William Shakespeare and Mark Twain to the stake in the very recent past. And Kurt Vonnegut's *Slaughterhouse Five,* itself a novel about fire, the fire-bombing of Dresden, was burned in the furnace of an American school on the instructions of the school's committee. As Bertolt Brecht said, at the end of his parable about Hitler, *The Resistible Rise of Arturo Ui,* "The bitch that bore him is in heat again."

It was yet another German, Heinrich Heine, who said that "he who burns books burns people," and in a way it is this proposition that Canetti takes to its extreme and renders grotesquely comical. For Peter Kien, books actually *are* people. He talks to them and even asks their advice. It is this little peculiarity of his that gives us our first clue that all is not as it should be within that noble cranium; as he chats to his books, more intimately than he could ever bring himself to converse with a mere human being, we hear the first fluttering of bats' wings in his belfry. By the end of the novel, the said bats are swarming out of his ears. When the books burn, he hears them scream.

When I reread *Auto-da-Fé* recently, the paradoxical nature of its method was what stuck me most forcefully. Kien is a bookman made mad by books; and the novel is an even stranger paradox: a consummately erudite warning against the perils of erudition. The erudition is genuinely awe-inspiring. Canetti appears to be almost as great an expert on ancient China as his hero; he also seems to know everything about everything else. But toward the end of the novel, in a long argument between Kien and his brother George, this overpowering learning is turned against itself. Peter and George argue in long diatribes during which everyone from Confucius to Clytemnestra makes a guest appearance; but the debate reveals them both to be almost totally ignorant of human nature—little more, in fact, than fools. The worm of learning turns, swallows its tail, and bites itself in half.

The novel, on rereading, changed in other ways as well. One of its most interesting new ideas was that other people are fictions we invent. In *Auto-da-Fé* more or less every character is completely misunderstood by at least one other character. Everyone in it sees in everyone else the people they wish them to be, not the people they actually are. Peter Kien marries his housekeeper because he persuades himself she loves his books; Therese, the housekeeper, marries Kien because she thinks he is a millionaire. She then falls in love with Mr. Brute, the furniture salesman, because she wants to believe his flirtatious sales talk; she wants to believe herself young. And it gets even worse than this: the characters even misunderstand themselves, inventing for themselves fictional characters even more fictional than the fictions they actually are. Fischerle, the hunchbacked dwarf, sees himself as Dr. Fischer, the World Chess Champion. Actually, he isn't very good at chess, and frequently cheats when he plays, but this minor detail in no way affects his opinion of himself . . . In *Auto-da-Fé*, when people see themselves in mirrors, they usually fail to recognize themselves. The fictions by which they live have become more real than the truth. So real that when Therese reads Peter Kien's will and finds a remarkably small sum mentioned there, she is sure he has made a mistake, and adds a few zeros to the figure until it looks right.

The reason that this notion is so frightening is that it is true. And this new *Auto-da-Fé*, the *Auto-da-Fé* of my thirties rather than my teens, seems to me a very scary book indeed. It is full of terrible things. There is the character of Benedikt Pfaff, the caretaker, for instance, a proto-Nazi monster whose flat boasts, among other notable features, a special peephole eighteen inches above ground level that enables him to spy, unobserved, on the passing world. There is the city's public pawnbroking establishment, whose name, the Theresianum, is an ironic echo

of Kien's persecuting spouse; in this nightmarish place lives—
or so Kien believes—a grotesque hog-man who actually devours books. Terrible things happen: Fischerle is murdered and
his hump is cut off by his wife's brutish lover. And Peter Kien,
possessed by an infinity of named and nameless fears, finally
brings upon himself and his library the thing that has been the
great fear of his days: he sets fire to his apartment and the
auto-da-fé begins.

You may be wondering why I called this book a comedy.
The answer lies in that black, ironic, and perhaps peculiarly
German tone of voice I mentioned earlier, which has the effect
of making us laugh with horror, and laugh louder and more
shrilly as the horror mounts, but to continue to laugh, until
the very last sentence, when the book itself joins in:

When the flames reached him at last, he laughed out loud, louder
than he had ever laughed in all his life.

Finally, one rather odd thing. The original German title of
this book has absolutely nothing to do with fire. *Die Blendung*
means, simply, "The Blinding," and it seems to me that, for
once, translation might actually have improved a title. I'm glad
I never read a book called anything as elliptical as *The Blinding;* I'm glad that by the time it reached me it had acquired
the resounding clarity of the title it really deserved.

I hope I've succeeded in persuading you to rush out and read
Auto-da-Fé. But, if I have, I shall also, like Peter Kien, have
brought upon myself the very thing I feared most: that is, I
shall have aided and abetted the Swedish Academy in their
fiendish campaign to rob me of the private pleasure of having
Elias Canetti all to myself.

Susan Sontag

Mind as Passion

I cannot become modest; too many things burn in me; the old solutions are falling apart; nothing has been done yet with the new ones. So I begin, everywhere at once, as if I had a century ahead of me.

—Canetti, 1943

The speech that Elias Canetti delivered in Vienna on the occasion of Hermann Broch's fiftieth birthday, in November 1936, intrepidly sets out some of Canetti's characteristic themes and is one of the handsomest tributes one writer has ever paid to another. Such a tribute creates the terms of a succession. When Canetti finds in Broch the necessary attributes of a great writer—he is original; he sums up his age; he opposes his age—he is delineating the standards to which he has pledged himself. When he hails Broch for reaching fifty (Canetti was then thirty-one) and calls this just half of what a human life should be, he avows that hatred of death and yearning for longevity that is the signature of his work. When he extols Broch's intellectual insatiability, evoking his vision of some unfettered state of the mind, Canetti attests to equally fervent appetites of his own. And by the magnanimity of his homage Canetti adds one more element to this portrait of the writer as his age's noble adversary: the writer as noble admirer.

His praise of Broch discloses much about the purity of moral position and intransigence Canetti aspires to, and his desire for strong, even overpowering models. Writing in 1965, Canetti evokes the paroxysms of admiration he felt for Karl Kraus in the twenties while a student in Vienna, in order to defend the value for a serious writer of being, at least for a while, in thrall to another's authority: the essay on Kraus is really about the ethics of admiration. He welcomes being challenged by worthy enemies (Canetti counts some "enemies"—Hobbes and Maistre—among his favorite writers); being strengthened by an unattainable, humbling standard. About Kafka, the most insistent of his admirations, he observes: "One turns good when reading him but without being proud of it."

So wholehearted is Canetti's relation to the duty and pleasure of admiring others, so fastidious is his sense of the writer's vocation, that humility—and pride—make him extremely self-involved in a characteristically impersonal way. He is preoccupied with being someone *he* can admire. This is a leading concern in *The Human Province*, Canetti's selection from the notebooks he kept between 1942 and 1972, during most of which time he was preparing and writing his great book *Crowds and Power* (1960). In these jottings Canetti is constantly prodding himself with the example of the great dead, identifying the intellectual necessity of what he undertakes, checking his mental temperature, shuddering with terror as the calendar sheds its leaves.

Other traits go with being a self-confident, generous admirer: fear of not being insolent or ambitious enough, impatience with the merely personal (one sign of a strong personality, as Canetti says, is the love of the impersonal), and aversion of self-pity. In the first volume of his autobiography, *The Tongue Set Free* (1977), what Canetti chooses to tell about his life features those whom he admired, whom he has learned from. Canetti relates with ardor how things worked for, not against, him; his is the story of a liberation: a mind—a language—a tongue "set free" to roam the world.

That world has a complex mental geography. Born in 1905 into a far-flung Sephardic family then quartered in Bulgaria (his father and his paternal grandparents came from Turkey),

Canetti had a childhood rich in displacements. Vienna, where both his parents had gone to school, was the mental capital of all the other places, which included England, where his family moved when Canetti was six; Lausanne and Zurich, where he had some of his schooling; and sojourns in Berlin in the late twenties. It was to Vienna that his mother brought Canetti and his two younger brothers after his father died in Manchester in 1912, and from there that Canetti emigrated in 1938, spending a year in Paris and then moving to London, where he has lived ever since. Only in exile, he has noted, does one realize how much "the world has always been a world of exiles"—a characteristic observation, in that it deprives his plight of some of its particularity.

He has, almost by birthright, the exile writer's easily generalized relation to place: a place is a language. And knowing many languages is a way of claiming many places as one's territory. Family example (his paternal grandfather boasted of knowing seventeen languages), the local medley (in the Danube port city where he was born, Canetti says, one could hear seven or eight languages spoken every day), and the velocity of his childhood all facilitated an avid relation to language. To live was to acquire languages—his were Ladino, Bulgarian, German (the language his parents spoke to each other), English, French—and be "everywhere."

That German became the language of his mind confirms Canetti's placelessness. Pious tributes to Goethe's inspiration written in his notebook while the Luftwaffe's bombs fell on London ("If, despite everything, I should survive, then I owe it to Goethe") attest to that loyalty to German culture which would keep him always a foreigner in England—he has now spent well over half his life there—and which Canetti has the privilege and the burden of understanding, Jew that he is, as the higher cosmopolitanism. He will continue to write in German—"because I am Jewish," he noted in 1944. With this decision, not the one made by most Jewish intellectuals who were refugees from Hitler, Canetti chose to remain unsullied by hatred, a grateful son of German culture who wants to help make it what one can continue to admire. And he has.

Canetti is reputed to be the model for the philosopher figure in several of Iris Murdoch's early novels, such as Mischa Fox in *The Flight from the Enchanter* (dedicated to Canetti), a figure whose audacity and effortless superiority are an enigma to his intimidated friends.* Drawn from the outside, this portrait suggests how exotic Canetti must seem to his English admirers. The artist who is also a polymath (or vice versa), and whose vocation is wisdom, is not a tradition which has a home in English, for all the numbers of bookish exiles from this century's more implacable tyrannies who have lugged their peerless learning, their unabashed projects of greatness, to the more modestly nourished English-speaking islands, large and small, offshore of the European catastrophe.

Portraits drawn from the inside, with or without the poignant inflections of exile, have made familiar the model itinerant intellectual. He (for the type is male, of course) is a Jew, or like a Jew; polycultural, restless, misogynistic; a collector; dedicated to self-transcendence, despising the instincts; weighed down by books and buoyed up by the euphoria of knowledge. His real task is not to exercise his talent for explanation but, by being witness to the age, to set the largest, most *edifying* standards of despair. As a reclusive eccentric, he is one of the great achievements in life and letters of the twentieth century's

---

* "What's odd about him?" he asked.

"Oh, I don't know," said Annette. "He's so—er—"

"I don't find him odd," said Rainborough, after waiting in vain for the epithet. "There's only one thing that's exceptional about Mischa, apart from his eyes, and that's his patience. He always has a hundred schemes on hand, and he's the only man I know who will wait literally for years for even a trivial plan to mature." Rainborough looked at Annette with hostility.

"Is it true that he cries over things he reads in the newspapers?" asked Annette.

"I should think it's most improbable!" said Rainborough. Annette's eyes were very wide . . .

imagination, a genuine hero, in the guise of a martyr. Although portraits of this figure have appeared in every European literature, some of the German ones have notable authority—*Steppenwolf,* certain essays by Walter Benjamin; or a notable bleakness—Canetti's one novel, *Auto-da-Fé,* and, recently, the novels of Thomas Bernhard, *Korrektur (Correction)* and *Der Weltverbesserer (The World Improver).*

Auto-da-Fé—the title in German is *Die Blendung (The Blinding)*—depicts the recluse as a book-besotted naïf who must undergo an epic of humiliation. The tranquilly celibate Professor Kien, a renowned sinologist, is ensconced in his top-floor apartment with his twenty-five thousand books—books on all subjects, feeding a mind of unrelenting avidity. He does not know how horrible life is; will not know until he is separated from his books. Philistinism and mendacity appear in the form of a woman, ever the principle of anti-mind in this mythology of the intellectual: the reclusive scholar in the sky marries his housekeeper, a character as monstrous as any in the paintings of George Grosz or Otto Dix—and is pitched into the world.

Canetti relates that he first conceived *Auto-da-Fé*—he was twenty-four—as one of eight books, the main character of each to be a monomaniac and the whole cycle to be called "The Human Comedy of Madmen." But only the novel about "The bookman" (as Kien was called in early drafts), and not, say, the novels about the religious fanatic, the collector, or the technological visionary, got written. In the guise of a book about a lunatic—that is, as hyperbole—*Auto-da-Fé* purveys familiar clichés about unworldly, easily duped intellectuals and is animated by an exceptionally inventive hatred for women. It is impossible not to regard Kien's derangement as variations on his author's most cherished exaggerations. "The limitation to a particular, as though it were everything, is too despicable," Canetti noted—*The Human Province* is full of such Kien-like avowals. The author of the condescending remarks about women preserved in these notebooks might have enjoyed fabulating the details of Kien's delirious misogyny. And one can't help supposing that some of Canetti's work practices are evoked in the novel's account of a prodigious scholar plying his obsessional trade, afloat in a sea of manias and schemes of orderliness. Indeed, one would be surprised to learn that Canetti doesn't have a large, scholarly, but unspecialized library with the range of Kien's. This sort of library building has nothing to do with the book collecting that Benjamin memorably described, which is a passion for books as material objects (rare books, first editions). It is, rather, the materialization of an obsession whose ideal is to put the books inside one's head; the real library is only a mnemonic system. Thus Canetti has Kien sitting at his desk and composing a learned article without turning a single page of his books, except in his head.

Auto-da-Fé depicts the stages of Kien's madness as three relations of "head" and "world"—Kien secluded with his books as "a head without a world"; adrift in the bestial city, "a headless world"; driven to suicide by "the world in the head." And this was not language suitable only for the mad bookman; Canetti later used it in his notebooks to describe himself, as when he called his life nothing but a desperate attempt to think about everything "so that it comes together in a head and thus becomes one again," affirming the very fantasy he had pilloried in *Auto-da-Fé*.

The heroic avidity thus described in his notebooks is the same goal Canetti had proclaimed at sixteen—"to learn everything"—for which, he relates in *The Tongue Set Free*, his mother denounced him as selfish and irresponsible. To covet, to thirst, to long for—these are passionate but also acquisitive relations to knowledge and truth; Canetti recalls a time when, never without scruples, he "even invented elaborate excuses and rationales for having books." The more immature the avidity, the more radical the fantasies of throwing off the burden of books and learning. *Auto-da-Fé*, which ends with the bookman immolating himself with his books, is the earliest and crudest of these fantasies. Canetti's later writings project more wistful, prudent fantasies of disburdenment. A note from 1951: "His dream: to know everything he knows and yet not know it."

Published in 1935 to praise from Broch, Thomas Mann, and others, *Auto-da-Fé* was Canetti's first book (if one does not count a play he wrote in 1932) and only novel, the product of an enduring taste for hyperbole and a fascination with the grotesque that became in later works more static, considerably less apocalyptic. *Earwitness* (1974) is like an abstract distillation of the novel-cycle about lunatics Canetti conceived when he was in his twenties. This short book consists of rapid sketches of fifty forms of monomania, of "characters" such as the Corpse-Skulker, the Fun Runner, the Narrow-Smeller, the Misspeaker, the Woe Administrator; fifty characters and no plot. The ungainly names suggest an inordinate degree of self-consciousness about literary invention—for Canetti is a writer who endlessly questions, from the vantage of the moralist, the very possibility of making art. "If one knows a lot of people," he had noted years earlier, "it seems almost blasphemous to invent more."

A year after the publication of *Auto-da-Fé*, in his homage to Broch, Canetti cites Broch's stern formula: "Literature is always an impatience on the part of knowledge." But Broch's gifts for patience were rich enough to produce those great, patient novels *The Death of Virgil* and *The Sleepwalkers*, and to inform a grandly speculative intelligence. Canetti worried about what could be done with the novel, which indicates the quality of his own impatience. For Canetti, to think is to insist; he is always offering himself choices, asserting and reasserting his *right* to do what he does. He chose to embark on what he calls a "life work," and disappeared for twenty-five years to hatch that work, publishing nothing after 1938, when he left Vienna (except for a second play), until 1960, when *Crowds and Power* appeared. "Everything," he says, went into this book.

Canetti's ideals of patience and his irrepressible feeling for the grotesque are united in his impressions of a trip to Morocco, *The Voices of Marrakesh* (1967). The book's vignettes of minimal survival present the grotesque as a form of heroism: a pathetic skeletal donkey with a huge erection; and the most wretched of beggars, blind children begging and, atrocious to imagine, a brown bundle emitting a single sound ("e-e-e-e-e-e") which is brought every day to a square in Marrakesh to collect alms and to which Canetti pays a moving, characteristic tribute: "I was proud of the bundle because it was alive."

Humility is the theme of another work of this period, "Kafka's Other Trial," written in 1969, which treats Kafka's life as an exemplary fiction and offers a commentary on it. Canetti relates the drawn-out calamity of Kafka's engagement to Felice Bauer (Kafka's letters to Felice had just been published) as a parable about the secret victory of the one who chooses failure, who "withdraws from power in whatever form it might appear." He notes with admiration that Kafka often identifies with weak small animals, finding in Kafka his own feelings about the renunciation of power. In fact, in the force of his testimony to the ethical imperative of siding with the humiliated and the powerless, he seems closer to Simone Weil, another great expert on power, whom he never mentions. Canetti's identification with the powerless lies outside history, however; the epitome of powerlessness for Canetti is not, say, oppressed people but animals. Canetti, who is not a Christian, does not conceive of any intervention or active partisanship. Neither is he resigned. Incapable of insipidity or satiety, Canetti advances the model of a mind always reacting, registering shocks and trying to outwit them.

The aphoristic writing of his notebooks is fast knowledge— in contrast to the slow knowledge distilled in *Crowds and Power*. "My task," he wrote in 1949, a year after he began writing it, "is to show how complex selfishness is." For such a long book it is very tense. His rapidity wars with his tenacity. The somewhat laborious, assertive writer who set out to write a tome that will "grab this century by the throat" interferes with, and is interfered with by, a concise writer who is more playful, more insolent, more puzzled, more scornful.

The notebook is the perfect literary form for an eternal student, someone who has no subject or, rather, whose subject is "everything." It allows entries of all lengths and shapes and degrees of impatience and roughness, but its ideal entry is the aphorism. Most of Canetti's entries take up the aphorist's traditional themes: the hypocrisies of society, the vanity of human wishes, the sham of love, the ironies of death, the pleasure and necessity of solitude, and the intricacies of one's own thought processes. Most of the great aphorists have been pessimists, purveyors of scorn for human folly. ("The great writers of aphorisms read as if they had all known each other well," Canetti has noted.) Aphoristic thinking is informal, unsociable, adversarial, proudly selfish. "One needs friends mainly in order to become impudent—that is, more oneself," Canetti writes: there is the authentic tone of the aphorist. The notebook holds that ideally impudent, efficient self that one constructs to deal with the world. By the disjunction of ideas and observations, by the brevity of their expression, by the absence of helpful illustration, the notebook makes of thinking something light.

Despite having much of the aphorist's temperament, Canetti is anything but an intellectual dandy. (He is the opposite of, say, Gottfried Benn.) Indeed, the great limit of Canetti's sensibility is the absence of the slightest trace of the aesthete. Canetti shows no love of art as such. He has his roster of Great Writers, but no painting, theater, film, dance, or the other familiars of humanist culture figure in his work. Canetti appears to stand rather grandly above the impacted ideas of "culture" or "art." He does not love anything the mind fabricates for its own sake. His writing, therefore, has little irony. No one touched by the aesthetic sensibility would have noted, severely, "What often bothers me about Montaigne is the fat on the quotations." There is nothing in Canetti's temperament that could respond to Surrealism, to speak only of the most persuasive modern option for the aesthete. Nor, it would seem, was he ever touched by the temptation of the left.

A dedicated enlightener, he describes the object of his struggle as the one faith left intact by the Enlightenment, "the most preposterous of all, the religion of power." Here is the side of Canetti that reminds one of Karl Kraus, for whom the ethical vocation is endless protest. But no writer is less a journalist than Canetti. To protest against power, power as such; to protest against death (he is one of the great death-haters of literature)—these are broad targets, rather invincible enemies. Canetti describes Kafka's work as a "refutation" of power, and this is Canetti's aim in *Crowds and Power*. All of his work, however, aims at a refutation of death. A refutation seems to mean for Canetti an inordinate insisting. Canetti insists that death is really unacceptable; unassimilable, because it is what is outside life; unjust, because it limits ambition and insults it. He refuses to understand death, as Hegel suggested, as something within life—as the *consciousness* of death, finitude, mortality. In matters of death Canetti is an unregenerate, appalled materialist, and unrelentingly quixotic. "I still haven't succeeded in doing anything against death," he wrote in 1960.

In *The Tongue Set Free* Canetti is eager to do justice to each of his admirations, which is a way of keeping someone alive. Typically, Canetti also means this literally. Displaying his usual unwillingness to be reconciled to extinction, Canetti recalls a teacher in boarding school and concludes: "In case he is still in the world today, at ninety or one hundred, I would like him to know I bow to him."

This first volume of his autobiography is dominated by the history of a profound admiration: that of Canetti for his mother. It is the portrait of one of the great teacher-parents, a zealot of European high culture self-confidently at work before the time that turned such a parent into a selfish tyrant and such a child into an "overachiever," to use the philistine label which conveys the contemporary disdain for precocity and intellectual ardor.

"Mother, whose highest veneration was for great writers," was the primal admirer; and a passionate, merciless promoter of her admirations. Canetti's education consisted of immersion in books and their amplification in talk. There were evening readings aloud, tempestuous conversations about everything they read, about the writers they agreed to revere. Many discoveries were made separately, but they had to admire in unison, and a divergence was fought out in lacerating debates until one or the other yielded. His mother's policies of admiration created a tense world, defined by loyalties and betrayals. Each new admiration could throw one's life into question. Canetti describes his mother being distracted and exalted for a week after hearing the *St. Matthew Passion*, finally weeping because she fears that Bach has made her want only to listen to music and that "it's all over with books." Canetti, age thirteen, comforts her and reassures her that she *will* still want to read.

Witnessing his mother's leaps and raging contradictions of character "with amazement and admiration," Canetti does not underestimate her cruelty. Ominously enough, her favorite modern writer for a long time was Strindberg; in another generation it would probably have been D. H. Lawrence. Her emphasis on "character building" often led this fiercest of readers to berate her studious child for pursuing "dead knowledge," avoiding "hard" reality, letting books and conversation make him "unmanly." (She despised women, Canetti reports.) Canetti relates how annihilated by her he sometimes felt and then turns this into a liberation. As he affirmed in himself his mother's capacity for passionate commitment, he chose to revolt against the febrility of her enthusiasms, the overexclusiveness of her avidity. Patience ("monumental patience"), steadfastness, and universality of concern became his goals. His mother's world has no animals—only great men; Canetti will have both. She cares only about literature and hates science; starting in 1924 he will study chemistry at the University of Vienna, taking his Ph.D. in 1929. She scoffs at his interest in primitive peoples; Canetti will avow, as he prepares to write *Crowds and Power:* "It is a serious goal of my life to get to know all myths of all peoples."

Canetti refuses the victim's part. There is much chivalry in his portrait of his mother. It also reflects something like a policy of his mother. It also reflects something like a policy of triumphalism—a steadfast refusal of tragedy, of irremediable suffering, that seems related to his refusal of finitude, of death, and from which comes much of Canetti's energy: his staunchless capacity for admiration and enthusiasm, and his civilized contempt for complaining.

Canetti's mother was undemonstrative—the slightest caress was an event. But her talk—debating, hectoring, musing, recounting her life—was lavish, torrential. Language was the medium of their passion: words and more words. With language Canetti made his "first independent move" from his mother: learning Swiss German (she hated "vulgar" dialects) when he went away to boarding school at fourteen. And with language he remained connected to her: writing a five-act verse tragedy in Latin (with an interlinear German translation for her benefit, it filled 121 pages), which he dedicated to her and sent, requesting from her a detailed commentary.

Canetti seems eager to enumerate the many skills which he owes to his mother's example and teaching—including those which he developed to oppose her, also generously counted as her gifts: obstinacy, intellectual independence, rapidity of thought. He also speculates that the liveliness of Ladino, which he'd spoken as a child, helped him to think fast. (For the precocious, thinking is a kind of speed.) Canetti gives a complex account of that extraordinary process which learning is for an intellectually precocious child—fuller and more instructive than the accounts in, say, Mill's *Autobiography* or Sartre's *The Words*. For Canetti's capacities as an admirer reflect tireless skills as a learner; the first cannot be deep without the second. As an exceptional learner, Canetti has an irrepressible loyalty to teachers, to what they do well even (or especially when) they do it inadvertently. The teacher at his boarding school to whom he now "bows" won his fealty by being brutal during a class visit to a slaughterhouse. Forced by him to confront a particularly gruesome sight, Canetti learned that the murder of animals was something "I wasn't meant to get over." His mother, even when she was brutal, was always feeding his flagrant alertness with her words. Canetti says proudly, "I find mute knowledge dangerous."

Canetti claims to be a "hear-er" rather than a "see-er." In *Auto-da-Fé,* Kien practices being blind, for he has discovered that "blindness is a weapon against time and space; our being is one vast blindness." Particularly in his work since *Crowds and Power*—such as the didactically titled *The Voices of Marra-kesh, Earwitness, The Tongue Set Free*—Canetti stresses the moralist's organ, the ear, and slights the eye (continuing to ring changes on the theme of blindness). Hearing, speaking, and breathing are praised whenever something important is at stake, if only in the form of ear, mouth (or tongue), and throat metaphors. When Canetti observes that "the *loudest* passage in Kafka's work tells of this guilt with respect to the animals," the adjective is itself a form of insistence.

What is heard is voices—to which the ear is a witness. (Canetti does not talk about music, or indeed about any art that is non-verbal.) The ear is the attentive sense, humbler, more passive, more immediate, less discriminating than the eye. Canetti's disavowal of the eye is an aspect of his remoteness from the aesthete's sensibility, which typically affirms the pleasures and the wisdom of the visual; that is, of surfaces. To give sovereignty to the ear is an obtrusive, consciously archaizing theme in Canetti's later work. Implicitly he is restating the archaic gap between Hebrew as opposed to Greek culture, ear culture as opposed to eye culture, and the moral versus the aesthetic.

Canetti equates knowing with hearing, and hearing with hearing everything and still being able to respond. The exotic impressions garnered during his stay in Marrakesh are unified by the quality of attentiveness to "voices" that Canetti tries to summon in himself. Attentiveness is the formal subject of the book. Encountering poverty, misery, and deformity, Canetti undertakes to hear, that is, really to pay attention to words, cries, and inarticulate sounds "on the edge of the living." His essay on Kraus portrays someone whom Canetti considers ideal both as hearer and as voice. Canetti says that Kraus was haunted by voices; that his ear was constantly open; that "the real Karl Kraus was the *speaker*." Describing a writer as a voice has become such a cliché that it is possible to miss the force—and the characteristic literalness—of what Canetti means. The voice for Canetti stands for irrefutable presence. To treat someone as a voice is to grant authority to that person; to affirm that one hears means that one hears what must be heard.

Like a scholar in a Borges story that mixes real and imaginary erudition, Canetti has a taste for fanciful blends of knowledge, eccentric classifications, and spirited shifts of tone. Thus *Crowds and Power*—in German, *Masse und Macht*—offers analogies from physiology and zoology to explain command and obedience; and is perhaps most original when it extends the notion of the crowd to include collective units, not composed of human beings, which "recall" the crowd, are "felt to be a crowd," which "stand as a symbol for it in myth, dream, speech, and song." (Among such units—in Canetti's ingenious catalogue—are fire, rain, the fingers of the hand, the bee swarm, teeth, the forest, the snakes of delirium tremens.) Much of *Crowds and Power* depends on latent or inadvertent science-fiction imagery of things, or parts of things, that become eerily autonomous; of unpredictable movements, tempos, volumes. Canetti turns time (history) into space, in which a weird array of biomorphic entities—the various forms of the Great Beast, the Crowd—disport themselves. The crowd moves, emits, grows, expands, contracts. Its options come in pairs: crowds are said by Canetti to be quick and slow, rhythmic and stagnant, closed and open. The pack (another version of the crowd) laments, it preys, it is tranquil, it is outward or inward.

As an account of the psychology and structure of authority, *Crowds and Power* harks back to nineteenth-century talk about crowds and masses in order to expound its poetics of political nightmare. Condemnation of the French Revolution, and later of the Commune, was the message of the nineteenth-century books on crowds (they were as common then as they are unfashionable now), from Charles Mackay's *Extraordinary Popular Delusions and the Madness of Crowds* (1841) to Le Bon's *The Crowd* (1895), a book Freud admired, and *The Psychology of Revolution* (1912). But whereas earlier writers had been content to assert the crowd's pathology and moralize about it, Canetti means to explain, explain exhaustively, for example, the crowd's destructiveness ("often mentioned as its most conspicuous quality," he says) with his biomorphic paradigms. And unlike Le Bon, who was making a case against revolution and for the status quo (considered by Le Bon the less oppressive dictatorship), Canetti offers a brief against power itself.

To understand power by considering the crowd, to the detriment of notions like "class" or "nation," is precisely to insist on an ahistorical understanding. Hegel and Marx are not mentioned, not because Canetti is so self-confident that he won't deign to drop the usual names, but because the implications of Canetti's argument are sharply anti-Hegelian and anti-Marxist. His ahistorical method and conservative political temper bring Canetti rather close to Freud—though he is in no sense a Freudian. Canetti is what Freud might have been were he *not* a psychologist: using many sources that were important to Freud—the autobiography of the psychotic Judge Schreber, material on anthropology and the history of ancient religions, Le Bon's crowd theory—he comes to quite different conclusions about group psychology and the shaping of the ego. Like Freud, Canetti tends to find the prototype of crowd (that is, irrational) behavior in religion, and much of *Crowds and Power* is really a rationalist's discourse about religion. For example, what Canetti calls the lamenting pack is just another name for religions of lament, of which he gives a dazzling analysis, contrasting the slow tempos of Catholic piety and ritual (expressing the Church's perennial fear of the open crowd) with the frenzied mourning in the Shi'ite branch of Islam.

Like Freud, too, Canetti dissolves politics into pathology, treating society as a mental activity—a barbaric one, of course—that must be decoded. Thus he moves, without breaking stride, from the notion of the crowd to the "crowd symbol," and analyzes social grouping and the forms of community as transactions of crowd symbols. Some final turn of the crowd argument seems to have been reached when Canetti puts the French Revolution in its place, finding the Revolution less interesting as an eruption of the destructive than as a "national crowd symbol" for the French.

For Hegel and his successors, the historical (the home of irony) and the natural are two radically different processes. In *Crowds and Power,* history is "natural." Canetti argues to history, not from it. First comes the account of the crowd; then, as illustration, the section called "The Crowd in History." History is used only to furnish examples—a rapid use. Canetti is partial to the evidence of historyless (in the Hegelian sense) peoples, treating anthropological anecdotes as having the same illustrative value as an event taking place in an advanced historical society.

Crowds and Power is an eccentric book—made literally eccentric by its ideal of "universality," which leads Canetti to avoid making the obvious reference: Hitler. He appears indirectly, in the central importance Canetti gives to the case of Judge Schreber. (Here is Canetti's only reference to Freud—in one discreet footnote, where Canetti says that had Freud lived a bit longer he might have seen Schreber's paranoid delusions in a more pertinent way: as a prototype of the political, specifically Nazi, mentality.) But Canetti is genuinely not Eurocentric—one of his large achievements as a mind. Conversant with Chinese as well as European thought, with Buddhism and Islam as well as Christianity, Canetti enjoys a remarkable freedom from reductive habits of thinking. He seems incapable of using psychological knowledge in a reductive way; the author of the homage to Broch could not have been thinking about anything as ordinary as personal motives. And he fights the more plausible reduction to the historical. "I would give a great deal to get rid of my habit of seeing the world historically," he wrote in 1950, two years after he started writing *Crowds and Power*.

His protest against seeing historically is directed not just against that most plausible of reductionisms. It is also a protest against death. To think about history is to think about the dead; and to be incessantly reminded that one is mortal. Canetti's thought is conservative in the most literal sense. It—he—does not want to die.

"I want to feel everything in me before I think it," Canetti wrote in 1943, and for this, he says, he needs a long life. To die prematurely means having not fully engorged himself and, therefore, having not used his mind as he could. It is almost as if Canetti had to keep his consciousness in a permanent state of avidity, to remain unreconciled to death. "It is wonderful that nothing is lost in a mind," he also wrote in his notebook, in what must have been a not infrequent moment of euphoria, "and would not this alone be reason enough to live very long or even forever?" Recurrent images of needing to feel everything inside himself, of unifying everything in one head, illustrate Canetti's attempts through magical thinking and moral clamorousness to "refute" death.

Canetti offers to strike a bargain with death. "A century? A paltry hundred years! Is that too much for an earnest intention!" But why one hundred years? Why not three hundred?—like the 337-year-old heroine of Karel Čapek's *The Makropulos Affair* (1922). In the play, one character (a socialist "progressive") describes the disadvantages of a normal life span.

What can a man do during his sixty years of life? What enjoyment has he? What can he learn? You don't live to get the fruit of the tree you have planted; you'll never learn all the things that mankind has discovered before you; you won't complete your work or leave your example behind you; you'll die without having even lived. A life of three hundred years on the other hand would allow fifty years to be a child and a pupil; fifty years to get to know the world and see all that exists in it; one hundred years to work for the benefit of all; and then, when he has achieved all human experience, another hundred years to live in wisdom, to rule, to teach, and to set an example. Oh, how valuable human life would be if it lasted three hundred years.

He sounds like Canetti—except that Canetti does not justify his yearning for longevity with any appeal to its greater scope for good works. So large is the value of the mind that it alone is used to oppose death. Because the mind is so real to him Canetti dares to challenge death, and because the body is so unreal he perceives nothing dismaying about extreme longevity. Canetti is more than willing to live as a centenarian; he does not, while he is fantasizing, ask for what Faust demanded, the return of youth, or for what Emilia Makropulos was given by her alchemist father, its magical prolongation. Youth has no part in Canetti's fantasy of immortality. It is pure longevity, the longevity of the mind. It is simply assumed that character has the same stake as mind in longevity: Canetti thought "the brevity of life makes us bad." Emilia Makropulos suggests its longevity would make us worse:

You cannot go on loving for three hundred years. And you cannot go on hoping, creating, gazing at things for three hundred years. You can't stand it. Everything becomes boring. It's boring to be good and boring to be bad. . . . And then you realize that nothing actually exists. . . . You are so close to everything. You can see some point in everything. For you everything has some value because those few years of yours won't be enough to satisfy your enjoyment. . . . It's disgusting to think how happy you are. And it's simply due to the ridiculous coincidence that you're going to die soon. You take an ape-like interest in everything. . . .

But this plausible doom is just what Canetti cannot admit. He is unperturbed by the possibility of the flagging of appetite, the satiation of desire, the devaluation of passion. Canetti gives no thought to the decomposition of the feelings any more than of the body, only to the persistence of the mind. Rarely has anyone been so at home in the mind, with so little ambivalence.

Canetti is someone who has felt in a profound way the responsibility of words, and much of his work makes the effort to communicate something of what he has learned about how to pay attention to the world. There is no doctrine, but there is a great deal of scorn, urgency, grief, and euphoria. The message of the mind's passion. "I try to imagine someone saying to Shakespeare, 'Relax!'" says Canetti. His work eloquently defends tension, exertion, moral and amoral seriousness.

But Canetti is not just another hero of the will. Hence the unexpected last attribute of a great writer that he finds in Broch: such a writer, he says, teaches us how to breathe. Canetti commends Broch's writings for their "rich store of breathing experience." It was Canetti's deepest, oddest compliment, and therefore one he also paid to Goethe (the most predictable of his admirations): Canetti also reads Goethe as saying, "Breathe!"

Breathing may be the most radical of occupations, when construed as a liberation from other needs such as having a career, building a reputation, accumulating knowledge. What Canetti says at the end of this progress of admiration, his homage to Broch, suggests what there is most to admire. The last achievement of the serious admirer is to stop immediately putting to work the energies aroused by, filling up the space opened by, what is admired. Thereby talented admirers give themselves permission to breathe, to breathe more deeply. But for that it is necessary to go beyond avidity; to identify with something beyond achievement, beyond the gathering of power.

Roberto Corcoll Calsat

Elias Canetti and Spain

As I share with many of my countrymen a profound admiration for Elias Canetti and his literary work, it afforded me
great satisfaction, as a Spaniard and as a scholar of German,
to be invited to contribute to this festschrift.

Canetti is not one who has won literary prizes and a wide
readership through eccentricities, partisan politics, or literary
sponsorship and patronage. What he has earned is based solely
and exclusively on the inner value of his diverse and far-reaching
literary work.

This is so much the case that in 1981, when the Swedish
Academy voted on the Nobel Prize for Literature, not a single
vote was cast against him. As Canetti was to receive the prize,
all were in agreement—clear proof of the degree to which his
work enjoys unanimous international recognition.

I share the apt view of Canetti's Spanish publisher, Mario
Muchnik, in whose opinion the literary world, at least in this
century, has produced two human types: the cicadas and the
ants. The cicadas don't miss a single cocktail, are forever giving interviews, air their opinions on this and that, and make
literary and all manner of other efforts to bag awards. They
may well be great writers, excellent public figures, or clever
polemicists, but nevertheless their skills in savoir faire have
nothing to do with the quality of their intellectual contribution.

The ants, on the other hand, resist all contact with the public. In general they are extraordinarily sensitive and have an unusual capacity for concentration, so that it is only with difficulty that they can go over from creative work to drawing-room conversation, or vice versa. Setting their inspiration in motion costs them great pains, and as soon as they succeed in this and their creative powers are at work—and that is all they really want—they are well able to protect their energies and avoid company.

Naturally Elias Canetti is one of the ants. In *The Tongue Set Free*, remembering his school days and a teacher who showed slides of Ghiberti's famous bronze doors for the Baptistery in Florence, which Ghiberti worked on for forty-nine years, Canetti writes: "Now I realized that one can devote a whole life-time to one or two works, and patience, which I had always admired, acquired something monumental for me. Less than five years later, I found the work to which I wanted to devote *my* life." A conscious resolution to devote one's life to one work is not commonly characteristic of the worldly cicadas: it is the business of the ants.

And it was this ant's work, not only persevered in but done well, a whole life's labors devoted to literature, that the Swedish Academy, with a certain instinct, honored in 1981. It should incidentally be said in the Spanish reading public's favor that Canetti was known and read in Spain long before receiving the Nobel Prize.

Between 1976 and the present, nearly all of Elias Canetti's works have been issued in good translations, most of them by Muchnik. The success and the positive reception the works met with from the start is due first and foremost to their indisputable literary quality, but also, to some extent, to the unusually fine Spanish translations, which have given readers the spirit as well as the letter of the German originals.

Further, it has to be added that Spain, where there is a sound Germanophile tradition, has many readers who do not need translations in order to read German works.

In the press too, Canetti's works have always met with a

kindly reception, and literary magazines, such as *Camp de l'Arpa,* have even devoted special issues to him. Eminent university professors and literary critics, among them Jaime Vandor, Lluis Izquierdo, Jordi Llovet, Eustaquio Barjan, José María Carandell, Robert Saladrigas, Luis Maristany, and others, have reviewed his works after their publication in Spanish, and have written essays and commentaries praising him.

The German departments of Spanish universities are increasingly dealing with Canetti's works too, and as I write the Barcelona German department is preparing a festschrift to be published in July 1985, with contributions from professors at all the Spanish German departments as well as from respected literary critics.

Aside from the interest in Canetti's work there is also interest in the author himself. We Spanish see in him not only an extraordinary writer working in German but also, to some extent, a Spaniard, or rather a descendant of Spaniards who in 1492 were done a great injustice and expelled from the country, as a result of Catholic Isabella's religious fanaticism.

For a relatively short number of years Spain has again, once and for all, been a democratic nation, a nation where people today have more freedom than in many other European countries, a nation which has put a final stop to intolerance. We Spanish of today feel a kind of remorse if we think of the religious intolerance of our ancestors. On the other hand, we are deeply satisfied by the fact that the Sephardim, in spite of the centuries that lie between and in spite of the terrible injustice they were victims of, still love Spain and eagerly preserve our language.

So it probably comes as no surprise that the most widely read book by Canetti, in Spain, is the first part of his autobiography, *The Tongue Set Free.* I do not believe a single Spanish reader of this magical book would fail to be moved on learning how the author's mother and the other Sephardim took pride in their Spanish origins, still spoke the language as a rule, and felt superior to other, non-Spanish Jews.

We know that Canetti is not Spanish, but, like his ancestors, we are proud that his deepest roots are in Spain, and as we are certain that Canetti himself feels greatly sympathetic toward everything Spanish, it is small wonder that we claim him as a part of ourselves.

In this connection an article that appeared in the newspaper *La Vanguardia* under the heading "Elias Canetti Sees Himself as a Spanish Writer" is interesting, and I here reproduce it in part:

The new winner of the Nobel Prize for Literature, Elias Canetti, a German-speaking Bulgarian, is in reality descended from Spanish Jews who were deported from the peninsula in 1492 but who jealously preserved the language of their forefathers through the centuries.

In a recent interview, Canetti himself explained the Spanish origin of his surname and the change in its form at the beginning of the last century under the influence of the Italian colony in Turkey, where the Sephardim had fled. "Originally," said the author of *Auto-da-Fé* and *Crowds and Power,* "my family was called Cañete. It is the name of a town between Cuenca and Valencia, which was fairly important in the Middle Ages and is now quite small."

On his father's side, Elias Canetti's ancestors lived for several centuries in Adrianopolis in Turkey, till his grandfather moved to Bulgaria, where Elias was born in 1905.

At the start of the nineteenth century one of the author's forebears Italianized the original surname by changing Cañete to Canetti. Nevertheless, the language he had inherited from his ancestors, Ladino, or the Spanish that was spoken on the peninsula in the fifteenth century, was the real mother tongue of the Nobel Prize winner. His second language was English, as his family moved to Manchester in 1911. Not until he was eight years old, before moving to Vienna, did he learn German, the language his whole oeuvre was written in.

In his thirtieth year, after Germany annexed Austria, Canetti again had to emigrate, this time to London.

"When I arrived in England, German had become far too important to me for me to do anything about it. Pride will have had something to do with it too. I wouldn't have anyone, least of all Hitler, tell me what language to write in. . . . Sometimes I feel like a Spanish author writing in German. If I read the old Spanish, say the *Celestina* or the *Sueños* by Quevedo, it's as if I were speaking through them."

Understandably, most of the Spanish tributes to Canetti have been paid in Cañete or Cuenca. Let me briefly mention the celebrations organized by the Academia Conquense de Artes y Letras which took place in Cuenca and Cañete on December 18–19, 1982, under the auspices of the Diputación Provincial of Cuenca and the Ministry of Education and the Arts.

A commemorative stone was erected in his honor in the main square of the little town, and after this there followed a literary ceremony with speeches by Professor Jaime Vandor of the University of Barcelona and Don Carlos de la Rica, secretary-general of the Academia. Then the meeting unanimously voted Canetti an honorary citizen of the town. The certificate, on magnificent historic parchment, is written in Hebraic characters but in Castilian, which resembles the Spanish spoken in the sixteenth century; the lettering and decoration were done by the poet and painter Carlos de la Rica. In view of its importance I shall give the wording of the text in full:

As we, the Lord Mayor of the noble town of Cañete, the town elders, and the town council in full assembly, motu propio and at the suggestion of literary people in our province and in the bishopric of Cuenca, honor Don Elias Canetti, eminent writer and 1981 Nobel Prize winner, because through him we honor his Sephardic race, which, one woeful long-gone day, was forced to abandon home and hearth in this same town and this kingdom of Spain by people who in turn were at the mercy of higher powers, we have decided, by virtue of the right invested in us and thanks to our liberty to exercise that right, and because we consider Don Elias to be one of our own, to name him a son and citizen of our town of Cañete, and herewith we proclaim the fact on this day of Our Lord the seventeenth of December nineteen hundred and eighty-two, as witnessed by people and citizens of Cañete, representatives of the Academia Conquense de

Artes y Letras, and further eminent public figures of the province and members of the Jewish communities of Madrid and Barcelona. We hereby hand over this document, signed, recorded and stamped, in the town and on the date mentioned ut supra.

In view of Cañete's, Cuenca's, and indeed Spain's claims to Canetti, I also reprint part of the address given by Don Enrique Dominguez Millán, president of the Academia Conquense de Artes y Letras:

The outstanding figure we have gathered here this evening to honor shares with us roots in the province of Cuenca, the identity of orgins. His and our roots meet in a distant past below this very soil that sustains us. It was with pleasure that we learned this one December day in 1981, scarcely a year ago. On that day, the press announced that the Nobel Prize for Literature had been awarded to Elias Canetti, a Sephardic writer, born in Bulgaria, resident in Zurich, the author of a manifold literary oeuvre written in German. Soon afterward our initial suspicions were proved correct: Elias Canetti is descended from Spanish Jews who lived in our province, or, to be exact, Jews of the province of Cuenca who lived in the Jewish quarter of Cañete. The Jews he is descended from lived in Cañete for centuries and, at least in the latter half of the Middle Ages, played an extremely important role in the life of the town, but one dark day had to leave Cañete when the religious and nationalist fanaticism of Catholic Isabella decreed the expulsion of their race.

Among the 35,000 Jewish families that were forced to take the hard road of emigration in 1492, the year of the fall of Granada and the discovery of America, was the family that in the course of time was to bring forth the admirable and admired figure of a Nobel Prize winner. It was a family so rooted in the province of Cuenca and so identified with their town that they took the name Cañete as their family name. And with this name they reached their exile, where changes and fashions transformed it into Canetti. As the exiled family remained faithful to its beliefs, principles, and traditions, it took with it many of the principles and traditions of that part of the world it had been forced to leave. And not only did they take them with them but they preserved them as a valuable treasure and handed them down from generation to generation, in spite of trials and tribulations and without regard to distances in space and time. As well as their language they preserved their longing, their memory of the Sephardic community they came from and where they had left behind their experiences and roots. And they preserved their character too. Of all the Jews of the diaspora, of all those who settled in the Jewish quarters of Amsterdam, Hamburg, Central Europe, the Balkans, Thessalonica, Istanbul, Smyrna, the Sephardim—that is to say, those Jews of Spanish birth—had a particular characteristic, a refinement that marked them with distinction. Four hundred years after they left, this distinctive feature or special mark was still visible in Elias Canetti's childhood. In his wonderful book *The Tongue Set Free,* Canetti himself tells us of it. Speaking of his family, and in general of the Sephardim or Spanish Jews, he emphasizes: "The thing that was most powerful, and irresistible for a child, was a Spanish attitude," and, above all: "With naïve arrogance, the Sephardim looked down on other Jews." Canetti tells us that in his community, the Sephardic community of Ruschuk in Bulgaria, marriage to a Jew of non-Spanish origin was frowned upon. These marriages, which he calls "mixed" marriages as if the partners had been of different races or religious faiths, were viewed with suspicion or disapproval or even naked antipathy. And even within the Sephardim there were classes. "The proudest words one could hear about a person were: *Es de buena famiglia,*" Canetti tells us—"he is of a good family."

What we see here is the survival of the old Castilian nobility. Elias Canetti's mother, who was to have so profound an influence on his life, boasted of her "good family," as she was of Spanish origin and well-to-do as well. Because of this, Elias's father had difficulty in winning her for his wife. His financial position was inferior to hers, although he was a man of means. But grandfather Canetti, who had a "butica," that is to say, a store, in Ruschuk, for his part boasted the greatest racial purity in the family: he had not married into a Turkish family as his counterpart father-in-law had. At all events, the future Nobel Prize winner came of Sephardic stock on both sides. We can say he was a nobleman of the kind his forefathers knew in the area around Cañete. As the period when those forefathers settled in the town is unknown, we do not know what prominent people they knew or met socially. Without question the last occupants of the Cañete house, those who were forced to emigrate, at least knew the oldest of them, Don Diego Hurtado de Mendonza, the head watchkeeper of Cuenca and a gentleman of Cañete. Quite probably they also knew Don Alvaro de Luna, before or after he was appointed Constable, and his brother Don Juan de Cerezuela, who is said to have held high office in the church of Castile—both of them sons of the noble town of Cañete. Maybe they knew Don Andrés de Cabrera and Doña Beatriz de Bobadilia, the Marquis and Marquise of Maya, when they saw the latter driving through Cañete on their way to their estates. It is a stirring thought, that the image of our simple, austere Cañete and that of those aristocratic inhabitants should have lived on in the Canetti family's memory and in their family history as something dreamlike, lost in dark origins but still remaining alive on some far corner of Bulgarian soil.

The emotion we felt on encountering the Conquense forebears of the illustrious Nobel laureate moved us not to be inactive in the face of this valuable discovery. The Academia Conquense de Artes y Letras immediately thought of making known the sensitive link between Canetti and Cuenca, Cuenca and Canetti, across the generations—a link whose roots are in this ancestral soil. The Academia is proud to make it known with undisguised satisfaction, and proud to pay public homage to a writer of genius who has written immortal pages—in German, the language his mother taught him without letting him forget Spanish, the inheritance he had received from his ancestors—and has inscribed on the covers of his books a name taken from our province: Canetti, Cañete. It is for this reason that I said at the outset that our tribute is based on roots. It is these roots, his but also our own, shared roots, divided roots, that we celebrate this evening as we celebrate Elias Canetti, winner of the Nobel Prize for Literature, famed throughout the world—Elias from Ruschuk, Elias from Zurich, yes, but, reaching back much further, Elias from Cañete, Elias from Cuenca.

The ceremonies at Cañete and Cuenca may stand as examples of the many tributes paid in Spain. If I have given some space to them, I have done so in order to show the author's

Spanish roots. Unfortunately Canetti could not attend the ceremonies for reasons of health. His Spanish publisher, Mario Muchnik, excused his absence to the committee and to the citizens of Cañete and Cuenca.

Professor Jaime Vandor took upon himself the task of informing the great Sephardic writer of the ceremonies attending his honorary citizenship of Cañete, and of putting together for him news documentation of the festivities in his honor. As was to be expected, Elias Canetti found the time to write an ample letter of thanks, with the request that it be passed on to the organizers of the amiable tributes.

I am sure the citizens of Cañete, Cuenca, and all Spain ardently wish that Señor Cañete's health may one day permit him to visit the town and country of his roots.

While we are awaiting his visit, or rather his return, Señor Canetti can rest assured that here in Spain he has countless readers, admirers, and friends who wish him from their hearts many, many years of life and health, in the hope that in the future he will delight us with many more of his exquisite literary works.

Johannes Edfelt

Introducing Elias Canetti

It was not until relatively late in life—to be exact, in the first half of the 1970s—that I acquired a greater and deeper knowledge of Elias Canetti's work. In other words, *Auto-da-Fé*, which doubtless occupies as weighty and important a position in European literature as Hermann Broch's *The Death of Virgil* and Robert Musil's *The Man Without Qualities*, escaped my attention when it first appeared in 1935. I was not the only one who failed to notice it. At that time the book won relatively little acclaim, as we know. It was only the later editions, after the end of the Second World War and during the 1960s, that brought full recognition and appreciation to the psychological truth and linguistic power and diversity of Canetti's novel.

As the fate and experience of Kien the sinologist occupied me more and more, it was quite consistent and inevitable that my interest should have extended to the writer's other works. I read them, pondered them, and decided to make them known to the Swedish public; and this I did by means of a study, and reviews which were published in the *Svenska Dagbladet*. What gripped me was not least the clear-thinking aphoristic work in Canetti's notebooks—marginalia which cannot be defined as maxims in the spirit of the French moralists but, far more, are preponderantly critical observations on the absurdities of the world. I translated into my own mother tongue a selection of these notes—which, in their accuracy of aim, diversity, and (in this pointed form) universal validity, in my opinion merit comparison with the classical aphorisms of Georg Christoph Lichtenberg. A selection appeared in book form in 1979, with an author's foreword. The Swedish title was a direct translation of Canetti's own title for the notebooks: *The Human Province: Notes, 1942–1972.*

What follows here is the introduction I wrote to the volume I translated, with only a few minor amendments, and represents a summary of my view of Canetti's work. To it has been added the bulk of a review of his second volume of memoirs, *The Torch in My Ear,* which was published in the *Svenska Dagbladet* not long after the original edition appeared.

It cannot be sufficiently emphasized that what I have written here on Elias Canetti is in the form of a presentation originally intended for a Swedish readership, introducing a great, original, and strangely gripping writer, a narrative and dramatic author who is also a highly independent and original investigator of the genesis, structures, and symbols of crowds and power. All I was out to do, then, was to communicate to the literary public in a Nordic country my opinion and subjective image of a writer who had appealed powerfully to my feelings and intellect. In other words, I made no other claim than to *introduce.*

It also seems appropriate to add that in 1982 I was entrusted with a similar task: I was requested by the Swedish Academy to give the *laudatio* on Elias Canetti in Stockholm's concert hall on December 10, the day he was awarded the Nobel Prize for Literature. Making the personal acquaintance of Elias Canetti on that occasion was for me as for many others an extraordinary pleasure. The memory of his clear-sighted, deeply human personality is one of those that abide through the years, as a point of light and a source of warmth.

I

There are writers who capture attention and fame at a blow. Others see their work winning readers and influence only gradually. Elias Canetti's work belongs in the second category.

He was born in 1905 in Ruschuk in Bulgaria, into a Spanish-Jewish family whose members were expelled in 1492 from Cañete, a town once of importance that lies between Cuenca and Valencia. For several centuries his ancestors then lived in Turkey. In 1911 Canetti came with his parents to England; after his father's death in 1913 the family moved to Vienna. From 1916 to 1924 Elias Canetti went to school in Zurich and Frankfurt-am-Main, and afterward studied natural sciences in Vienna, concluding his studies with a doctorate in 1929. Since 1938 he has lived in London.

Canetti's imaginative masterpiece is without doubt the great novel *Auto-da-Fé*. That it was an extraordinary test of his powers is beyond question. It is written in a style whose hallmarks are above all clarity and precision: it is no accident that Elias Canetti has called Stendhal one of his masters. Yet the novel has fantastic and daemonic elements which we necessarily associate with Gogol and Dostoevsky: Canetti himself has expressed a debt of gratitude to the two Russian writers. Of twentieth-century writers, the ones he is linked to by elective affinity are Robert Walser and Franz Kafka.

A Vienna apartment block is the main setting of the novel's action, which is full of the grotesque and macabre. *Auto-da-Fé* struck various critics as one vast metaphor of Man's threat to himself in the age of the masses. Seen from a different angle, the novel appears as a study of a human type, a man who specializes in self-satisfied isolation and perishes because of it.

The protagonist is the sinologist Peter Kien, a "Jakob Burckhardt of oriental culture." He lives in an ivory tower—consisting in his case of a library of many thousand volumes. Wholly absorbed in his philological pursuits, he is helpless when confronted with the world of harsh reality. He falls into the hands of his housekeeper, Therese, the very personification of grasping greed, bourgeois moral hypocrisy, erotic lust, and extreme vulgarity. She appears as the symbol of the human masses, as does the brutal caretaker Pfaff, who drives his own daughter to her death and in the end tyrannizes Kien too.

Expelled from his home by Therese, whom he has married, Peter Kien makes a veritable descent into hell, through a criminal world dominated by the figure of Fischerle. This pimp character resembles Kien in being a manic individual on his own level. Kien's cry for help finally reaches his brother George, who is a psychiatrist in Paris; but he, when he joins his brother, can no longer put a halt to Peter Kien's spiritual disintegration and final downfall. The conflagration puts a stop to Peter Kien's life, a life lived in contempt and fear of the masses, a life in which specialization has meant isolation and an end to any genuine human communication. It is difficult to imagine a more loveless world than that revealed in *Auto-da-Fé*. Peter Kien's brother George, the psychiatrist, has his own definite conception of the "crowd": he sees it as an integral part of us all. One passage in the novel, the great value of which as an independent, powerfully executed epic creation is beyond doubt, links up with Elias Canetti's second major work, *Crowds and Power* (1960):

We wage the so-called war of existence for the destruction of the mass-soul in ourselves, no less than for hunger and love. . . . "Mankind" has existed as a mass for long before it was conceived of and watered down into an idea. It foams, a huge, wild, full-blooded, warm animal in all of us, very deep, far deeper than the maternal. In spite of its age it is the youngest of the beasts, the essential creation of the earth, its goal and its future. We know nothing of it; we live still, supposedly as individuals. Sometimes the masses pour over us, one single flood, one ocean, in which each drop is alive, and each drop wants the same thing. But it soon scatters again, and leaves us once more to be ourselves, poor solitary devils. In memory we can hardly conceive that we were ever so great, so many and so much one. "Disease," says one overburdened by intelligence; "the beast in man" soothes the lamb of humility, and does not guess how near to the truth is its mistake.

II

Elias Canetti's thoughts began early on to dwell upon the world of mass movements. *Crowds and Power,* the fruit of various and profound experience, is the work of a polyhistorian. Philosophy and psychology, anthropology and sociology are united in it, and an immense abundance of points of view on Man as a creature of the crowd are accommodated. Canetti shows how a primeval fear of being touched is dispelled among human beings when, either under pressure or on suggestion, they are absorbed into a crowd, a herd. He examines the character of "open" or "closed" crowds and constantly emphasizes the fundamental drive of the crowd, to multiply. His field of research includes not only real crowds but also the invisible: the hosts of spirits, devils, angels that populate so many religions. He studies collective movements in modern mass society, and the wielding of power in and through them. Like Gustave Le Bon in his crowd psychology, Canetti sees the root factors in the formation of the masses in the modern era. But Canetti differs from his various predecessors in introducing the concept of "the pack," which is not foremost a quantitative concept—a group, that is to say, of considerably limited extent; from this he evolves such concepts as "the hunting pack" (which in our times becomes the "baiting crowd"), "the war pack," "the lamenting pack," "the increase pack," etc.

Canetti's theories about the origins, constitution, and behavior of crowds, from the primeval times of primitive tribes to modern times, are intimately bound up with his analysis of the genesis and nature of power and commands. He sees the command to flee as the original, fundamental use of power. According to Canetti, the threat of death is profoundly present behind every order. He also examines crowd symbols and their function, not least national symbols.

I can indicate only a few of the themes in *Crowds and Power,* which is so alive with ideas, and an assessment of its scholarly value is beyond my competence. But it should be noted that the work has aroused lively and widespread interest. Theodor W. Adorno and Joachim Schickel are among those who have devoted exhaustive attention to *Crowds and Power.* One thing is clear: *Crowds and Power* is a work written with a radiant clarity, vividness, and linguistic power.

III

Elias Canetti has described his plays as "acoustic masks." They are absurd plays—and at least the first of them, *The Wedding* (1932), was written before absurdist theater became a fashionable movement. Canetti's three plays are all based on experiment with a thought, on what Canetti himself calls an "idea."

In *The Wedding* Canetti shows us the inhabitants of an apartment block and presents their often unbounded egoism, and the greedily erotic foundations of their relationships. Money and love are the driving powers in their lives. The prototype is the senile, dissolute Dr. Bock. The catastrophe for the house and its occupants, prophetically caused by the idealist Horch, leads to a hectic flaring-up of passions all round, and of the basest utterances.

The *Comedy of Vanity* (1950), in three acts, is based on the "idea" that a state decree requires the removal of all mirrors and photographs, in order to counteract vanity. The death penalty awaits those who break the law. But mankind needs its vanity and cannot give it up. Director Garaus expresses the idea of this absurd play when he says in the course of a monologue, "What after all *is* a man nowadays? A man is his image.

. . . Yes, and a man without his image will get nowhere." Even looking at one's reflection in water is a crime that everyone fears to commit. Nonetheless, the law is constantly being broken. The last act presents a kind of magic cabinet where people view their mirror images in order to gain their identities, to live.

The Numbered (1956) shows us people whose names represent their predetermined life spans: at birth, each one of them receives a locket which supposedly contains the date of his or her death. In cases of death the Keeper opens the lockets. A man named Fifty robs two old women of their lockets, opens them, and finds they are empty. The people rebel against the idea of the lockets: they all want to live in that freedom which uncertainty about the hour of death can give. One woman expresses the situation of the characters in the play in this way: "They are all heartless. . . . First of all because a man like that knows one thing for certain: he will outlive everyone around him. . . . How can he love anyone?"

IV

Canetti's sensitive awareness of complex psychological situations and his extremely acute perceptiveness of external modes of behavior bear excellent fruit both in his exotic travel book *The Voices of Marrakesh* (1967) and in his numerous essays. Of the latter, *Kafka's Other Trial* (1969) deserves special mention: in it Canetti examines Kafka's relationship with Felice Bauer and, with confident insight and penetration, illuminates Kafka's need for admiration, his self-punishing conduct, and the reflection of this erotic relationship in his novel *The Trial*.

But Canetti's lively intelligence and his intensive commitment to essential philosophical and sociological problems are no less clearly expressed in his various volumes of notes. In my opinion their content has rarely been surpassed in contemporary aphorisms, and thus they represent one of Canetti's most important contributions to modern literature. His hatred of death, of the very fact of death, is a constant theme in Canetti's notebooks. This hatred, though, is of course only the other side of his love of real life.

One of Canetti's most recent works is *Earwitness: Fifty Characters* (1974). The fifty human types which, following Theophrastus and La Bruyère, he here presents show Canetti to be a truly witty satirist; he etched his portraits with the exactness of a caricaturist, and with an absurd humor. A wide knowledge of human nature can be seen in the compendium of idiosyncrasies and phobias Elias Canetti presents us with.

V

Canetti has recorded his memories of childhood and youth in *The Tongue Set Free* (1977), a book which, through its clear yet nuanced style and through its numerous vivid portraits of both milieux and individual people, offers us an unusually rewarding reading experience.

Ruschuk, a small town on the Danube, is the backdrop for Canetti's earliest memories. In the midst of the town's busy life we see the teeming Canetti family, particularly the grandfather, a wholesale grocer and figure of authority in the town, who in Canetti's remembrance becomes the focus of a magnificent study. He describes the colorfulness of Ruschuk, peopled by a wide range of ethnic groups: Turks, Greeks, Armenians, and gypsies gave the town its flavor. Canetti's father and mother had both gone to school in Vienna and both had intellectual interests. His father subscribed to the *Neue Freie Presse,* and his mother, like his father, had dreamed of a stage career—a dream she had had to relinquish.

When Elias is about six years old the family moves to Manchester in England, where his father becomes a businessman. Grandfather, who remains behind in Ruschuk, curses his son for moving. On hearing the news of the outbreak of the Balkan War, Elias's father, who is only thirty, dies of a stroke. This event leaves a permanent mark on the son's psyche: he has never been able to reconcile himself to the thought of death, and his whole world of thought and of feeling is infected by it. His mother's shouts "pushed Father's death into me, and it has never left me since," we are told in the memoirs.

It is now the mother's task to care for Elias and his two younger brothers alone. One move follows another: Lausanne, Vienna, Zurich, where Elias goes to school. But he learns most, and at an amazingly early age, from his mother. Elias Canetti's picture of her is one of the most curious portraits we are likely to come across. She has had to arm herself against life's blows; she is immensely dominating; her derision can take veritably abominable form—yet at the same time she is impressive in her endeavor to extend the frontiers of her own knowledge and to share her experience with her son. At an age when most boys are reading Leatherstocking or Buffalo Bill, Canetti's mother reads Shakespeare or Dickens with her son. Her son's appetite for reading is enormous; precocious as he is, he picks up the demanding and complex too.

His relationship with his mother is a principal theme in Canetti's book of recollections. In all its ambivalence, its mixture of hatred and love, it is filled with a persuasive truthfulness in every nuance. Canetti brings the same succinct evocativeness to bear on the the teachers and fellow pupils he once knew in Zurich. It is a milieu where anti-Semitism is rampant, but Canetti, together with other pupils of Jewish family, hands the headmaster of the *Gymnasium* a petition which proves in time to have a lasting effect on the baiting.

Elias Canetti is a cosmopolitan writer. By no means the least remarkable feature of his memoirs is his ability to convey the atmosphere of totally different milieux. But above all he is a very fine human portrait artist, clear-sightedly perceptive and incorruptible in his allotment of light and shadow.

The compendious intellectual register, the truthfulness of his portraiture of milieux and of people, and his concision of style make Canetti's autobiographical writings a highly unusual literary experience.

Two

John Bayley

Canetti and Power

Henry James writes of a very grand lady that she had an air of keeping, at every moment, every "advantage." Paradoxically, the same would be true of the literary personality of Elias Canetti. Behind its approachable modesty, its avoidance of every publicity and image-making process, there is a loftiness, an assurance, a stance of absolute superiority. Indeed the modesty and the dignity make the same point: why make a fuss about your greatness?

Great writers usually do, nonetheless. "Fame wants to find safety," as Canetti has put it. Thomas Mann was notorious for his self-importance and his suspicion of anyone whom he felt might be detecting signs of weakness in him; Thomas Hardy spent his last days writing venomously bad verses against fellow authors whom he felt had patronized him. Across the Atlantic the Hemingways and Mailers positively seethe with anxiety about their status and reputations. Such unease does not mean they are not great: it just shows the extreme vulnerability which usually goes with true creative powers.

Canetti's superiority is reverenced and proclaimed by his disciples, who feel something different from enthusiasm for an admired writer. He is sage and master of an art which only the initiated can fully perceive. The American firm which has begun to publish all his books—the novel, the essays, the play— simply prints "Canetti" in big black letters on top of the jacket, as it might be "Socrates" or "Confucius," and the full name and title in smaller print below. A critic writes of his memoir *The Tongue Set Free* that "all readers—even those not yet exposed to the writings of Elias Canetti—will appreciate this self-portrait." The idea of such an "exposure"—a magic ordeal yet to come—is typical. Nor, in this case, does it seem absurd.

The novel which emerges, *Auto-da-Fé,* has been seriously called the most remarkable of this century. A meaningless judgment, and yet what could be said is that it is the most remarkable attempt at an intellectual imagination of the true nature of the twentieth century, an apotheosis of the immensely weighty and serious Faust tradition of German letters. It could only have been written *in* German, and yet it could hardly have been written *by* a German, a man too physically at home in the *gemütlichkeit* of his native speech. Canetti's use of the language is enormously mental, magical, and dynamic. During a thirty-year residence in England after his return in 1938, he often suffered what he called "word attacks," a compulsive urge to make lists and patterns of German words as if they were counters in a spell to conjure, or to abjure, power. He also began to keep the extended diary of thoughts and aphorisms now published as *The Human Province.* Full of fascination but verging on the portentous as such compilations in an English translation unavoidably do, it contains such comments as "So long as there are people in the world who have *no power whatsoever,* I cannot lose all hope," and "I have never heard of a person attacking power without wanting it." Portraits of the powerful in history rekindle his hatred of power, "and warn me of my own power over people."

Everything Canetti writes is obsessed with and transformed by this abstract passion, even his academic but strangely haunting play *The Numbered,* written in England after the war. His own creative dynamism comes from the love-hate relation with power, and from "confronting" its special nightmare in our own century. *The Human Province* is a sort of Caesar's

Commentaries on power geography. One of Canetti's strengths is that he never discriminates between the public and the private spheres of power, just as he never admits, even tacitly, a division between his own abstraction of it and the thing itself. A profound admirer of Hobbes, he wastes no time on the anatomy of modern power systems—Communism, Fascism—which absorb the individual into an ideal of overall social cohesion. He sees the crucial area both of power and of freedom in the private life, the area which Hobbesian authority exists to encourage and protect. Yet it is here also that the worst abuses take place, as is shown by the vision of a father and daughter relation in the chapter of *Auto-da-Fé* called "The Kind Father."

For Canetti, it is self-evident that *Auto-da-Fé* engrosses as a novel the most central significances of our time, and in his other writings he speaks of it as Goethe spoke of *Faust*. What about such a novel as *Ulysses?* That would be by comparison a piece of random jewelry, a plaything with the popular appeal of such a craft object. The same with *A la Recherche du Temps Perdu,* even with *The Magic Mountain.* They are essentially independent of their time, floating above it: they are *literature.* In art Canetti had, as he tells us, a contempt for "salvation and joy," for anything that was "relaxing." Art should have the atmosphere of revolution, the excitement, as in Goethe, of a potential, "manifest in each of its moments." A favorite text of Canetti is Stendhal's account of growing up in the French Revolution, *La Vie de Henri Brulard.* Dostoevsky, Büchner, Kafka also point the way to *Auto-da-Fé.* Writers who don't, even great ones like Tolstoy, are of minor interest; Canetti's essay on Tolstoy, one of his very few pieces lacking in compulsive interest, merely makes the point that Tolstoy at the end of his life became like the hero of *Auto-da-Fé.*

"Truly to confront the age"—great art does not often do that so self-consciously. Stendhal does it with lightness and élan; the painter Beckmann did it after the First World War with mythic violence and horror. Beckmann's painting is probably the closest parallel in art to Canetti's novel. Canetti does not mention him, but when writing his novel he surrounded himself with reproductions of Grünewald, who also inspired Beckmann. And apart from the intention, an art that confronts the age must not give way to it. It must be highly organized technically, to survive its own picture of disintegration.

The thought came to me that the world should not be depicted as in earlier novels, from one writer's standpoint as it were; the world had *crumbled,* and only if one had the courage to show it in its crumbled state could one possibly offer an authentic conception of it. . . . When I ask myself today where I got the rigour of my work I come to heterogeneous influences. . . . Stendhal it was who made me stick to clarity. I had just finished the eighth chapter, now titled "Death," when Kafka's "Metamorphosis" came into my hands. Nothing more fortunate could have happened to me at this point. There, in utmost perfection, I found the antipode to literary non-commitment which I hated so much; there was the rigour that I yearned for. There, something was achieved that I wanted to find for myself. I bowed to this purest of all models, knowing full well that it was unattainable, but it did give me strength.

Kafka seems to be not so much an influence on *Auto-da-Fé* as totally absorbed by it, almost as Shakespeare's sources were absorbed by Shakespeare, and it is revealing to find out that Canetti discovered him in the actual process of writing his novel. But the greatest formative influence in Vienna at that time was Karl Kraus, the extraordinary nature of whose achievement—partly because it was histrionic, acted out in his recitals—can probably never be adequately presented to an Anglo-Saxon readership. Indeed, it would probably not be too much to say that *Auto-da-Fé,* which has been effectively translated, and which contains beside the potent forces of Canetti's internationalism, even his "Englishness," his Shakespearean side, gives the best intuition that a non-Germanist can get of Kraus's peculiar genius.

It is, above all, a genius of commitment—to language and to emotion. That was the same with Kafka. How to combine, in art, a pure, fastidious rigor with the simplest feeling of rage and sorrow against the dreadfulness of life, the domination of the powerful, the torture of beetle Gregor by his family, of Woyzeck by the captain, of Jews by Nazis, Russians by Communists, Oliver Twist by Bumble, of Smike by Squeers (*Nicholas Nickleby* was one of Canetti's early and passionate enthusiasms)? For such an artist, the inner world, the world of his invention, cannot and should not be any different from the world of human and historical reality. In his study of Kafka Canetti writes that his strength was increased by the horror with which he saw the "mass events accompanying the outbreak of war." The rigor, the totality of his art is a direct expression of the wholeness of that sense of horror, the "bond between the external hell of the world and his inner hell." "He did not have for his private and interior processes that disregard which distinguishes insignificant writers from writers of imagination. A person who thinks that he is empowered to separate his inner world from the outer one has no inner world from which something might be separable."

Canetti has written nothing more significant than that. Most people do, in fact, feel empowered to achieve a normal equilibrium by separating their own world from the outer one. What is more, most art exists to aid, comfort, and satisfy that natural urge. Our inner world is supported and confirmed by it against the outer world—which is the reason thoughtful Nazi officials could read Goethe and Schiller, and listen to Mozart, while going about their business of persecution and domination. Many artists of real honesty will admit the fact, tacitly or openly. Jane Austen, possibly not a genius in whom Canetti takes much interest, writes in a letter about a bloody battle in the Napoleonic war: "How dreadful that so many poor fellows should be killed, and what a mercy that one cares for none of them." There speaks the voice of a certain kind of common sense, the kind that most of us have to live by.

Not Canetti's great masters, however. Shakespeare may not have wept over King Lear, may indeed have written the play in a passion of relish, but he *suffered:* the play is a correlative of his total capacity to suffer. That is perhaps self-evident and tautologous. In a climate of pseudo-scientific structuralism, a bloodlessly mechanistic approach to literature, Canetti's insistent emphases are decidedly salutary. In what sense, though, is Kafka for him the "purest of all models"? That in which suffering is most absolute, most evident? But the message of great works of art is more ambiguous than that, and in a sense more comforting. As Auden wrote in Jane Austen vein: "You can only tell them parables, from which each according to his immediate and peculiar needs may draw his own conclusions." And as with the client's need, so with that of the artist himself. Kafka suffers all in himself, but by writing he accepts and takes possession of that suffering. By becoming a beetle, his hero paradoxically has found how to keep, "at every moment, every advantage." There is nothing "pure" in the spectacle of Kafka's pleasure in discovering the perfect way of separating himself from his hated family: for the reader, it is too touching for that, too "human, all too human."

That vulnerability is not to be found in Canetti's novel, a work of pure schematic power and ferocity, in which every sentence crackles with violent intelligence, violent humor. "There was not *one* voice that he did not hear, he was possessed by every specific timbre of the war and rendered it compellingly. Whatever he satirically foreshortened was foreshortened effectively; whatever he exaggerated was exaggerated so precisely that it only first existed in this exaggeration and remained unforgettable . . . unsparingly, uncomfortingly, without embellishment, without reduction, and above all and most important, without habituation. Whatever was repeated . . . remained horrifying through every single repetition." What Canetti wrote of Kraus's play *The Last Days of Mankind* is true of his own novel. As the First World War "completely entered" Kraus's play, so a horrifying sense of the modern world completely enters his novel. But it is not in the slightest degree a self-consciously "black" work, like Céline's; nor does it parade a ready-made metaphysic of gloom, like the novels of Graham Greene and Patrick White. It is not apocalyptic but dreadfully and intently domestic, like Dickens's world of Todgers.

It is divided into three parts: "A Head without a World," "Headless World," and "The World in the Head." Kien, the hero, a recluse and a distinguished sinologist, with an enormous library, is the head; the library his inner world. His housekeeper, Therese, the most memorable portrait in the book, is a world without any head. Everything in the novel can be distinctly "heard," Therese and her speech particularly so. Having no contact with life, Kien has no speech, only an interior utterance. But he (and his creator) are painfully sensitive to what Canetti apropos of Kraus calls "acoustic quotations": the sense that everything in the world—newspapers, people, and now radio and television—has a *voice*, its own sort of unique propaganda, which the artist must render unsparingly. He must "let everybody speak," though most artists do not know how to listen: "It is the hereditary vice of the intellectual that for him the world consists of intellectuals." This no doubt is why the greatest acoustic artists, like Dickens and Shakespeare, are not in the German sense "intellectuals"—they are naïve rather than reflective. And it is perhaps the greatest achievement of Canetti to fuse in himself as artist the massive endowment and consciousness of a modern European thinker with an absolutely precise and humble sense of other people, their irreducible, untranslatable utterance of being.

Significant, then, that the speech reality of the novel is in its headless world of Therese, the red-haired porter Benedikt Pfaff, the chess-playing dwarf Fischerle, his prostitute wife the Capitalist, and the other denizens of the café called The Stars of Heaven. Kien, a profound student of Confucius, becomes aware that Therese, whom he finds wearing white gloves to read a tattered book he has given her, *The Trousers of Herr von Bredow,* has a greater respect and feeling for books than he has. Amazed and humbled by this revelation, he decides to marry her. The sequence is one of the funniest in the novel and echoes the range of meaning in its German title *Die Blendung,* a noun which combines the literal with the metaphorical to signify blinding, dazzlement, delusion, deception. The married Kien is crumbled willy-nilly into the horrors of the headless world, beaten, driven out, and forced into the company of the denizens of The Stars of Heaven—particularly the dwarf Fischerle, who sets out to exploit him (there is a sort of grotesque reversal hereabouts of the adventures of Little Nell and her father).

Unhinged, Kien is convinced that he has removed his entire library into his head, whence it has to be laboriously unpacked when he lies down at night, and repacked again in the morning. "Anything that appears in reality is seen in terms of the delusion as a whole." This fantasy is remarkably like that set forth in a "real" madman's book—*Denkwürdigkeiten,* by Schreber, a former president of the Senate of Dresden, whose paranoia was examined by Freud in an essay of 1911. Canetti suggests, rightly, that Freud has missed the point, and that Schreber's is really a very typically twentieth-century case of what he calls "Power and Survival." Schreber's delusion was that he was the one man left alive after some vast catastrophe—the nuclear bomb, as it might now be. He was aware of other people around him in the asylum, but he explained their presence away by knowing that they were "fleetingly sketched men," not real, manikins whom he can repack into his head as and when he needs, as Kien repacks the books, though for Kien books are the only reality, which is why in the headless world his survival depends on his continuing to hold them in his head. Kien, like Schreber, has entered, though by another route, what Canetti calls the extreme phase of power—the certainty of onlyness. Power is, ultimately, nothing but the refusal to believe that other people exist, and to act on that belief.

Kien is thus, by a grim paradox, reduced simultaneously to the state of ultimate survival power and of total degradation and powerlessness. As Gogol's Akaky can only apprehend the world through the reality of a new overcoat, so Kien survives by haunting the state pawnshop, "releasing" by purchase all the books which headless people have brought to pawn, and repacking them in his own head. This is, among other things, a parable of the way in which we try to serve the world and come to terms with it, while retaining our own kinds of solipsism. The most important and terrifying statement of Kafka, says Canetti, is that fear and indifference made up his deepest feeling toward human beings. "If one thinks about it with a little courage, our world has indeed become one in which fear and indifference predominate. Expressing his own reality without indulgence, Kafka was the first to present the image of *this* world. "The head without a world can only feel those emotions toward it, and it is the task of the artist like Kafka to bring the world into the head, to compel the two into coincidence. That is also what happens in the last section of *Auto-da-Fé*. Reunited with his library, Kien sets fire to it and perishes in the flames. The world has got into his head and he has voluntarily joined the crowd, the mass, the headless world, as Gregor in "The Metamorphosis" joins it by his humble death as an insect, something dry to be swept up off the carpet. Canetti records that his ending was suggested by the burning of the Justice Palace in Vienna by crowds protesting against the shooting of some workers, and against the acquittal of those responsible. He himself witnessed the scene and, like his puppet Kien, felt at last truly one with and a part of the crowd.

Schematic as it certainly is, the novel's extraordinary richness, the density of its wit and style, can only be travestied by such a brief sketch of its contents. It is not without faults, though these are more evident in the English version than in the German original. Even though it was translated by the historian Veronica Wedgwood "under the personal supervision of the author," English linguistic forms and models cannot quite accommodate themselves to an outburst of *Kunstprosa* that was in every sense *intended* for the German language. There its fierce abstractness, its almost paralyzing intelligence, are wholly at home: even the tedium which it by no means lacks seems, as it were, a wholly genuine and necessary tedium, an essential, and even dynamic part of its massive mental specification. For the Anglo-Saxon reader accustomed to less demanding works of fiction, even the endless multiplication of the grotesque can be a little wearing, as if a computer had been programmed to turn out an infinite series of scarifying intellectual jokes, sometimes at its own expense. An example would be Kien's comment to a student who brings a set of Schiller to pawn. "Why Schiller? You should read the original. You should read Immanuel Kant." In classic German literature there is nothing opaquely "original": the prismatic radiance of intellect is reflected from one work to another. Canetti's novel seems, in one sense, like the pinnacle of every brilliant and transparent work in its language: in another sense, as if it was already immanent in all of them. Exhilarating as it is, and also so physically disturbing that some of the author's friends and fellow writers hated it and couldn't bear to read it, it is at the same time a purely intellectual and philosophic exercise. This tension between a mental and physical plane is by no means unique in German literature, and it continues today in massive fantasy novels probably influenced by *Auto-da-Fé*, like those of Günther Grass.

It is also a tension unknown in naïve art—art which slips without a purpose into a particular perfection of its kind. *The Bronze Horseman*, or *The Golden Bowl*, are just as much graphic studies of power as *Auto-da-Fé*, but they are also halcyon structures of consummated art, by their very natures tranquil and uninsistent. The high-pressure blast of ruthless clarity in *Auto-da-Fé* seems to blow away the whole world of art. This may be the reason some of its greatest admirers, though they may also admire Proust or Musil, tended in England to be intellectuals to whom it would never occur to read and enjoy the standard English poets and novelists. Like Voltaire or Nietzsche, Canetti seemed to them quite separate from the mere banal arts of literature.

Nonetheless, it may be that the predicament of *Auto-da-Fé*'s puppet hero, although he has none of the physical reality and emotional pathos of Gogol's Akaky or Kafka's Gregor Samsa, has for intellectuals not only a strong masochistic appeal, but conventional fiction's charge of fascination and suspense. Canetti has himself written, as any good novelist might do, that "true writers encounter their characters only *after* they've created them": and yet his hero is obviously and by intention not a character in this sense. While the book was in progress, he was called simply B, or Bookman, and later Kant (the novel had the provisional title *Kant Catches Fire*), finally becoming the combustible Kien (Pinewood) when the conflagration nears which ends the novel. Therese was based on Canetti's first impression of his Viennese landlady.

The finally completed novel was dispatched out of the blue to Thomas Mann, the author being confident that he would recognize it for the masterpiece it was. Mann replied apologetically that he found himself unable to read it. It remained in manuscript for a further four years and was published in 1935, achieving an immediate success. To Canetti's amusement, Thomas Mann wrote a warmly enthusiastic letter. But Canetti wrote no more novels: in that form there was no other subject for him. He had always been obsessed by the need to write his theoretical study of power and the mass, for which he had never ceased to read omnivorously. It was written mostly in England, and was finally published in Germany in 1960.

Crowds and Power could be said to ingest history, all stories about themselves and their behavior which human beings have told, in the same way that *Auto-da-Fé* ingested the works of art that told in their different way the truths about power that Canetti was seeking. His favorite historian is Herodotus, a storyteller, with whom it hardly matters whether the story told is factuallly true or not, because it is always true to the psychology of the society it relates to. Conversely, he has little use for Aristotle the rationalist, who is more interested in the processes of knowledge than in those of suffering, of who does what to whom. As an analyst of the power process, Canetti is equally contemptuous of the empirical and factual historian and of the men-of-destiny school, noting that both are on the side of power and have a vested interest in it, either because of their theories or from their very function as investigators. "Muhammad Tughlak has been defended by modern Indian historians. Power has never lacked eulogists, and historians, who are professionally obsessed with it, can explain anything, either by the *times* (disguising their adulation as scholarship), or by *necessity*, which, in their hands, can assume any and every shape." He is instructive, as I have already indicated, on the psychology and powers of the survivor, and has two chapters on the paranoia of Schreber, which are far more illuminating than any of the "explanations" of Freud. (We might note that Canetti is implacabaly hostile to Freud's view of literature as both a substitute for life and a way of achieving power in it. For him, great literature is the truest expression possible of the predicament of living and of its need to understand and renounce power.)

The survivor may be detested, as in the example of Muhammad Tughlak, who killed all those returning from an unsuccessful expedition, or he may be credited with almost magical powers, as in the case of Josephus, or Hitler. Josephus probably the only historian to have actually been in this physical sense a survivor, drew lots with his soldiers in a cave after the fall of the fortress he was commanding. They were to kill each other on this basis, but Josephus cooked the deal in such a way that he and one other man were left alive. "This is precisely what he brings the Romans: the enhanced sense of his own life, feeding on the deaths of those he had led." This power he is about to sell, as it were, to Vespasian and his son Titus, in the form of a prophecy that they will become Emperors of Rome. Josephus's distinction as a survivor is so great that it quite outweighs his betrayal of his fellows and desertion of his country.

Surviving the crowd implies having been once a part of it. Hitler's survivor complex was based on the amazing deliverance from his enemies of Frederick the Great. When Roosevelt dies a few weeks before the end of the war, Hitler is convinced he is saved, as Frederick had been saved by the sudden death of his arch-enemy the Empress Elizabeth of Russia. This clutch of a precedent shows an almost pathetic stupidity—and the paranoiac's ignorance of and separation from the realities of the outside world. Yet Hitler had once been truly a part of that world, and of the German and European crowd at the beginning of the First World War. "He described how, at the outbreak of war, he fell on his knees and thanked God. It was his decisive experience, the one moment at which he himself honestly became part of a crowd. He never forgot it, and his whole subsequent career was devoted to the re-creation of this moment, but *from outside.*"

Hitler's response had been that of the crowd, which was given the same expression by men like Péguy and Rupert Brooke. His paranoia devotes itself to re-creating that erstwhile solidarity, and his immediate instrument is the crowd: he perceives how to turn the old *closed* crowd of the German Army, now forbidden under the Treaty of Versailles, into the *open* crowd of the National Socialist Party. The orders, exercises, and expectations essential to German psychology had to be procured again at all costs. "Every closed crowd which is dissolved by force transforms itself into an open crowd to which it imparts all its characteristics."

The many categories which Canetti makes—invisible crowds,

double crowds, crowds as packs—claim no quasi-scientific status. So clearly and forcefully does he set them out that we seem to be recognizing something we have always known, as Molière's hero discovers that he has been speaking grammar all his life. The human condition in history is seen as Montaigne might have seen it, in pictures and conversations: the mode of discourse is itself entirely open. This very openness can lead to a sense of repetitiveness: the reader may feel that he has got the point quite early on. But it is the strength of Canetti's mode of creative exposition that he is not out to prove anything and that his terminology does not imprison inquiry. *Masse* and *Macht* are more resonant and more menacing than their English equivalents—the word "crowd" suggests flower shows and football matches rather than the forces inherent in a human mass—and the material of Canetti's book is mythic and historical rather than contemporary, though it can also be curiously prophetic, as is indicated by cant modernisms like "student power" and "gay power."

The nemesis of such an undertaking, steadfastly nurtured through so long a period of intellectual growth, must be that its director becomes himself charged in its emotional field. To study the operation of power is in some sense to love it; and Canetti's scorn for historians who enjoy the spectacle of power involuntarily and aesthetically cannot dissociate him entirely from their predicament. As a character of Saul Bellow's observes, the deepest ambiguity in intellectuals is that they despise the civilization which makes their lives possible, and prefer to contemplate one, or to create one mentally, in which this would cease to be so. But Canetti never commits that particular *trahison*. His calm, which is never ironic, can be directed against himself (he repeatedly queries the possibility of self-knowledge and praises Kafka for having come as near to it as a writer can). Some of the best things in *Crowds and Power* are detached essays or meditations, like that on immortality, the last infirmity of power, and the way a walk among the silent crowd in a cemetery feeds the sensation of it ("We draw from them the strength to become, and to remain forever, *more than they are*"). Stendhal is again a favorite here, the least pretentious aspirant to immorality: such a writer "will still be here when everyone else who lived at the same time is no longer here." To live forever in this way is Canetti's own expressed ambition.

His aura of extreme exclusiveness seldom irritates; even when, in his most brilliant essay, he does not so much explain Kafka as absorb him, the process seems biologically natural and benign—Kafka was the thinnest of men and Canetti is corpulent. *The Other Trial,* first published in Germany in 1969, analyzes Kafka's correspondence with Felice Bauer, to whom he was twice engaged. Canetti sees these letters as decisive in Kafka's writing life: by writing to her, he discovered both how to love her and how himself to be a writer. Two nights after his first letter he writes "The Judgment," the first tale which liberates his characteristic genius, in a single ten-hour sitting, by night, and a day or two later, "The Stoker." He produces six chapters of *Amerika,* and after an interval his finest short story of all, "The Metamorphosis." It is a *mensis mirabilis* comparable to Pushkin's Boldino autumn, the most fertile writing period in Kafka's career.

He can feel she expects something of him, and he in turn expects of her an equal precision in recording her days and her feelings. "He succeeds in imposing upon her his own obsession," his own way of being in love, which he would later transfer to her friend Grete Bloch. Felice has given him what she could, but he cannot give her marriage in return. He confronts her family and the two girls in Berlin, at what he called the "Tribunal," with the war already impending, and a little later he begins *The Trial,* with its culminating scene of the two executioners leaning over Josef K like the two girls, their cheeks touching.

Canetti uses the word "obduracy" to describe the way Kafka

protected "the tremendous world he felt to be in his head"—a new world in which the human situation appears in art in a new way. Canetti rejects any idea that Kafka is exploring the nature of God or the Divine Law: it is power itself, in its ultimately and impersonally human shape, which executes Josef K and oppresses the hero of *The Castle*. The implication of Canetti's short book, which reads like one of Kafka's own compelling stories, is that the truest and most significant modern literature can be seen as a withdrawal from power, even from literature's own magnificent pageant of mastery as it appears in the great creations of naming, recording, and enjoying, in the worlds of Homer, Shakespeare, Milton, or Dante. Kafka must find mastery in minuteness, in disappearance.

Kafka's sovereign perspective on psychoanalysis ought to have helped critics to detach from its constricting domain his own person at least. His struggle with his father was essentially never anything but a struggle against superior power as such. . . . Since he fears power in any form, since the real aim of his life is to withdraw from it, in whatever form it may appear, he detects it, identifies it, names it, and creates figures of it in every instance where others would accept it as being nothing out of the ordinary. . . . *Macht* and *mächtig* are his unavoided, unavoidable words.

Marriage is out of the question. The place of smallness in it is usurped by children, whom Kafka envied and disapproved of because they are not actually small beings who want to dwindle and disappear, as he wants to, but "false smallnesses" who want to grow bigger. Himself an expert on Chinese literature, where the idea of smallness—in insects or animals—is subtly explored and imagined, Canetti claims that Kafka "belongs in its annals," and quotes for this the authority of Arthur Waley, for whom Kafka was the one Western prose author to be read with passionate attention.

Canetti's feeling for the Orient is perceptible in *The Voices of Marrakesh,* a unique travel book and, together with *Kafka's Other Trial,* the most formally satisfying of his works. A sentence referring to Kafka's letters gives the clue to the way he enters into and conveys to us the baffling and yet familiar quality of strangers met in such a scene: "They are so enigmatic and familiar to me that it seems they have been mental possessions of mine from the moment when I first began to accommodate human beings entirely in my mind; in order to arrive, time and again, at a fresh understanding of them." That sort of accommodation is the key to Canetti's creative vision, with its peculiar blend of intense abstraction and equally stunning physical reality, constantly creating images of power where others would see "nothing out of the ordinary."

Though he is a scholar and a man of the mind, Canetti's sense of human societies and his gift—as in the Marrakesh book—for familiarizing out-of-the-way places have something in common with the art of another and earlier Nobel Prize winner, Rudyard Kipling. But the timely comparison and contrast is with a more recent winner, the Polish poet Czeslaw Milosz. Both authors have written in a wide range of forms and both are exiles—Milosz in America—though in Canetti's case exile is itself a mode made for genius, for his country is the entire European tradition. Milosz's wonderful record of a Polish-Lithuanian childhood, *The Issa Valley,* should be enjoyed together with Canetti's *Geschichte* of his own early years in Bulgaria and England, Switzerland and Vienna. Both are subtle analysts and historians of national fixations and complexities. There are, it is true, poems by Milosz—one of the great poets of our time—which move the reader more directly than anything by Canetti, who is by adoption a German *Dichter* but not in the naïve and direct sense a poet. He enchants and enlightens but does not make the tears flow. But what a pair! The fact that two such remarkable writers should have won it in recent years almost makes one believe in the prize as an "award" to literature.

Edgar Piel

Putting an End to Power: Canetti's Archetypal Images and New Myth

I

Time and again we encounter in Canetti images and thoughts we cannot cope with. In his notebooks in particular we are frequently confronted with passages whose fundamental hopelessness for humankind leaves us speechless, indeed quite helpless. But we can arrive at an understanding of the meaning of Canetti's work as a whole—and moreover, I suspect, of Man, of the human condition, of ourselves—only if we do not bluff our way through those straits where everything seems impossible and all the signs point only to meaninglessness.

One of those texts whose hopelessness can scarcely be surpassed is the following note, written at the end of 1947:

On the last day of the month I go down into my ruin, the ridiculous lamp in my right hand, and, the deeper down I go, tell myself: it's all for nothing. What belief is there that could penetrate to the earth's core? Whatever you or someone else or any of us may do, it is all in vain. Oh, the vanity of all endeavor—the victims are still falling in their thousands and millions—this life, whose sacredness you feign belief in, is sacred to no one and nothing. There is no secret power with the wish to preserve it. Perhaps there is no secret power that wishes to destroy it either, but it is destroying itself. How should there be value in a life that resembles an intestinal tract? The plant kingdom may have been better off—but what do you really know of the torments of suffocation?

Oh, the nausea goes on without end, and it is a nausea that comes from eating. Everything is contaminated with eating, everything is addicted to eating. That day of peace some experience is hypocritical—a day torn apart is more truthful. The peaceful cover the earth with the leaves and the slowness of plants, but their nets are weak and, even where they win, the fleshly destruction continues beneath their green covers. The powerful man struts and swaggers, with the biggest of stomachs, and the vain man is resplendent in all the colors of his entrails. For those who are digesting, and gagging, art strikes up its dance tune. Art always makes things better again, and its heritage is guarded as the most precious of possessions. There are some who flatter themselves with the thought that it could all end, and they work out one catastrophe after another—but the deeper intentions of this torment lie in eternity. The earth is still young and life on earth is multiplying, and new, complicated, more extreme and perfect kinds of misery are being devised. And one man implores his neighbor: help me, make it worse![1]

A more drastic critique of the conditions of our existence and of a civilization that only obscures those conditions is inconceivable. Again: "Everything is contaminated with eating, everything is addicted to eating." Though anyone with eyes in his head is naturally familiar with this necessary fact of (our) life, we generally find little occasion to let the fact of eating spoil our appetites or even moods. Quite apart from the fact that the thought cannot alter a jot of what is inevitable, beliefs and ideologies of every conceivable kind have trained us well enough to distinguish the satisfaction of our needs from ourselves and the way we see ourselves. Only on rare occasions do skepticism and pessimism break through. And only in very few cases do such skepticism and pessimism lead to realism, that is to say, closer to life: often what is produced is the contrary. High on a massive dose of cynicism, the skeptics and pessimists readily dissociate themselves: "The Lord of Creation, the Swine, Man—"

Benn's sarcastic phrase has primarily achieved one thing only: it has supplied a vindication for those who would view the world and this senseless toing-and-froing of Man which we call history only from the outside. From the outside. Of course, we need to keep our distance, if possible to wear the dermatologist's rubber gloves, if we are to make that great fermentation process Life bring forth on its surface the shiny resplendent bubbles we call works of art.

In the face of such endeavors to cream off art from the despised process of Life, Canetti has never turned his back on the experiments that bring knowledge, not even at the time he wrote the note on life as eating. That note, which so repels us, was used by Canetti in his work as a hard, sharp-edged, deep-cutting tool to slit open the soft skin of our animal natures and to cut apart the psychic armor plating of our imagined harmlessness and harmony with life. The findings of this vivisectional process are available in his compendious work *Crowds and Power*.

II

One of the chapters in *Crowds and Power* is headed "The Entrails of Power." In this chapter, Canetti's premise for his investigation and thinking is made clear with an uncompromising and indeed offensive harshness. Put briefly, this premise goes as follows: Nothing affects us more directly, and is thus more directly of concern to us, than what we eat. That we have to incorporate everything we are or will become determines the very last fiber of our real existence. Canetti's final and pithiest observation runs: "Nothing has been so much part of one as that which turns into excrement."[2]

What looks like a superficial crashing banality when divorced from its context is intended to point up the insight that the simple eating process that animals and Man have in common means more in Man's case than a physiologist might suppose. "The constant pressure which, during the whole of its long process through the body, is applied to the prey which has become food; its dissolution and intimate union with the creature digesting it; the complete and final annihilation, first of all functions and then of everything which once constituted its individuality; its assimilation to something already existing, that is, to the body of the eater—all this may well be seen as the central, if most hidden, process of power. It is so much a matter of course, so automatic and so far beyond consciousness, that one underrates its importance."[3] The reason for the meticulousness with which Canetti describes the passage of the prey through the body is that here Canetti is envisioning a model of that process through which Man, exposed and helpless in a hostile environment, made sure of his survival, and appropriated both reality and power. The stages in this process are plainly recognizable in the spiritual realm too. The prey which is gradually consumed provides Man not only with essential vitamins, minerals, and nutriments but also with its entire being. In eating the bear, those who had fought and overcome the bear themselves became bears. The heap of excrement as the final point in the process of digestion needs to be understood as the sealing of a seizure of power.

In his chapter "The Entrails of Power," Canetti describes in minute detail the connection between seizing and incorporating and Man's ability to cope with reality. Man's imagination is forever occupied with the stages of incorporation: lying in wait, pursuing, touching, seizing, crushing, ripping, grinding, and digesting his prey. "The gaping jaws of the large beasts which threatened him have pursued him even into his dreams and myths. Voyages of discovery down these jaws were no less important to him than those over the sea, and certainly as dangerous."[4]

Taken together, the interlinked, merging processes of seizure, incorporation, and digestion constitute for Canetti that process which is fundamental to the copiousness of Man's psychic, spiritual, and social being, and also to his culture. Through continually renewed transfers, transpositions of this one process into other spheres, beyond Nature (which was out to devour Man) into Man's own flexing of teeth, muscles, and nerves, and thence into the psychic, social, and political realms—through all of this adaptation and metamorphosis of a single paradigmatic process, the prehuman creature became Man, and Man in turn has in the meantime become his own worst enemy. Starting from this primeval scene still animal in character and wholly dictated by violence, Canetti has evolved an anthropology that renders comprehensible not only our dreams of Man but also the brutality, manifest at every moment in this century, which Man has shown to Nature, to animals, and to his fellow man.

Why it was that the entirety of occidental culture and civilization were unable to afford protection from the relapse into the barbarity of mass extermination and world wars seems only to become apparent once we grasp that civilization is by no means simply a wonderful antithesis to the realm of bestiality and natural violence, nor does culture as such represent the conquest of the jungle. An intuition of an indissoluble connection between culture and the animal digestive process appears in Canetti as early as 1947—in other words, in the same year as his note on life as eating:

How is it possible that we put in our mouth something that has been torn apart, that we go on tearing it apart by chewing, and that then words should come from that very same mouth? Would it not be better to have another orifice for food, and to keep the mouth only for words? Or does this intimate mixing of all our utterances with the lips, teeth, tongue, throat, all those parts of the mouth that serve the business of eating—does this mixing tell us that language and eating forever belong together, that we can never be nobler and better than we are, that basically, however it's disguised, all we say is the same terrible and bloody thing, and that revulsion and our gorge only rise if something is wrong with our food?[5]

In *Crowds and Power* too—the extensive anthropological investigation through which he tried to "take our century by the throat"—Canetti discovers the bloody primeval scenes of eating and being eaten not only at the threadbare or fragile points in present-day culture; indeed, he locates the tensions, threats, and sense of jeopardy which characterized the archetypal situation of Man in culture itself—in the ceremonies, forms of style, topoi, the architecture and the signs that surround us. For example, harmless pleasure in symmetry and order, which almost seems innate in Man, is for Canetti readily explained by fear of being struck and bitten by the stronger. This fear is allayed only if the distances separating each man from his neighbor are regulated and kept to. "Every man, even the least, seeks to prevent anyone else coming too near him. Every form of social life established among men expresses itself in distances which allay the ceaseless fear of being seized and caught."[6]

III

The posing and description of the problem in *Crowds and Power* evolves from this experiential sentence: "There is nothing that man fears more than the touch of the unknown." Both power (the full destructive potential of which we have seen in this century) and the powerlessness of the masses, who have given life (literally their own lives) to power, are viewed in this work, which is meant for our century and the present, as deriving from that primeval mortal fear. "Even clothes give insufficient security: it is easy to tear them and pierce through to the naked, smooth, defenceless flesh of the victim. All the distances which men create round themselves are dictated by this fear."[7]

Crowds and Power, a condensation of over twenty years of research into dreams, myths, past rituals, religions, and strange, in part primitive customs, was written in the 1940s and 1950s; but the primeval images it describes can also be found in Canetti before that time, in his early plays of 1933–34 and in his novel, *Auto-da-Fé*, which was written at the start of the 1930s.

The basic position of the characters both in *Auto-da-Fé* and in the play *The Wedding* is that of lying in wait. In the prologue to *The Wedding*, Toni, the granddaughter, is waiting, watching her aged grandmother. She can hardly wait for the old woman's death and her own inheritance. In the next room, Professor Thut and his wife, ears to the wall, are equally in wait, keeping everything that happens in old grandmother Gilz's room under their surveillance. They too are after her house, which they plan to do her out of before she dies. In the main scene of the play we are shown a wedding party where almost everyone is out to make everyone else a sexual prey, and everyone is on the run from everyone else.

Auto-da-Fé, surely one of the great city novels of this century, is wholly determined by archetypal images of lying in wait, devouring and being devoured. The protagonist, Peter Kien, finds that his housekeeper of many years, Therese, turns out to be a demon incarnate after he has finally married her, a wild animal stalking and attacking him and his money as if they were precious prey. "She was quiet and, in spite of her bulk, flexible. Or was it something to do with the room, that she so suddenly appeared and vanished? Her eyes had an evil glitter; they were cat's eyes. When she wanted to say something, but interrupted herself before she could get it out, it sounded like a cat spitting."[8] Kien soon begins to suspect that he had admitted a "bloodthirsty tiger" to his library, a tiger that is "not even young and beautiful" but "instead of a shining skin . . . wore a starched skirt."[9]

After Therese has conquered the territory of Kien the scholar, and has expelled him from his library and flat, Kien hallucinates a heroic murder committed to save scholarship from the demon. "For weeks I left her alone. Convinced that she must die of hunger, I passed night after night at hotels. . . . Instead of me—for by many a secret assault she brought me near to death—she now lay there, devoured by her own mad hunger. She did not know how to help herself. . . . Piece by piece of her body fell a prey to her greed. . . . The flesh which she had torn off in strips from her body stank to heaven."[10] While they still lived together in the flat, Therese tried to make her husband's a dog's life, and now, at the close of his murder fantasy, he lets loose a hound on her bodily remains: "No man can harm a skeleton; the mob dispersed. Only a bloodhound would not let go. He sought for flesh, but found none. Enraged, he tore the coffin to the ground and bit the blue skirt into small fragments. These he devoured, without pity, to the last morsel."[11]

At the beginning of the 1970s, in an essay on Alfred Hrdlicka's cycle of etchings related to *Crowds and Power,* Canetti emphasized that the entire work of his friend the painter and sculptor presupposed a world populated by predatory beasts. In a wholly literal sense, this is true of the greater part of Canetti's own work too. The motif of the predator and the prey can be traced back as far as his accounts of childhood—for example, to the wolves his mother would tell him of, or the wolf which one night stood at the narrator's bed. "One night, when I had dozed off," writes Canetti, "I was awakened by a giant wolf leaning over my bed. . . . I screamed as loud as I could: 'A wolf! A wolf!' No one heard me, no one came; I shrieked and yelled louder and louder and cried. Then a hand slipped out, grabbed the wolf's ears, and pulled his head down. My father was behind it, laughing."[12]

The fright the child Elias got from this wolf went so deep that afterward he had nightmares night after night and was considered a particularly sensitive child whose imagination should not be overexcited.

The further back we follow the motif of predator and prey, eating and being eaten, in Canetti's work or life, the clearer it becomes that, for Canetti, this constitutes a vivid and lifelong obsession. Nonetheless, as we reach this conclusion we must unavoidably ask the question which so far we have refrained from asking in our consideration of this horrific Canetti motif: What has this obsession, plainly of an individual and private nature, to do with us and the reality we live in? Why should one repeatedly remind oneself of the inevitable basic facts of life and, as Canetti does in his essay on Hrdlicka, envisage life itself as one single, terrible, ugly process of destruction in which the most wonderful creatures fall prey and are torn limb from limb,[13] if all that this results in (cf. the note from *The Human Province*) is doubting the value of a life that is like an intestinal tract? Is this not merely a particular hypersensitivity, the overexcitable imagination which Canetti suffered from even as a child?

In fact, of course, an individual obsession can be a reaction to something which concerns us all. Probably that is indeed more often the case than we would like. For the sake of a quiet life we tend to accept as "natural" facts of life the things we ourselves see as indisputable. For Canetti, however, the spur for his lifelong occupation with the bloody primeval underground realm beneath everyday life is his conviction that life could be different if we at least tried to bring the whole of our attention and powers of resistance to bear on the hidden violence of life. Even if, in his attempt to examine power in every last detail, Canetti was almost overwhelmed by the agonies of his labors, *Crowds and Power* was nonetheless "written" (as he tells us in the essay on Hrdlicka) "in the undisguised hope of putting an end to power."

IV

"Everything is contaminated with eating, everything is addicted to eating." Again: what has this to do with us and the reality we live in? I have said that Canetti means to draw our attention to the hidden violence and power that still affect us now. We have already noted that the process of seizure, incorporation, and digestion is in Canetti's view identical with the process of taking power. If we are to use the key Canetti has given us, in his portrayal of primeval hunting and eating, in order to understand the current social and political situation, we shall have to read his insight in reverse. To read it in reverse means, in relation to power, something like this: that power, whatever form it takes, is primarily motivated by a compulsion to incorporate fellow human beings (or Nature), by an impulse to exploit and to destroy totally. Canetti himself, in *Crowds and Power* and in his essays, has provided us with a model of this method of reading, in order to grasp what has happened in this century and to expose the roots of Fascism.[14]

To this end, the author of *Crowds and Power* presents a meticulous investigation of one case of paranoid megalomania. Paranoia, he writes, is by its very nature a "disease of power," so that through it we gain insight into the nature of power as we do nowhere else. Since Canetti sees in the paranoiac an exact counterpart image of the powerful, he has interpreted the self-penned case history of the megalomaniac *Senatspräsident* Daniel Paul Schreber (of the Dresden Senate) as a study parallel to those mass dictators of the twentieth century, Stalin and Hitler.

When the paranoiac is considered what becomes clear first and foremost is the connection between the feeling that one has been driven into a corner, and is oneself the prey, and the resultant irrepressible urge to incorporate the whole world, the whole of reality, into oneself. Fear, and this sense of impotence, give rise both in madness and in political reality to a feeling of total omnipotence, of needing to have everything in one's power, the reins in one's hands—ultimately, a sense that the ego extends almost cosmically and everything (the world) is being digested as prey by this ego. While the world in this way becomes nothing to the paranoiac, his own sense of himself develops into something tantamount to Deity. With specific reference to the political paranoiac Hitler, Canetti writes: "One cannot fully picture the destruction occurring in the mind of a paranoiac. His opposition, serving to extend and immortalize him, is aimed at this very infection by destruction. Yet it is within him, for it is part of him; and if it suddenly appears in the outer world, on whatever side, it cannot in any way surprise or astonish him."[15]

At the end of his account of the case of Schreber, Canetti summarizes his general diagnosis: "It is difficult to resist the suspicion that behind paranoia, as behind all power, lies the same profound urge: the desire to get other men out of the way so as to be the only one; or, in the milder, and indeed often admitted, form, to get others to help him become the only one."[16]

V

From this observation concluding his analysis of paranoia we see that the primeval images of lying in wait, seizing, and incorporating which Canetti has revealed not only provide a model for clinical or political paranoia but, indeed, this primitive process proves quite plainly to be deeply rooted in Man's nervous system from the start. Very early on, Man somatically and psychically adopted this process, and now it is having a terrible effect, even in everyday life.

We can see this clearly through Canetti's commentary on commands, which today remains one of the best pieces of work written on the subject. Commands, according to Canetti, need to be understood as a suspended threat of death. "The basic situation in nature arises from the fact that many animals feed on other animals. Those they feed on belong, however, to species different from their own and thus most animals feel threatened by creatures of a different kind; it is strangers and enemies who command them to flee." [17]

In mankind commands have developed considerably beyond this biological origin in the course of social evolution. In the context of human community, be it the state or the family, commands still play an essential part, but naturally they take on a very different character from those necessary in the wild. Little or nothing remains of the threat of death or of the command to flee—quite the contrary: "A master calls his slave and the latter comes although he knows he will receive an order. A mother calls her child and it does not invariably run away; although she rains orders of all kinds on it, it continues on the whole to trust her." [18]

How are we to explain this social transformation, this domestication of commands, that they seem to be rendered harmless? Canetti locates the explanation in "the fact that in the three basic relationships I have cited a kind of bribery is practised." [19] A kind of reversal has been accomplished, he believes. According to Canetti, the power of the command no longer anticipates success through some bestial threat of incorporation, but instead by guaranteeing food. A close link has gradually been forged between the provision of food and the command. This denaturing of the biological command to flee educates men, like pets, into a sort of voluntary imprisonment, which can be seen at every possible grade and level. This imprisonment, though, never entirely changes the essence of the command, which ultimately still consists in the threat of death.

Socially and politically, Canetti's explanation has an explosive force which has if anything increased since *Crowds and Power* was written. It is a forceful explanation because in it he exactly describes the role of commands and power in a welfare and consumer society—that is to say, in circumstances we take so much for granted that we are barely able to review them anymore. The reversal of the command which Canetti is focusing on can be reconstructed historically and politically as an event of the recent past.

From Hobbes to the present day, the modern state has drawn its capacity to function not from the placing of any general taboo on force but from the monopolization of the use of force. However, the way that the willingness to obey orders is instilled has changed significantly since Hobbes. According to the absolutist conception of the state, the state itself, as all-powerful master and commander-in-chief, was not simply the only one that might force other men to do something on pain of death, but indeed required a glad recognition that it was the one that kept in check the violent, wolfish nature of Man—the common urge of the state's subjects to fight, tear, and devour.

"Power discharges commands like a hail of magical arrows," writes Canetti; "those who are hit must surrender themselves. The command wounds them and also summons and guides them to the seat of power."[20]

That this could not go on indefinitely not only has been demonstrated historically but is also readily explicable in retrospect using Canetti's analysis of the nature of commands. Every command, Canetti tells us, leaves behind a sting in Man. This being so, the threat of death, institutionalized and permanent in the absolutist state, must have had horrifying effects on mankind. The insecurity caused in its recipient by a command, the humiliation, the approach to nothingness, cannot be outweighed only by that domestic peace which the state guarantees. In the long run, the masses, wounded by countless commands and stings, will be literally stung to rebellion.

Commands leave no sting behind only in cases where the threat of death contained in them, though meant seriously, can be passed on by the recipient of the order. The perfect recipient of commands is the one who will kill when ordered to do so. No sting is left behind in him because he is passing on sting, threat, death, the lot. In the act of killing he gains his recompense for the debasement suffered in taking the order. By striking and surviving his victim, he partakes of the strength and the glory of the master who wields the power.

It may now sound somewhat provocative if we say that the progress in the domestication of the command which we have achieved, from the absolutist state to the consumer-oriented welfare state of today, seems to be the unwitting result of this very passing-on experience. In the consumer society, at last, everyone (including those not in power) participates to a large extent in the incorporating consumption of reality, that reality that is served up to us day after day after day as our prey—in little tidbits and big helpings, till we cannot manage any more—by a worldwide supply system ever approaching closer to perfection.

Those who, in this society, are out for opportunities to have men obey their orders—that is, to exercise power—must see to it that a general mood of festiveness is kept up. When a population loses its faith in economic growth (as happened in West Germany in 1982), a change in the powers-that-be is on the way: that is to say, those who would command have not only to see to it that appetites are satisfied but, paradoxically, must also be constantly whetting appetites, so that the stings which a "mild welfare state dictatorship" implants (like any other) can be passed out of the system in an unbroken process of incorporation and digestion.

The Konstanz sociologist Horst Baier recently spoke of a "mild welfare state dictatorship" in assessing the social and political reality of 1984, the Orwell year. Other than in Orwell's novel, the art of political technocracy today really consists not in opposing or ignoring Man's needs, drives, and passions (when large-scale social systems are being run) but in harnessing them as potential motivation. It is only this "physical-cum-organic substratum," built into highly sophisticated "symbiotic mechanisms,"[21] that keeps the operation going.

The uninhibited avowal, by the powerful in modern times, of what "is the case"—that is, of Man's instinctive drives, of his greed to devour, and of the intestinal—has been called by the philosopher Peter Sloterdijk "a shameless, 'dirty' realism."[22] When Canetti spoke in his note of life as an intestinal tract he was giving expression to a generally depressed sense of existence. He could not have suspected that the image which then repelled him would become a valid description of a society which at that time could not even be glimpsed on the horizon: the society of survivors, those who had survived the catastrophe of the Second World War and the extermination orders of the all-consuming paranoiac Hitler.

No doubt the fact that in this new society the stalking, hunting, and clawing down of the prey, the whole frenzy, is rejected, represents progress. That the primeval images have by no means been put behind us, however, is shown by excrement, which stinks pungently and evilly. In the chapter "The Entrails of Power" we read: "The excrement, which is what remains of all this, is loaded with our whole blood guilt. By it we know what we have murdered. It is the compressed sum of all the evidence against us. It is our daily and continuing sin and, as such, it stinks and cries to heaven."[23]

Dirt and waste that befoul everything are a sign of the power—the omnipotence, the all-destroying power—of a society which plunders Nature, a society in which, along with consumption, there come a depressive ennui[24] and a dark suspicion that we ourselves are no longer anything but the helpless prey of a catastrophic future.

VI

"How should there be value in a life that resembles an intestinal tract?" Canetti tells us that in his lifelong preoccupation with the bloody underground realm of our everyday life he was inspired by the hope of "putting an end to power." It is true that inspecting the archetypal, primeval images he has repeatedly put before us in his work has heightened our attentiveness to hidden power in the present day too. But where are we to find the strength to resist a reality whose superficially peaceable character is historically unique and whose covert violence seems to derive from the nature of Man, indeed from Nature itself? In his image of life as an intestinal tract, Canetti is not only drawing our attention to the fact that everything is food, ready for consumption or in process of being prepared; he is also saying that everything, every bodily form, even the most beautiful, will be dissolved and pass away into nothing. The image of intestinal life implies that everything is doomed to die—and so far no one has conquered Death.

In these reflections on what seems to be a veritably overweening confidence on Canetti's part in his repellent scenes and images, Death puts in a wholly natural appearance; yet surely there has never before been any society that so resolutely shut its eyes to Death, and repressed the thought of Death, as our own—which is reminded by Death and the destruction of natural life all too graphically of the unintended goal of its own activity. The very determination with which every individual human being creates in himself, through incessant consumption, a sense of eternal life, of having the power to live, makes the masses easy to manipulate, and it is this too that makes the command, the tune everyone dances to, the technical/industrial rhythm of violence, the destruction of Nature and of Man, unending.

For Canetti, though, what makes us bad, or bestial, or indeed, in the last analysis, pets well fed with meat, is not Man's violent nature but Death. He finds it absurd to despise Man on account of his bestiality, which has been demonstrated time and again. Canetti the Jew has never, not in a single word, turned Nazi-hunter, even though the Nazis were not without influence on his life.

In his opinion it is only Death that makes people bad—Death, which not only threatens the lives of all living beings but also reduces either to resignation or to a grotesque, hypocritical noise all our endeavors to end our wickedness and be good:

I cannot explain why a vivid sense of the wickedness of this life always accompanies an alert passion for it in me. Perhaps I feel that it would be less wicked if it were not capriciously torn up and cut off. . . . Death would not be so unjust if it were not decreed *in advance*. Each of us, even the worst, still has the excuse that nothing he does can touch the wickedness of this advance verdict.[25]

Canetti's work as a whole is not merely a documentation of the wickedness that has resulted up to the present from the primeval needs to prey and eat, from Man's lust for power; far more, from the word go it is an impressive documentation aimed against Death. The struggle against the powerful, against every form of power among men, and against violence in life, is essentially one single struggle—against Death. Death as the origin of all worldly evil well-nigh takes on physical shape in Canetti, and seems in his work to have become the mythic incarnation of an evil deity.

But how are we to escape Death? Naturally Canetti never gives us any answer to this question—unless we assume the answer to be that the question has never occured to him. What concerns him is the fight we put up against Death, if need be to our dying breath. "The aim is not to parrot the banality that so far all human beings have died: the point is to decide whether to *accept* death willingly or stand up against it."[26]

The world is approaching a catastrophe: this is, on the one hand, something we have to fear, and believe ourselves right in perceiving. But, as Canetti has repeatedly stressed since the 1960s, the future has split: on the other hand, it is (thus Canetti) the very clarity of our view of catastrophe, of the death of all life, of nothingness, that may convert mankind to Life.

Many things which for thousands of years could not conceivably be realized were nonetheless anticipated in the ancient myths and have today long since become a reality we take for granted. However, as far as our ability to originate new myths and wishes is concerned, we are in a lamentable way (says Canetti). If in these times the writer still has any special task, there is none more important than breaking out of the circle of perpetual repetition and mere chatter. It is writers who are best in a position to cast off resignation to Death—which can, in any case, never be their business. "Any fiction that makes the living better in their behavior to each other is all right with me,"[27] we read in *The Human Province*.

Putting an end to Death. Mankind has got into a situation where it must decide either to continue along the course it has started on, and go on rehearsing, over and over again, for the grand finale, the scenario of violence long since started in the distant past, or at last to seek the workable mean which will make possible a life free of violence and power. In this critical situation, Canetti has opted for myth. Myth, for Canetti, is a narrative where something that is perhaps only a wish, a fabrication, a fiction, or simple necessity, is communicated as irrefutable certainty. "Whatever it is that one experiences in myths, as incredible as it would have to appear in some other context, here it remains free of doubt, here it has a single unalterable shape."[28] In the past, myths were forever presenting Man with the most implausible metamorphoses. But it was only this that enabled Man to conceive himself remaining alive in situations of the utmost despair, even, if need be, undergoing a transformation himself. Today, at a time when Man must once more either change or be annihilated, the human race has a chance only if we are no longer kept under the spell of false myths, the myths of resignation and Death.

Canetti's myth, which makes up his entire oeuvre, is the myth of mortal enmity—that is, of the fight against Death, who holds sway at the core of the work like the Devil himself. It is only when they catch a glimpse of this dark figure that threatens to tear everything asunder that the living come together. But the hero of this myth is Canetti himself,[29] whom we encounter in more shapes than we can number in his almost hopeless fight with Death: as the child, keeping his mother alive merely by existing and being there; as writer and dramatist, bringing the most outlandish types and characters to life; as an exemplary reader, who breathes his own breath and life into the figures of literature; as ethnologist, historian, and traveler, bringing to life for us the remotest of myths, strange customs, alien existences unknown to us, and a thousand voices; and, at last, as an old man, remembering a long, good life and recalling to life all the other lives that have entered into him.

It is a fact that one would prefer to avoid the "bitter, persistent, incurable torment" of parts of Canetti's work. But only if we clearly understand these parts do we recognize the sources of courage and hope that still exist for us. "We can take our hope only from the darkest of knowledge; otherwise it will be no more than a mocking superstition and will accelerate the catastrophe whose threat comes ever closer."[30]

NOTES

1. Elias Canetti, *Die Provinz des Menschen*, pp. 139 ff. In my monograph *Elias Canetti*, Munich, 1984, I deliberately gave particular attention to this passage. It now seems to me that the understanding of this note will cancel any distance remaining between us and Canetti's oeuvre, and it is that understanding that the present paper hopes to create.
2. Elias Canetti, *Crowds and Power* (translated by Carol Stewart), London, 1962, p. 210.
3. Ibid.
4. Ibid., p. 209.
5. *Die Provinz des Menschen*, p. 138.
6. *Crowds and Power*, p. 207.
7. Ibid., p. 15.
8. Elias Canetti, *Auto-da-Fé* (translated by C. V. Wedgwood), London, 1946 et seq., p. 154.
9. Ibid., pp. 154–55.
10. Ibid., pp. 315–16.
11. Ibid., p. 318.

12. Elias Canetti, *The Tongue Set Free* (translated by Joachim Neugroschel), New York, 1979 and 1983, p. 20.

13. Elias Canetti, "Das Chaos des Fleisches," in Alfred Hrdlicka, *Acht Radierungen zu Elias Canettis "Masse und Macht,"* Stuttgart, undated (1973), p. 21.

14. Elias Canetti, "Gespräch mit Horst Bienek," in *Die gespaltene Zukunft,* p. 98.

15. Elias Canetti, *The Conscience of Words* (translated by Joachim Neugroschel), New York, 1979, p. 165.

16. *Crowds and Power,* p. 462.

17. Ibid., p. 307.

18. Ibid.

19. Ibid.

20. Ibid., p. 305.

21. This is Niklas Luhman's term for those sociocultural arrangements which aim at the physical-cum-organic substratum to stabilize social structures: sexuality/love, money/consumption, violence/power. Cf. Niklas Luhman, "Symbiotische Mechanismen," in Horn, Luhmann, Narr, et al., *Gewaltverhältnisse und die Ohnmacht der Kritik,* Frankfurt, 1974. Cf. also Edgar Piel, "Sophistik und die 'alles penetrierende Verwaltung.' Gedanken zum Irrationalismus im Gefolge gesellschaftlicher Rationalisierung," in *ZfP,* 1979 (1), pp. 52 ff.

22. Peter Sloterdijk, *Kritik der zynischen Vernunft,* vol. 1, Frankfurt, 1983, p. 365.

23. *Crowds and Power,* p. 211.

24. Cf. Edgar Piel, "Langeweile. Ein Schicksal?" in Elisabeth Noelle-Neumann and Edgar Piel (eds.), *Allensbacher Jahrbuch der Demoskopie 1978–1983,* Munich, 1983. In this study I attempt, on the basis of empirical social data and chronological series, to show the sociopsychological results of the depressive ennui which is growing among us.

25. *Die Provinz des Menschen,* p. 166.

26. Elias Canetti, *The Torch in My Ear* (translated by Joachim Neugroschel), New York, 1982, p. 50.

27. *Die Provinz des Menschen,* p. 176.

28. *The Conscience of Words,* p. 244.

29. "The quite concrete, serious, and avowed goal of my life is my anticipation of Man's immortality. There was a time when I gave this anticipation to the central character in a novel, a character I called the Enemy of Death. But during the war it became clear to me that convictions of such moment, which are really a religion, need to be uttered directly and without disguise. So now I record everything to do with death in the way I want to communicate it to others, and the Enemy of Death has been thrust quite into the background. . . . In the novel his hubristic undertaking was to be his downfall; he was marked out for an honorable death; he was to be struck by a meteor. Perhaps the thing that today disturbs me most is that he was to fail. He mustn't fail. But I cannot have him triumph, either, if mankind is still dying in millions. Either way, what is meant in deadly earnest becomes mere irony. I had better make *myself* the object of ridicule—shoving some character forward in a cowardly fashion is no solution. It is fitting for me

to fall on this field of honor—let them bury me like some nameless cur, or denounce me as a madman, or avoid me like some bitter, persistent, incurable torment." *Die Provinz des Menschen,* pp. 52–53.

30. Ibid., p. 241.

Barbara Surowska

Writing from Conviction

It was the year 1927, as we know, that prompted Canetti to his involvement with the phenomenon of crowds and power: the events of July 15, 1927, shook him deeply. We have a description of them in *The Torch in My Ear* and in *The Conscience of Words,* and here too we meet that figure that is to occupy us further: an intellectual lamenting the burning of court records. Canetti portrays himself as a participant in the protest march, he shares the indignation of the multitude, but he is the only one who notices this man who cannot come to terms with the destruction of that dead paper. His anger at this civil servant, who is at bottom pigheaded and wholly engaged in his world of files, reflects his unsatisfied expectation that a man of the intelligentsia, whom we count among those who know, ought really to have a humanitarian sensibility. On that July 15 he ought to have been lamenting the human losses and not the lost records.

At that time Canetti did not yet suspect that this figure would provide an inspiration for the conception of Kien, the protagonist of *Auto-da-Fé*. Out of this man obsessed with records he created a bookworm and misanthrope whom he has go up in flames together with his library in the end. Canetti has repeatedly declared that intellectuals with no sense of responsibility mean nothing to him, do not exist for him, that he exiles them into the void.

The events of July 15 occupied him for some time to come. The workers had protested spontaneously and were right to do so, since their sense of justice had been wounded. The task of literature, of this higher authority, would now have been to take a stand quickly and unequivocally; yet the illustrious men of Vienna remained silent. One alone spoke out, Karl Kraus, who took upon himself the role of the just man in order to avert catastrophe: "Under the impact of the massacre on that day," Canetti writes in *The Torch in My Ear,* "he put up posters everywhere in Vienna, demanding the voluntary resignation of Police Commissioner Johann Schober, who was responsible for the order to shoot and for the ninety deaths. Kraus was alone in this demand; he was the only public figure who acted in this way. And while the other celebrities, of whom Vienna has never had a lack, did not wish to lay themselves open to criticism or perhaps ridicule, Kraus alone had the courage of his indignation. His posters were the only thing that kept us going in those days. I went from one poster to another, paused in front of each one, and I felt as if all the justice on earth had entered the letters of Kraus's name."[1] Karl Kraus's public activity filled him with satisfaction; his "idolization of him was at its highest level then. This time it was gratitude for a specific public deed; I don't think I have ever been so grateful to anyone for anything."[2]

That the young Canetti made high demands of literature and expected an ethical position of the intelligentsia will surprise no one. Behind this lies the tradition of his parental home, his education, and his constant dealings with books. At the same time, he attained his maturity in a time when there was a good deal of talk of the role of the mind. It was also in 1927 that Karl Mannheim, the originator of the expression "unbound intellect" (*freischwebende Intelligenz),* confronted the intelligentsia with the demand that they preserve "watchfulness in the face of the historical present." In the same year, the pamphlet *La Trahison des Clercs,* published by the Frenchman Julien

Benda, provided the basis for a widespread discussion of the thesis that the intellectuals had betrayed their responsibility as critics of the powers that ruled the world. In a word, it was a time when many were considering the role of the intelligentsia in crisis situations where the masses appear to have the say.

Canetti will have been familiar with these matters, at least from hearsay. For him, though, Karl Kraus was the intellectual phenomenon that obscured all else, as I have said. He was fascinated by him to such an extent that he placed blind faith in his judgments. He associates with him "the sense of absolute responsibility"[3] which in the future he was to take over from him. "I had it before me in a form bordering on obsession," he wrote in 1965, "and nothing less seemed worth devoting a life to. That model is before me even today, so powerful that all subsequent formulations of the same demand would have to appear inadequate. We have that miserable word *engagement* [commitment], for example, which was destined for banality from birth and is now rampant everywhere like some weed. It sounds as if one were an employee of the most important things. True responsibility is infinitely more difficult, for it is sovereign and self-determining."[4]

One reason why Canetti felt so strong an attraction to Kraus was that the latter was a staunch opponent of war. The reader of Canetti's autobiography will surely have noted how very much he hated and abhorred war from early youth. After "death," "war" must be the most frequently used word in his writings. Whenever he speaks of Karl Kraus, Canetti makes certain to emphasize that the editor of *Die Fackel* and author of the play *The Last Days of Mankind* was against the First World War and opposed it to the full extent of his powers. According to Canetti, he was one of the few who immediately recognized the calamity. "Most intellectuals got along by swimming with the general current."[5] They simply failed.

In 1928 Canetti went to Berlin, which at that time was a citadel of the intelligentsia. In contrast to Vienna, which seemed to him quite "sterilized," the German capital impressed him as a place "where contacts of any sort, incessant, were part of the very substance of living."[6] Above all, he felt at the mercy of the hectic, exaggerated, crisscrossing kinds of various currents, tendencies, and individual characteristics: "The animal quality and the intellectual quality, bared and intensified to the utmost, were mutually entangled, in a kind of alternating current. If you had awakened to your own animality before coming here, you had to increase it in order to hold out against the animality of other people; and if you weren't very strong, you were soon used up. But if you were directed by your intellect and had scarcely given in to your animality, you were bound to surrender to the richness of what was offered your mind. These things smashed away at you, versatile, contradictory, and relentless; you had no time to understand anything, you received nothing but strokes before the new ones showered upon you. You walked around Berlin as a tender piece of meat, and you felt as if you still weren't tender enough and were waiting for new strokes."[7] There were too many impressions for him to have been able to capture them all in his autobiography later; he remains content with the general observation that what came out of it was "books, paintings, plays, one against the other, crisscross, zigzag."[8]

Wieland Herzfelde brought famous people to his attention, those people who then constituted the intelligentsia. But there were too many names: "The names *rubbed* together, that was their goal. In a mysterious osmosis, one name tried to filch as much radiance as possible from another name, after which it hurried off to find yet another one very quickly, in order to repeat the same process. The mutual touching and sloughing of names had something hasty to it, but also something arbitrary; the fun of it was that you never knew which name would come next. This hinged on chance; and since names that were out to make their fortune arrived from everywhere, anything seemed possible."[9] Canetti plays a literary game with the names, he breathes life into them and sets them in action, rushing about, bumping into each other, eliminating others from the game, appearing in an unfamiliar light. These names seem to belong to no one, they have taken on independent lives of their own, they are enterprising and vigorous, yet in fact without physical substance.

For Canetti, Brecht becomes a central figure—Brecht, whom he admires as the author of the *Hauspostille (Domestic Breviary)*. The premiere of *Die Dreigroschenoper (The Threepenny Opera)* is just being prepared: the whole of Berlin is waiting for this sensation. Canetti, however, is disappointed, indeed repelled; he can quite simply not believe the social criticism of a Brecht interested in material things. He was "devoted to the purity and rigor of Karl Kraus" and could place no trust in a man who cynically asserted that of course he was writing for money. The premiere of *Die Dreigroschenoper* left him with the impression that "everyone knew himself to be Mack the Knife and now he was at last openly declared as such and approved and admired for it."[10] Canetti was outraged at Brecht and the entire audience: "It was a cunning performance," he writes, "coldly calculated. It was the most accurate expression of this Berlin. The people cheered for *themselves:* this was they and they liked themselves. First came their grub and then their ethics: not one of them could have put it better, and they took it literally. Now it had been spoken, they felt as snug as a bug in a rug."[11]

What Brecht had here put on stage was, in Canetti's eyes, an admiring self-portrait and by no means a satirical, chastising mirror image. Canetti expresses this very clearly: "If it is the task of satire to lash people for the injustice that they devise and commit, for their evils, which turn into predators and multiply, then, on the contrary, this play glorified all the things that people usually conceal in shame: what was most cogently and most effectively scorned was pity. To be sure, everything was merely taken over and spiced up with various new kinds of coarseness, but this coarseness was precisely what made it so authentic."[12]

Die Dreigroschenoper serves Canetti as his touchstone for the hypocritical and bogus in art. And from now on he sought to escape this "lure of the empty."

The sole positive figure in Berlin seems to have been the modest Isaac Babel, who felt just as repelled as Canetti by the "peacock ways of the artists" and their "heartless vanities." Babel becomes a kind of counter-figure to the cyncial Brecht. Canetti writes of the Russian: "Cynicism was alien to him because of his strenuous conception of literature. If he found that something was good, he could never have *used* it like other people, who, in sniffing around, implied that they regarded themselves as the culmination of the entire past. He never felt superior to others because he knew what literature was. He was obsessed with literature, not with its honors or with what it brought in. I do not believe that I saw Babel any differently from what he was because he spoke to me. I know that Berlin would have devoured me like lye if I hadn't met him."[13]

Canetti's subjects of conversation with Isaac Babel were Stendhal, Flaubert, and Maupassant, and not *Red Cavalry* or *The Odessa Tales,* which were published in German by the Malik publishing house he worked for and which were well known to him. "The latter" he had even read "more than once." If Canetti's aversion to Brecht had not been so great, he might have had something to say on the similarity of the subject of *Die Dreigroschenoper* to the Babel story "The King," for both works have in common the basic idea of integrating gangsters into "polite society." We see this at the wedding of the forty-year-old goitrous sister of the hero, Benya Krik, "gangster and king of gangsters," when she weds a weed of a lad who has been paid to marry her: both the aristocrats of Moldavanka and the Odessa gangsters and beggars attend, in rare harmony, and even the police, who had intended going so far as to disrupt Benya Krik's celebrations, recognize that the gangster king must be treated as a person to be respected. Babel's tale is at once wild and charming; the patina of a vanishing era lies transfiguringly upon it. The gangster is not the unscrupulous man of modern society but one who, it is true, lives at odds with the law yet who nonetheless holds on to certain fundamental principles of honorable conduct. He goes down along with his society. It is only in the story that he lives on as the characteristic and highly picturesque figure of the daredevil and likable robber. Brecht's Mack the Knife is in comparison far too calculating. As a critic of a society dependent on capital, Brecht had little interest in an affectionate treatment of human weaknesses: he was after a brutal, merciless portrayal. Canetti is absolutely right when he says Brecht has no compassion for humanity. Babel, by contrast, shocks no one with his story. Here the dread is part of the wit. His tale is not biting and unsentimental, and its effect is in fact comic and cheerful, even if it does not take any especially amusing societal conditions as its targets.

When Canetti writes that in his Berlin days he was impressed by Stendhal's *Scarlet and Black* and Babel's *Red Cavalry* and *The Odessa Tales,* we should not therefore suppose that he borrowed any motifs from these works; nor are there any particularly striking points of comparison between them and *Auto-da-Fé.* What links Canetti to them is the excellent style, the disciplined work with the word, and above all the honest, scrupulously moral authorial attitude.

One of Canetti's disappointments in Berlin was his acquaintanceship with George Grosz. From Grosz he received as a gift the famous *Ecce Homo* folder. Canetti, at heart a puritan, accepted the folder (which was banned as obscene) with "an odd mixture of horror and approval." He recalls: "These were dreadful creatures of Berlin's night life that you saw here, but they were here because they were viewed as dreadful. I regarded my disgust at them as the artist's disgust."[14] Once personal experience made it clear to him that Grosz was definitely out to enjoy freedom in sexual matters in Berlin's artistic scene, he felt a sense of horror at being confronted with an artist without morality.[15] With his somewhat "extravagant notions of literature," Canetti could not countenance an artist criticizing something without refraining from it himself. In his eyes, Grosz's drawings could not be genuine satires if obscenity did not repel their author but in fact, as it turned out, fascinated him.

Canetti's great authorities were done with for the moment. Even his idol Karl Kraus had disappointed him; he began to have ever greater doubts about the infallibility of his judgments. After Canetti's return to Vienna, which took on the character of flight, he tried to come to terms with his Berlin experience. "I had overcome none, absolutely none, of the things that had been filling me with horror and dreadful forebodings since Berlin. What could the outcome be if not dreadful conflagration? I felt how pitiless life was: everything racing by, nothing really dealing with anything else. It was obvious not only that no one understood anyone else, but also that no one *wanted* to understand anyone else."[16]

We might suppose that this impression resulted from the excitable rashness of a young, sensitive person then twenty-three years old. Canetti himself frequently speaks in *The Torch in My Ear* of his naïveté, lack of experience, and innocence at that time. But if we consider beside it another document of the age, the testimony of the thirty-seven-year-old Kurt Tucholsky, we are astonished by the similarities in their assessments of the intellectual climate in Berlin. On June 12, 1927, Tucholsky writes the following words to Maximilian Harden, in order to explain the reason for his flight from Germany: "Germany— as I do not need to explain to you, of all people—is none too friendly territory. I do not enjoy life there, and I fear that this has been apparent in my work too. If one is neither vain nor know-all, there is little joy to be had from the things I should have to do there—unless one felt some kind of vocation. And that is scarcely in demand in 1927."[17] And some years later, on January 18, 1931, he explains in a letter to his brother Fritz: "I'm fed up with it. As you will have gathered from my permanent silence apropos a number of monstrous things currently going on. . . . You wouldn't believe how the country looks from outside: a heap of neurasthenic madmen who are all, every man jack of them, in his own way, wrong. Such misunderstandings, all talking at once and all at cross purposes . . . no, my dear fellow, it's not what I was born for. . . ."[18]

His Berlin visit had afforded Canetti the valuable insight that the milieu of the artists and literati did not come up to his high expectations. And although he slightly pokes fun at himself too in his account, he has never abandoned his rigor, nor indeed even lessened it.

When he went to Berlin for the second time he avoided the company of the famous. He was attracted to the quieter parts of the city. Over against the big names he wanted to set those who had no name, who were "poor in name." He discovered simple people: "I wanted to see and hear *everyone*. . . . The freer I became for this and the more time I devoted to it, the greater my astonishment at this variety, and right in the poverty, banality, the misuse of words, not in the braggadocio and bumptiousness of the writers."[19]

In the things he observed and overheard there was a wealth of material out of which his scenes and figures grew. But he did not follow in the steps of Babel; he did not set about presenting the events of everyday life as vividly as he had experienced them, if possible without distortion. True, Babel had infected Canetti with his interest in "the *people,* and indeed all kinds of people, not those who hung out in the artists' restaurants and the fancy pubs," and had taught him an intensity of vision: "I have never met anyone who looked with such intensity. . . . He rejected nothing when seeing, for he felt equally serious about everything; the most usual as well as the most unusual things were important to him."[20] But Canetti does not see with Babel's eyes, and he also developed his own manner of reporting on the things he had seen, in literature. His strength lies not in realistic presentation but in distortion and in outsize exaggeration. He belongs beside Kafka, though his effect is more surreal than Kafka's.

At that time, Canetti must already have experienced the world as heterogeneous, incoherent. His ambition was to make clear the "centrifugal pull" of things: "they strove apart, leaving one another at top speed. Reality was not at the center, holding everything together as if with reins; there were many realities, and they were all outside. They were wide apart from one another, they were unconnected; anyone attempting to harmonize them was a falsifier."[21]

For this reason, Canetti required a subtle form that would point to a plurality of characters living at one and the same moment but of various natures and gregarious ways.

He set about writing an eight-volume opus, a *Comédie Humaine*. The Steinhof mental asylum and Grünewald's Devil constantly before his eyes, he forced himself to be strict and to exercise the most severe working discipline. He thought up figures for the cycle, figures with a fundamental trait, each "invented in terms of his main preoccupation." They had "a completely personal view of things" and moved in a linear mode, in a fixed direction. They "could no longer cast about promiscuously, but could only feel and think along certain channels."[22] Doubtless it could not be foreseen where their craving for admiration would finally lead them, but both the stable framework of their characteristics and their unmistakable language were to keep them moving in circles. Canetti, who began to be fascinated by the idiosyncrasies of the insane, wanted neither to heal his figures nor consign them to death. After a year's work on these characters, however, "none had evolved far enough for [Canetti] to foresee his end." To use death as a conclusion was ruled out from the start; Canetti "saw them together in the pavilion ward, which [he] had saved for them.

Their experiences, which I viewed as precious and unique, were to be preserved there. The ending I had in mind was that they would talk to one another. In their individual isolation, they would find sentences for one another, and these peculiar sentences would have a tremendous *meaning.*"[23]

Putting this idea into practice would have lent the whole a contrived, utopian-positivist aspect, as Canetti himself explains: "If the speakers of these individual languages had anything to say to one another, anything meaningful for them, then there was still hope for us ordinary people, who lacked the dignity of madness."[24]

It remains to be asked why it was not possible to carry out this idea. What became of it in the end? I believe the project foundered on its mutually contradictory premises. On the one hand, the author had decided to leave the goal his figures were driven toward in the dark; on the other hand, he wanted to save them. Although they were opposed to each other, they were to come together in some way or other. Out of dark there was to come forth light—which, if Canetti was to abide by his severity, was impossible.

The stringency of the author, which some of his readers find a torment, in my opinion benefited the literary quality of his work, which in the end was condensed into one book, *Auto-da-Fé.* The mercilessness of the whole, and the somber close, the auto-da-fé of the Bookman, is appropriate to the reality of our world.

None of the figures created for the novel cycle proved more viable than the Bookman, Kien, and it need by no means surprise us that Canetti took pleasure in him and preferred him to the other characters. A bookworm who confines himself to his library, to seek refuge from everything that interferes with his dealings with books; who becomes so practiced, for so long, at turning a blind eye to things which hold no interest for him that at last he quite loses his eye for reality and in the end is defeated by that disdained and underestimated reality—such a character was particularly well suited for castigating the egoism and smug complacency of intellectuals. Through the characteristics of this Bookman, the principal vices of the intelligentsia could be shown in exaggerated form, and handed over to the criticism of the general public. This work (in contrast to Brecht's) was to give no occasion for self-satisfied contemplation. Kien was not intended as a portrayal of any individual: he represented a caricature of the intellectual per se.

We have here before us, as it were, a living catalogue of the sins of the intellectual. Peter Kien naturally considers himself the authority in his field. The title of professor, which he owes to no university faculty but to the caretaker Benedikt Pfaff, he accepts as a matter of course, as if it were his due. He describes himself as a genius and, in doing so, emphasizes the value for his scholarly work of his phenomenal memory. We do not, though, come upon any trace of independent, authoritative thought, of abilities in critical analysis; all that is foregrounded is his pedantry and his pronounced sense of order. He is in a position to command a good overview of systematized masses of learning. Nor does it cost him any effort to master languages: "He knew more than a dozen oriental languages. And naturally a few of the western ones. No branch of human literature was unfamiliar to him. He thought in quotations and wrote in carefully considered sentences."[25] He shows a good deal of technical skill. Above all, he is skilled in the reconstruction of old texts: "Countless texts owed their restoration to him. When he came to misreadings or imperfections in ancient Chinese, Indian or Japanese manuscripts, as many alternative readings suggested themselves for his selection as he could wish. Other textual critics envied him; he for his part had to guard against a superfluity of ideas."[26] His ease in working with source material is at odds with his meticulous caution in presenting treatises of his own. Kien also takes care not to appear before an audience. "He had not, he averred, been born to be an orator." He has left teaching at all manner of schools to "unproductive popularizers." He is known for his refusal to attend congresses; but his absence by no means damages his reputation, as people talk about him.

What he has achieved is rated as invaluable. He does not write an excessive amount, as he wants to present only results that are certain: "The papers which he had hitherto published, few in number, yet each one the starting point for a hundred others, had gained for him the reputation of being the greatest living authority on sinology. They were known in every detail to his colleagues, indeed almost word for word. A sentence once set down by him was decisive and binding. In controversial questions he was the ultimate appeal, the leading authority even in related branches of knowledge. A few only he honoured with his letters. That man, however, whom he chose so to honour would receive in a single letter enough stimuli to set him off on years of study, the results of which—in the view of the mind whence they had sprung—were foregone conclusions. Personally he had no dealings with anyone. He refused all invitations. Whenever any chair of oriental philology fell vacant, it was offered first to him. Polite but contemptuous, he invariably declined." [27] In this portrait, it is not only he who is the object of irony, but also his colleagues in the field, for their scholarly work rests primarily on the support of material already familiar. All of these scholars have for years been keeping going, surely and smugly, a mechanism of dead knowledge. Everything remains within clear confines, nothing reaches over into other areas of life. Kien, the great authority, does not clear any new paths. He has renounced doubt. He is proud of the size of his cranium, wherein he preserves an impressive number of data which are proven and valid once and for all.

The "genuine, creative research workers" (of whom he naturally counts himself one) ought in his view to devote themselves exclusively to their work. In this way he also rationalizes his urge to isolate himself in his library: his interest is only in his books, and they mean the world to him—and all in all there would be nothing to be said against this, if only his pleasure in intellectual activity had also borne intellectual fruit. As a scholar, however, he cannot be taken seriously, but is instead a grotesquely comic figure. His hours of diversion with his books turn out to be aberrations of reason. The only fruit they bear is illusion and sham.

Kien's conception of truth scarcely differs from his conception of scholarly work. "You draw closer to truth," he reasons, "by shutting yourself off from mankind."[28] He believes himself in possession of the truth, considering the everyday to be "a superficial clatter of lies." The maxim that determines his behavior is framed as follows: "*Esse percipi*, to be is to be perceived. What I do not perceive, does not exist."[29] From a general statement he formulates a particular: the familiar philosophical insight* does not lead him to conclude that that which cannot be perceived has no being, but rather that that which *I* do not perceive does not exist. For him, a great deal does not in fact exist, for he has achieved expert proficiency in not seeing all of those things that do not fit his world. No experience can shatter his convictions. He remains forever true to himself. Fixed in his views and immutable as he is, he consigns himself irremediably to insanity.

The portrait of Kien would not be complete if it lacked the trait of spitefulness. His deeds always originate in feelings of hatred or triumph. Every kind of empathy is alien to him. No manner of noble feelings can be expected of him. His misanthropy has destroyed them. He mobilizes all his intellectual powers for attacks on his opponents, and for that alone. In order to anticipate their expected offensives and outwit them, he at length sets fire to his library, although in doing so he negates himself; yet he is no longer filled with anything but hatred. It is hatred that leads him on in the last stage of his holy war against the book-philistines, to a deed which, in his

---

*The most familiar and classic expression of this insight is in I, 3, of Berkeley's *Treatise Concerning the Principles of Human Knowledge.* —Trans.

ardent speech to the books, he has previously condemned in passionate terms. He told them of the book burning which the Chinese Emperor Shi Hoang Ti, on the advice of his minister Li Si, ordered in 213 B.C. With satisfaction Kien reported that for this the minister was sawn in two. Kien, however, destroys his library not out of considerations of power, like the Emperor, but in the promptings of a blinded illusion which, as I have said, leads to his own downfall.

Canetti, as has been noted, had wished for a different conclusion to his novel cycle: the characters were to be brought together. Discovery of the power of hatred, however, brought this to naught: he could not have the extreme characters of *Auto-da-Fé* come together. Their lives ran parallel without any communication; they talked past each other, devised means of outwitting each other, and combated each other—and this in the end led to mutual destruction and the fire. A fire, to cap it all, with a festive mood.

After his Berlin experiences, Canetti must necessarily have concluded that the intelligentsia as such had failed. They were not in a position to be the moral conscience of society, as he had hoped when Karl Kraus and Grosz were still his ideals. For this reason he could create only the grotesquely comic (not even tragicomic) figure of a member of the intelligentsia. His writing, obeying the promptings of conscience, became tantamount to an account of the absence of conscience.

NOTES

1. Elias Canetti, *The Torch in My Ear* (translated by Joachim Neugroschel), New York, 1982, p. 246.
2. Ibid.
3. Elias Canetti, *The Conscience of Words* (translated by Joachim Neugroschel), New York, 1979, p. 34.
4. Ibid.
5. Ibid., p. 226.
6. *The Torch in My Ear*, p. 269.
7. Ibid., pp. 299–300.
8. Ibid., p. 300.

9. Ibid., p. 301.

10. Ibid., p. 307.

11. Ibid., p. 306.

12. Ibid.

13. Ibid., pp. 293–94.

14. Ibid., p. 283.

15. Canetti's judgment is not quite fair to Grosz. As we learn from Hans Hess, Grosz was well aware of the conflicts in his existence as an artist: "Morally he was in a curious position, since he had a poor opinion of the art market and dealers. He despised the pompous claims of art, for long before most he had seen through what he called 'ideological humbug.' And yet he was by temperament and tradition an artist with a highly personal conception of torment and hell. At the same time, though, he also had obligations to his political convictions, so that he worked consistently for Communist periodicals: *Die Pleite, Der blutige Ernst, Der Knüppel,* and at times *Die rote Fahne.* He also remained associated with Herzfelde's publishing house, Malik. He was aware of the delicate role of the artist in society, and in the artist he saw first and foremost the swindler, deceiving and shooting his mouth off and clowning—in this his view resembled Thomas Mann's equation of the artist with the con man. The power of his views becomes apparent in a letter to the actor Vladimir Sokolov: 'All of us wanted to win bicycle races or become itinerant clowns. Somehow or other you did become a clown, and so did I. Don't we both earn our living with rabbits, the kind you pull out of nowhere from out of a top hat?' This ambiguity in the artist's position, which Grosz was so acutely aware of, also becomes apparent in his social life. He personally was equally acceptable to the upper and the lower levels of society: the upper crust welcomed him, and he consorted with equal familiarity with scoundrels. Grosz ate with bankers, drank with tramps, and discussed the next issue of *Der Knüppel* with Party members. His work at that time reflects his own experience, and if he lacked unity in his style and direction the same is true of his life. He saw himself not only as an artist or satirist but as one who played many parts." (Hans Hess, *George Grosz,* Dresden, 1982, pp. 119 ff.)

16. *The Torch in My Ear,* pp. 322–23.

17. Hans-Albert Walter, *Bedrohung und Verfolgung bis 1933. Deutsche Exilliteratur 1933–1950,* vol. 1, Darmstadt and Neuwied, 1972, p. 109.

18. Ibid., p. 110.

19. *The Torch in My Ear,* p. 363.

20. Ibid., p. 291. Just as Karl Kraus was Canetti's master in the art of hearing, so Babel was his master in the art of seeing.

21. Ibid., pp. 318–19.

22. Ibid., p. 321.

23. Ibid., pp. 323–24.

24. Ibid., p. 324.

25. Elias Canetti, *Auto-da-Fé* (translated by C. V. Wedgwood), London, 1946 et seq., p. 17.

26. Ibid.
27. Ibid., p. 18.
28. Ibid., p. 15.
29. Ibid., p. 71.

Gerhard Neumann

Revoking the Fall:
Elias Canetti's Aphorisms

I

*Every work constitutes a rape by its sheer mass. We have to
find other, purer means of expressing ourselves as well.*[1]

Aphorisms are the creative moments of language, the true shape
taken by thought on our origins; they are concerned with the
Creation of the world and the character given it by the Fall;
they are at once language's hereditary flaw and its healing. In
their notes, both Franz Kafka and Elias Canetti, each in his
own way, retraced the path to those evil origins. The Old Testament, as we know, offers two different accounts of the Creation of the world: one (Genesis 1:28) centers on the Father's
blessing on His creatures, a second (Genesis 3:14 ff.) on His
curse. As if it were a matter of course, both Kafka and Canetti[2]
take the second version as the basis of self-evaluation: Man's
history begins with a ban.

"God's wrath against the family of Man. The two trees, the
unexplained prohibition, the punishment of all (serpent, woman
and man) . . ."[3] we read in Kafka, and

Original sin, the old wrong done by Man, consists in the reproachful
accusation he has raised, and will not stop making, that he himself
was wronged, that the original sin was committed against him.[4]

Analogously, one of Canetti's notes reads:

The Old Testament is the history of the power of God. . . . God's power, it is true, begins with Creation itself, and without doubt it is the tale of this Creator's demands that gives the Bible its uniqueness.[5]

And further:

The story of the tower of Babel is the story of the second Fall. After mankind had lost their innocence and eternal life, they aspired to climb high up to Heaven by means of their own artistry. First they had eaten the fruit of the forbidden tree and now they were copying its ways and growing straight up. In retribution they were deprived of what had remained theirs after the first Fall: the unity of language. God's deed was the most devilish act ever committed. The confusion of names was a confounding of His own Creation, and it is impossible to comprehend why He should still have saved anything from the Flood.[6]

The biblical myth of the Fall describes the birth of Man from out of a prohibition: that birth derives from the power of God, and is overshadowed by fear. In transgressing against God's ban and eating the forbidden fruit of the Tree of Knowledge, Man attains knowledge and thus definition of the self through the Other, which has the twofold form of a counterpart sex ("wo-man") and Death. Expulsion from the home territory and acquiring the language of knowledge are two sides of the same coin. Paradisaic experience of the body has been replaced by experience of the Law, by means of the establishment of permission and taboos as the system from which all the guidelines in future human intercourse will derive.

What determines Canetti's understanding of this primitive human myth is that he sees it developing in two stages, first a loss of innocence and of eternal life, and then a loss of authentic language. It is not Man's being marked for death that signals his true destruction by God, but the withdrawal of the unique feature of his language—only the confounding of his language represents the real death of Man. If the paradisaic truth of his language were confirmed it might grant him victory over Time and thus restore him to power over Death. This is the one great thought Canetti's oeuvre is built on.

Starting from this perception of the life-sustaining power of language, Canetti's aphorisms, like Kafka's, are forever circling and approaching this problem of Man's origins in the Divine prohibition, and the difficulties that result from this for God and Man. These are from the outset difficulties related to the phenomenon of power. Power is based on fear of death, on the games played with this fear, and it is this fear that separates God from Man, at once parting and uniting them. "To be God, and then to reject it as if it were nothing at all. Have we been rejected like that?"[7] we read at one point in Canetti. And elsewhere he ponders the possibility of another, true God without fear (which is a correlative of power):

If God existed He would be the one being without fear; who acted without fear, and rested without fear; who created and commanded without fear; who punished and rewarded without fear; who promised without fear, and forgot without fear. That would be God, a tremendous, strong God. The rest of them, the supposed gods, squirm and fall apart for fear. What makes them anything more than us?[8]

Two possible conclusions may be inferred from this confounding of Creation by power, by the might of that ban which stood at its beginning, and Canetti moots them in two mutually opposed notes:

A God who kept His Creation *secret*. "And behold, it was not good."[9]

God's longing for the world as it was before He created it.[10]

A failure of Creation, or God's longing for that moment that came before the act of Creation—these are two "forgotten" aspects of the situation of the Creation, and it is art that is able to make us aware of them, for a brief moment, in the form of a counter-Creation. Art alone represents the unending struggle between Fear and Death; art is the very antithesis of power, a counterpart power. Thus Canetti locates moments in music where this paradisaic condition preceding the Creation of the world seems to have been captured:

In Haydn's *Creation,* God has accomplished everything including the human couple. The Fall is still to come. God is still innocent. . . . God Himself does not yet know what He has done, and He *believes* that it is good.[11]

And in this way the Old Testament becomes, for Canetti, the documentary repository of that myth whence springs Man's struggle against the power which originally was posited with him. In reading the Bible, Canetti experiences a mixture of "outrage" and "attraction": Holy Scripture becomes for him quite simply the history of the human condition, and the Fall is the paradigm of that condition:

It is the worthy image and model of Man, a magnificent thing, at once vividly clear and mysterious; it is the true tower of Babel, and God knows it.[12]

For those manifold increases in power that have become apparent in the history of our own times, the biblical myth of the birth of Man from out of the Divine prohibition functions as a "model" against which the dimensions of evil can be measured: "It is curious that only the Bible is potent enough to compass what is happening now,"[13] Canetti writes in 1943. Shortly before, we read, "The Bible is appropriate to Man's misfortunes,"[14] and then the complementary question: "What would the Bible have needed to be like to prevent mankind from destroying itself?"[15]

Canetti's tireless review of the myths of all the peoples of the world serves one single end and hope: to find a story where the problem of the origins of power is solved, or quashed. The biblical tale of the twofold Fall—on the one hand Man's origin (the birth of language out of confrontation with sexuality and death) in God's Word, on the other the confusion of languages [16] at the tower of Babel—very closely approaches this "story of all stories" that Canetti seeks. Repeatedly he formulates it anew, now with respect to the history of Man (in *Crowds and Power*), now with respect to his own life history *(The Tongue Set Free)*.

Man's aporia, the dilemma of being allowed access to discourse on the self only by way of a prohibition on the body's eating, only by way of the totally Other, Death, is rediscovered by Canetti in the myth of his own childhood too. First it is in his "earliest memory," [17] where (a first Fall) at the moment he gains the faculty of speech the two-year-old is threatened with the loss of his tongue, by force, experiencing the way his power of speech can be jeopardized by others, how its hours may be numbered. [18] Then it is in the experience of speech (acquired through the Word) as something which is not itself actual but is a mere "translation" of a wordless, paradisaic speech that cannot be grasped—Canetti himself considers this "mysterious translation" [19] of an indefinable actuality in speech into post-Fall discourse "the oddest thing" he can think of in his childhood. Further, it is in the experience of the death of his beloved father, the keeper of the script, [20] a death which seems to result from his grandfather's Word, his curse on Father as they fled the family paradise. [21] It is also in the boy Elias's struggle for the script, which goes as far as attempted murder—writing contains the power of language in two ways, as a life-sustaining but also as a life-destroying principle. [22] Finally, a second Fall, it is in the compulsory literalness of repeating sentences aloud when, under artificially contrived circumstances, he learns his parents' language, German, [23] with his Mother's Word ruling him: "You must not forget a single sentence." [24]

Thus what stands at the beginning of every story as a fact of human history is here repeated in memories of childhood as the birth of human discourse out of the tension of twofold violence—the prohibition on speech expressed in the threat to cut out his tongue, and the compulsory, literal, word-perfect speech-as-script. The "spasm of that birth"[25] of language is dominated by the struggle against fear, against death, and against the irredeemable unactuality of language.

II

> *"Culture" is brewed up by the vanities of patrons. It is a dangerous love potion that distracts attention from death. The purest expression of culture is an Egyptian grave, where everything is gathered about in vain—utensils, jewelry, food, pictures, sculpture, prayers—and still the deceased is not alive.*[26]

The reenactment of the biblical myth of the twofold Fall, through experience of death and through the confusion of language, explains Canetti's lifelong fascination with the phenomenon of power. He tries to do justice to its claims in two ways, through acts of survival and of metamorphosis. Both are attempts to revoke the Fall, by victory over Death, and by a free use of language and its power to create identity. His tool in these enterprises is literature, which, according to Canetti, is the only effective weapon in the struggle.

Through the original prohibition, the power of God took shape in Man as the faculty of speech, the ability to speak of death and love, of the dying of another and of desire of another. The paradox of this situation rests in the fact that it was only the Fall that made it possible to speak of paradise; and it is from this paradox that literary discourse, the reenactment of the Creation, derives. We can view the writer's fantasies and inventions only in the light of this paradox. Writing his way into the myth, the writer must succeed in converting the ban which originated his speech into free discourse. The myth is the most durable of all Man's creations; there is not a single tool that has so fully retained its shape throughout the millennia as certain myths. Their sacredness gives them protection and their representation gives them immortality, and he who is able to fulfill mankind through a myth has achieved more than the boldest inventor.[27]

If the writer's writing-in process fails, if the transformation of the language of prohibition into the language of freedom does not come off, the world falls apart: the "split future"[28] threatens. Only insistence on the paradox of our origin as handed down by myth can link freedom to prohibition and hope to the curse:

There is no end to the creative thought of Man. In this curse resides the sole hope.[29]

And so Canetti is also able to note:

I often feel as if everything I learn and read were made up. But what I myself invent always seems really to have been there already.[30]

Yet this placing of all hope on the creative power of human inventiveness, that power to survive and undergo transformation, is nothing other than an attempt to evolve from out of the Fall itself the terms of its own reversal, to reconstruct from the language of law and power learned in the Fall that language of paradise and freedom which existed before the Law—in order to cancel out Death and the power by which Death instills fear. This is the very procedure of the aphorism. In it, those "presentiments of writers" are imaged forth which depict the "forgotten adventures of God."[31] It is the serpent in the garden that represents this fidelity (in the form of a falling-off) to God's thoughts of Creation prior to the decreeing of the Law:

God Himself set the serpent on Adam and Eve, and everything depended on the serpent's not betraying Him. The poisonous creature has remained true to God to this day.[32]

With this, Canetti enters a long tradition that conceives the Fall an act of enlightenment, a process serving Man's maturing and his discovery of himself.[33] Hegel, in his *Lectures on the Philosophy of Religion,* wrote:

The account we are given of original sin tells us that Adam ate the fruit of the Tree of Knowledge, and so forth. This means that knowing equals that breach or separation in which for the first time Good is available to Man, but Evil too. . . . God remarks to Himself, "the man is become as one of us." So the serpent was not lying; God confirms what it said. Great labors have been lavished on the elucidation of this passage and some have gone so far as to declare it ironic. But the higher explanation is that it is the second Adam—Christ—who is meant. Knowledge is the principle of intellectual endeavor, but also, as we have said, the principle that heals the wound caused by the breach.[34]

Kafka too sees in the serpent a dialectical agent—the temptation of Man through Evil to Good:

The serpent was needed as go-between: Evil can tempt Man, but it cannot be made human flesh.[35]

The language of the aphorism attempts to put the serpent's "deceitfulness" to work as "fidelity," within the Law—to make visible to systematic violence the freedom of the unspoken,[36] the condition of Creation:

Every spoken word is false. Every written word is false. Every word is false. But what is there but words?[37]

Thus Canetti pens an aphorism which sets out to view the history of Man in the area of tension between the system of the

Law and the moment of Creation; the aphorism presents that very serpent, in its representation of deceitfulness as fidelity, and relates its fidelity to a Law which produces systematized compulsions (biting itself in the tail) and its deceitfulness to creative metamorphoses (shedding its skin):

Those who went before are laughing themselves silly at me. They are satisfied to have their thoughts bite hard into their own tails. They think they have really comprehended something, and yet it is only their own solitary thought biting its own tail yet again! The more often it does so, the more correct they think it must be, and if it feeds off its own body they go crazy with ecstasy. But the only fear that I have is that my thoughts will come out right too soon—and even then I leave them the time to reveal their entire falsehood, or at least to shed their skin.[38]

Aphorisms are attempts to revoke the Fall. In taking up the fight against Death as a fight for survival, and in trying to reverse the confusion of language, they illustrate two aspects of one problem: the conquest of Death by means of language, which originated in knowledge of Death. Kleist's farewell letters attest this, as does Kafka's fantasy of names, "A Dream." "So long as death exists," writes Canetti, "any utterance is an utterance against it."[39] In *The Human Province* there are many statements of this kind that aim to force the individual to survive through the power of language and invention: "A writer ought constantly to be able to invent his life, and thus he would be the only one to *know* where he is."[40] By inventing himself, the individual can succeed in wresting his identity from the grasping clutch of Death, from inclusion in universal mortality. Books, demands Canetti, ought to be gathered together that express and preserve "hatred of death": "An anti-death Bible of this kind could give strength to many when they are growing weary."[41] In addition to sentences expressing this anti-death invention of the self there are others advocating the restoration of pure naming (beyond the Word that led to the Fall) as a form of survival in paradisaic language: "In order to exist one needs a supply of undoubted names."[42] The name, conceived as the undoubted word of a "wild discourse," has its opposite counterpart in systematized thought and rigid nomenclature:

All arithmetical connections, proportions, elliptical fates and tracks, leave me indifferent; all the connections established by names excite me and are true.
My god is the Name, the breath of my life is the Word. Places are of no consequence once their names fade. I have been nowhere I wasn't drawn to by the name.[43]

It is against the Name that the power of survival must then be measured. To this day it remains the only real form of survival.[44]

Conquest of death, then, through the creative uniqueness of names accumulated in the writer's inventions; in the profoundest sense, books of aphorisms are collections of sentences that turn against death the language that has been won from death— they assert names against the destructive might of death. Repeatedly Canetti's notes return to that primitive story of the Fall and the possibility of revoking it through writing and creative imagination. Revocations of this kind take the form of reversals of the received myth:

What do you mean, you're made of clay, said Adam to Eve, and cast her aside. I'm your rib, she said, my clay comes from yours. He didn't believe her and took a bite out of the apple. Then he knew she was telling the truth; he kept her, and made a present of her to the serpent.[45]

God replaced the rib in Adam's side, snuffed out the breath of life in him, and fashioned him back into clay.[46]

III

The deserted earth, overloaded with letters, smothered in knowledge, and not a living ear left on it to listen out into the cold.[47]

In Canetti's creative world, aphorisms occupy a central position. The speech Canetti gave in November 1936 on Hermann Broch's fiftieth birthday presciently and with notable consistency outlines the thematic thrust of his own work, which is dominated by the novel and the aphorism: the incomprehensibility of the human invention of signs and thence the communicative power of writing; the incomprehensibility of the stories of the gods; the incomprehensibility of human sexuality; and the incomprehensibility of death.[48] Canetti's notebooks, which were begun six years later and have continued to the present, tend more and more to rewrite these four themes into the core elements in a story—the Old Testament myth of the Fall, of the painful birth of human discourse on death and sexuality out of God's ban on eating the fruit of the Tree of Knowledge. In 1976, in his address "The Writer's Profession," Canetti offered a late answer to the issue raised in 1936: "It cannot be the writer's task to deliver mankind over to death."[49] Rather, writing is an attempt at a continuing protest against death, taking the part of the Name against its threatened extinction. Aphorisms fill the gaps left by the Law—the Law, which speaks of the death of all mankind. A Bible has to be written against the library of the world, a Bible that will make possible discourse against death.

It is this polarity of library and Bible, of systematized knowledge and the "fearful magic'" of the Name (and of each individual word), that has plainly governed Canetti's writing from the start. It is expressed as a polarity of two ways of writing, the novel and the aphorism. Canetti's great novel was meant to show the "crumbled state"[50] of the world, its immense system breaking down in an auto-da-fé, figured forth as a library fire. And then there are the notes, written while Canetti was working on *Crowds and Power,* which essays a theoretical reconstruction of his central thinking on power and the converse of power, fear: these notes are aphoristic attempts to release from the individual word or sentence the paradisaic world that existed before the Law, where the thing and the word were still unseparated and it seemed possible to conquer death:

He is looking for the one sentence. He thinks a hundred thousand sentences to find the one.

Which language would the one sentence be in? Are the words of the one sentence heavenly bodies? Hearts? Deaths? Animals?

The one sentence is the one he himself will not repeat, nobody will repeat.[51]

The precondition of the possibility of such sentences, aimed at the Law and its standardizing powers, is paradoxically that they are forgotten,[52] that they are changeable;[53] aphorisms are constantly renewed attempts to find another word which will "vindicate and justify all words."[54] In the last analysis it is no doubt a matter of rediscovering that "wild language"[55] which must have existed before the prohibition. In an address of 1969, Canetti gives the term "word attacks"[56] to this kind of irruption of amorphous energy clusters into the systematic fabric of established language. They lead, as do dreams, to the lighting-up of the "colors of paradise, and in the terror of them one is baptized in unheard-of names."[57] They are fantasy images of those sentences which were uttered before the prohibition: "To speak as if it were the last sentence allowed one."[58]

It is surely no accident that Canetti tries to characterize the polarity of Bible and library, individual sentence and cultural system, aphorism and novel, by means of that pair of opposites paradise and hell. Thus, speaking of the notes that were written while he was working on *Crowds and Power,* he tells us:

Every outside sound seems to come from a forbidden paradise; whereas every word one joins to the labor that one has been continuing for so long, every such word, in its pliant adjustment, its servility, has the color of a banal and permitted hell.[59]

From the confrontation of spontaneous creation and the compulsions that accompany systems there arises the terrifying vision of a retrospective correction and recording of everything that has been spoken, a codifying of spontaneity (the lightning flashes of paradise) through the law which is based on the Fall:

He imagines that he has to alter every sentence he has ever spoken or written. It is not enough to tackle the sentences that are within reach; he has also to find all the ones that have been lost; he has to track them down, seize them, and bring them back. He is allowed no rest until he has them all. —An infernal punishment for all false believers.[60]

Out of this compulsion to heed a system, the law that derives from God's prohibition, there arises the constant invention of new hells, resisted by the writer's counter-inventions.[61] These hells take the form of a paranoid system in which death and the will to power merge in a fascistic myth: in the historical example of the unbalanced *Senatspräsident* Schreber, Canetti has outlined the preconditions and consequences of a model along these lines.[62] It is the task of aphoristic ways of thinking to break asunder all compulsions, to rethink the power system into a language of freedom. Received myths (as the analysis of Schreber's way of thinking shows, where the Christian Creation myth was used as a palimpsest) are on the border between the compulsions of systems and freedom of invention, always in danger of being appropriated by the system, always awaking hopes of clearing a way to untrammeled thought.[63]

Old myths are forever bringing us up short; there are so many of them; there are myths for everybody. Is that the reason why nothing really creative has been achieved in the world for so long? Were the old myths all we could manage?[64]

And then, by way of contradiction:

It ought to be possible to rule the world through only a few stories. But they would need to be the right ones; one would have to avoid confusing them; and many more, the majority, could never be told. —The superstition of the writer.[65]

By enlisting the aphorism as a special linguistic form of invention without system, a flaring-up of creative energy as before the Fall, Canetti enters a European tradition of transcendental morality;[66] his aphorisms continue the attempts of a Pascal or Lichtenberg, a Novalis or Musil, to preserve the rights of a sense of open possibilities in spite of the establishment of necessities, to put what has not yet been thought, the utopia of the left-out,[67] in the place of genealogical compulsions.

Basically the genealogies that Canetti sees determining thought since the Fall are two: first, the genealogy of Nature in the shape of Darwinism:

Nature has been cramped by the theory of evolution. It would be good to find the intellectual moment when Nature was least cramped, was at its widest and richest. Even as a strictly genealogical undertaking, the theory of evolution is dismal and petty, because it relates everything to Man, who has gained power over the whole earth anyway. It legitimates his claim by placing him at the end.[68]

And then, second, the genealogy of culture in Aristotelian shape, the total classification of things, the total deciphering of all texts:

Fear of the Aristotelization of my thoughts, of categorization, definitions, and suchlike vacuous playing-about. To rediscover the old strength that seizes its object and looks at it for the first time. Who will give me that strength?[69]

Soon no old text will remain undeciphered, and no further texts will turn up to be deciphered. And when that point is reached the sacred quality will have been taken from the script.[70]

What is expressed here is a clear insight into Man's origins through the prohibition, through the establishment of permission and taboos, where definitive reality replaces unlimited possibilities, a close-circuit system replaces endless creation, and a chain of necessities replaces the creative moment. The hallmark of this genealogical order of things is the written script, as a way of giving fixed finality to what has been thought. The script of Nature and the script of culture are simply two aspects of the same thing—of the origin of Man in the Law which was confirmed through his Fall. Seen like this, the aphorism, as a form of reversal or revocation, can develop its full force only through secret, silent methods, through disobedience of the Law—Canetti recorded his notes in illegible shorthand and suspended their publication. A form of discourse needs to be found that is rooted in the time before script, that is to say, before the Law—in "the time of calling out."[71]

His conception of happiness: to live a whole life long in tranquillity, and to write without ever showing anyone a word of it, without ever publishing a word. To leave everything one has written down in pencil, and change nothing, as if it were there for no purpose: like the natural course of life, which does not serve any cramping ends but is wholly itself and is recorded just as one walks or breathes, of its own accord.[72]

Aphoristic discourse as a form of protest against the Fall can only be conceived paradoxically as a "forgetting" of thoughts, as an "unthought thought."[73] Thus a 1947 note reads:

The man who has grown accustomed to his own thinking can be saved from despair by only one thing: the communication he withholds from the rest, which he records for himself and then forgets, which he later rediscovers with amazement. . . . He can remain free only by thinking in vain. . . . There is one thing that can help him: the chaos, created by himself, of his own thoughts insofar as they have remained isolated and undeveloped, and forgotten.[74]

Two basic anthropological categories are associated with the polarity of system and continual metamorphosis that Canetti envisions in the dichotomy of library and Bible, novel and aphorism: the paranoid option, seen by Canetti in the madness of *Senatspräsident* Schreber as a paradigm of power,[75] and the schizoid option of constant metamorphosis of the self, such as we find quite superbly—as the fine art of making oneself inconspicuous, and of wriggling out of confrontations with power—as a paradigm of counter-power in Kafka and his writings.[76] Aphoristic strategies of discourse would thus, as the very opposite of paranoia's power-obsessed *idée fixe*, be the epitome of anti-power. Only the aphorism's metamorphic flexibility[77] makes possible moments of paradisaic transformation of the self and of release from death, a reenactment, feasible for a few brief moments, of the "forgotten adventures of God."[78]

IV

What I find most off-putting in philosophers is that their thinking is a process of emptying out. The more often and the more skillfully they use their key words, the less remains of the world about them. They are like barbarians in some great, spacious house full of magnificent works. They stand there in their shirt sleeves and, methodically and unwaveringly, throw everything out of the window—armchairs, pictures, animals, children—till nothing is left but totally empty rooms. From time to time the doors and windows are tossed out too. The naked house is all that is left standing. They imagine that things look better with all this desolation.[79]

The leap into generalization is so dangerous that it has to be
practiced time and again, and from the same point.[80]

What is incomparable and, in the history of the European aphorism, unparalleled in Canetti's notes is his attempt to use the linguistic form of the aphorism as a weapon against death, as a "thinking" and "life" against death. Canetti himself has given very precise definition to his own special position in the tradition of aphoristic thought:

In one question, which for me is the most important, the question of death, I have found among all the thinkers only opponents.[81]

The reason for this is that Canetti sees the represenation of life not as continuous time but as leaps,[82] not as a system but as metamorphosis:

Many have tried to grasp their lives in an intellectual context, and those who have succeeded in the attempt will scarcely grow older. I should wish that some would record life thorugh the leaps it makes.[83]

Canetti substitutes for the approach of autobiography that of the aphorism. This means that he replaces history with myth, and the unyielding "chains of the script" with the metamorphic power of the living individual sentence. "History," he writes,

is forever bound up in the chains of the script. To the falsest, most lying, basest documents it holds out the promise of centuries to come. No one can sign a contract today without it still being known in a thousand years. No one can be born unnoticed—at the very least he is numbered in statistics. No one can think, no one can breathe; history pollutes his pure breath and twists the words in his brain.[84]

Written history, with its impertinent manner of defending everything, makes the situation of Man, which in any case is desperate, all the more desperate through its addition of lying handed-down accounts.[85]

This stifling power of a system of written records, a system which was given its perfect and most desperate expression in the paranoid world of *Senatspräsident* Schreber, is answered by Canetti with the possibility of a mythic power of speech, the life's breath of the living voice:

I have not yet lived in a single moment on earth without being contained in this or that myth. Everything always has meaning, even despair. It may have changed its appearance from one moment to the next, but it was always a meaning that went on growing. I may not even have perceived it; but it perceived me. It may have remained silent; but later it spoke out. It spoke in a strange language, and I learned it.[86]

Myths are stories without history, language without its chains, the words of life with their metamorphic powers. In Canetti's sense, they are *lived* aphorisms:

Of course, one could think only about words rather than about myths, and as long as one refrained from defining them all the wisdom could be extracted from them that Man has accumulated. But the myths are more *fun*, because they are full of metamorphoses.[87]

In quest of this mythic, in a sense musical power of aphorisms—"music is the true, living history of Man"[88]—Canetti confronts his predecessors in the tradition of the aphorism. "Which sentences one finds in a book of aphorisms does one write down for oneself?"[89] asks Canetti, and hits upon a number of possibilities: aphorisms "that confirm oneself," that are "funny," that "call up an image," that "make one ashamed," and finally those "untouchable or sacred sentences" that one does not dare write down.[90] It is these that provide the strength to overcome death; they take on the character of "names," and from them comes a wealth of immediacy and the potential for survival:

For me, Gérard de Nerval would rank as a poet if only because he believed he came from Nerval.

All arithmetical connections, proportions, elliptical fates and tracks, leave me indifferent; all the connections established by names excite me and are true.

My god is the Name, the breath of my life is the Word. Places are of no consequence once their names fade. I have been nowhere I wasn't drawn to by the name.[91]

It is against the Name that the power of survival must then be measured. To this day it remains the only real form of survival.[92]

Repeatedly Elias Canetti is occupied with the possibility of condensing the whole breath of life into one single sentence, of preserving for language the inviolability of dreams:[93]

Only one single sentence is pure. Simply one more takes something away from it.[94]

The necessity of isolated sentences: they pounce from a steeper angle; they hit and make their mark deeper; but not without first flaring up and illuminating an entire landscape which has never been seen in its entirety in this way before and will never again be totally dark.

The receptive moment for a sentence of this kind cannot be predetermined. It simply happens.[95]

He is looking for the one sentence. He thinks a hundred thousand sentences to find the one.[96]

What dominates Canetti's poetology of the aphorism is its distinction from system-thinking, that species of language that puts in the place of metamorphosis and the living sentence a sum total, which is an aspect of the power of death.[97] The Pre-

Socratics and Chinese thinkers,[98] Kafka[99] and Lichtenberg[100] are opposed to all varieties of Aristotelian.

Minds that illuminate and minds that order. Heraclitus and Aristotle as extreme cases.

The mind that illuminates is like lightning, moving rapidly and covering great distances. He leaves everything aside and makes straight for the one thing he himself does not know before illuminating it. His effectiveness begins with his striking. Without some destruction, without terror, he cannot take on a shape for mankind. Brightness alone is too unlimited and too shapeless. The fate of the new knowledge depends on the place he strikes. Man is on the whole still territory that has not been struck by this lightning.

What has been illuminated is then left to those who order. Their operations are as slow as the others are fast; they are the cartographers of the lightning strike, which they mistrust, and they try to take measures to prevent it from striking again.[101]

Canetti's hatred of death is also a hatred of systems, which— by chaining and by sealing up—are irreversibly made into forms of power:

I hate those people who rapidly erect systems, and I shall see to it that mine is never quite accomplished.[102]

With every thought what matters is what remains unspoken, how great is its love of what is unspoken, and how closely the thought approaches the unspoken without making contact. Some things are said so that they can never be said again. *Bold* thoughts are of this kind; if repeated, their boldness is gone. They say lightning doesn't strike the same spot twice. The electric charge it carries is its blessing, but its light is only brief. Where a fire starts it is no longer lightning.

Thoughts that unite into systems lack respect. They gradually exclude the unspoken and leave it behind, till it dies of thirst.[103]

The ingenious pigeonholing we have evolved is filled with everything that attracts curiosity. It is sufficient that something is found—in there it goes, and in its pigeonhole it had better act dead and keep quiet. Aristotle is omnivorous; he proves to mankind that nothing is inedible as long as one can categorize it. The things in his collections, living or not, are without exception objects and useful for something or other, if only to demonstrate how harmful they are.[104]

To see that all the conceptual hair splitting and systems of the philosophers must still become true, that nothing has been forced together or thought in vain—the world is a torture chamber of thinkers.[105]

Systematized thinking of this kind, which is a "wielding of power,"[106] is repeatedly revoked by Canetti in ever-new attempts: "What offers hope in any systsem resides in what it excludes."[107]

The antithetical concept opposed to "system" is that of the myth, in regard to the three characteristics which, in Canetti's sense, constitute his aphoristic quality: birth from out of the living single sentence, reversal, and metamorphosis. Reversals have always been a strategy in the traditions of aphoristic form. That they also release symbolic energy in a myth was perhaps first emphasized by Canetti, when he linked them to the mythic figure of the "Trickster," who unites within him all aspects of anti-systematic and anti-disciplinary existence:

In him, the effects of the command and of metamorphosis meet, and we can discover in him the nature of freedom as we can in no other human figure. He starts out as a chief, issuing orders which are obeyed. But he takes his people's obedience ad absurdum and so loses it. . . . There is no reversal he does not exemplify for us.[108]

Metamorphosis indeed becomes *the* key category in Canetti's aphoristic work. In place of an evolution of generative, civilizing invention, such as the systematized thought of the Enlightenment demanded, Canetti puts the moments of creation and the endless metamorphoses of myth.[109] His great historical model for this form is Ovid's *Metamorphoses:* in them, everything is anticipated which "most interests writers to this day"[110] and the "liberating breath of transformation"[111] blows through them. For Canetti, it is in animals that this creative moment, lost to Man's thinking, still resides. It would be of the essence to "take apart" Man "into the animals that make him up"[112] and to reintroduce the animal into history[113]—this would restore beauty,[114] safety,[115] and love,[116] which in turn would mean restoring power to the miracle as the vital principle of counter-violence:

Miracles, the pitiful remainders of those old metamorphoses bursting with energy.[117]

NOTES

1. Elias Canetti, *Die Provinz des Menschen*, Munich and Vienna, 1973, p. 93.
2. There is frequent testimony to Canetti's affinity to Kafka; see *Die Provinz des Menschen*, pp. 56, 64, 230, and 306.
3. Franz Kafka, *Tagebücher 1910–1923*, Frankfurt, 1954, p. 502.
4. Franz Kafka, *Beschreibung eines Kampfes*, Frankfurt, 1946, pp. 295 ff.
5. *Die Provinz des Menschen*, p. 206.
6. Ibid., p. 16.
7. Ibid., p. 143.
8. Ibid., p. 125.
9. Ibid., p. 126.
10. Ibid., p. 125.
11. Ibid., p. 194.
12. Ibid., p. 35.
13. Ibid., p. 58.
14. Ibid., p. 53.
15. Ibid., p. 71.
16. Ibid., p. 16.
17. Elias Canetti, *The Tongue Set Free* (translated by Joachim Neugroschel), New York, 1979 and 1983, p. 3.
18. "Not today, tomorrow": ibid., p. 3.
19. Ibid., p. 10.
20. Ibid., pp. 26–27.
21. Ibid., pp. 32–33.
22. Ibid., pp. 29–30.
23. Ibid., pp. 65 ff.
24. Ibid., p. 68.

25. Ibid., p. 74.
26. *Die Provinz des Menschen*, p. 35.
27. Ibid., p. 24.
28. Ibid., pp. 90 ff., and cf. Canetti's book title *Die gespaltene Zukunft (The Split Future)*, Munich and Vienna, 1972.
29. *Die Provinz des Menschen*, p. 92
30. Ibid., p. 224.
31. Ibid., p. 12.
32. Ibid., p. 15.
33. On the interpretation of the Fall in the history of philosophy, cf. Jürgen Strutz, "Der Mythos vom Paradies. Anmerkungen zu seiner Rezeption bei Kant und Hegel," in Olav Münzberg and Lorenz Wilkins (eds.), *Aufmerksamkeit. Klaus Heinrich zum 50. Geuertstag*, Frankfurt, 1979, pp. 575–88, but particularly Odo Marquard, "Felix Culpa? Bemerkungen zu einem Applikationsschicksal von Genesis 3," in Manfred Fuhrmann et al. (eds.), *Text und Applikation. Theologie, Jurisprudenz und Literaturwissenschaft im hermeneutischen Gespräch*, Munich, 1981, pp. 53–71 (this includes important bibliographical references to books by M. Metzger, E. Lämmerzahl, H. Wimmershoff, and W. Schmidt-Biggemann).
34. Georg Wilhelm Friedrich Hegel, *Werke*, 17 (Lectures on the philosophy of religion, II: lectures concerning the proofs of the existence of God), Frankfurt, 1969, p. 258.
35. Franz Kafka, *Hochzeitsvorbereitungen auf dem Lande und andere Prosa aus dem Nachlaß*.
36. *Die Provinz des Menschen*, p. 43.
37. Ibid., p. 202.
38. Ibid., p. 40.
39. Elias Canetti, *The Conscience of Words* (translated by Joachim Neugroschel), New York, 1979, p. 7.
40. *Die Provinz des Menschen*, p. 298.
41. Ibid., p. 309.
42. Ibid., p. 62.
43. Ibid., p. 199.
44. Ibid., p. 201.
45. Ibid., p. 168.
46. Ibid., p. 332.
47. Ibid., p. 78.
48. *The Conscience of Words*, pp. 2–3.
49. Ibid., p. 246.
50. Ibid., p. 210.
51. *Die Provinz des Menschen*, p. 343.
52. Ibid., pp. 132, 138, 292.
53. Ibid., p. 139.
54. Ibid., p. 174.
55. *The Conscience of Words*, pp. 48–49.

56. Ibid., pp. 140–44.
57. *Die Provinz des Menschen*, p. 76.
58. Ibid., p. 215.
59. *The Conscience of Words*, p. 42.
60. *Die Provinz des Menschen*, p. 139.
61. Ibid., p. 229.
62. Cf. Elias Canetti, *Crowds and Power* (translated by Carol Stewart), London, 1962, pp. 434–62.
63. For further information on the madness of *Senatspräsident* Schreber, cf. Samuel M. Weber (ed.), *Daniel Paul Schreber. Denkwürdigkeiten eines Nervenkranken*, Frankfurt, Berlin, and Vienna, 1973; Morton Schatzman, *Die Angst vor dem Vater. Langzeitwirkung einer Erziehungsmethode. Eine Analyse am Fall Schreber*, Reinbek, 1974; William G. Niederland, *Der Fall Schreber. Das psychoanalytische Profil einer paranoiden Persönlichkeit*, Frankfurt, 1978; Roberto Calasso, *Die geheime Geschichte des Senatspräsidenten Dr. Daniel Paul Schreber*, Frankfurt, 1980.
64. *Die Provinz des Menschen*, p. 102.
65. Ibid., p. 101.
66. For the broader context, see my book *"Indeenparadiese." Untersuchungen zur Aphoristik von Lichtenberg, Novalis, Friedrich Schlegal und Goethe*, Munich, 1976.
67. *Die Provinz des Menschen*, p. 88.
68. Ibid., p. 64.
69. Ibid., pp. 198 ff. and 45 ff.
70. Ibid., p. 74.
71. Ibid., p. 122.
72. Ibid., pp. 217 ff.
73. Ibid., p. 179.
74. Ibid., p. 132.
75. Cf. *Crowds and Power*, pp. 434–62.
76. Cf. "Kafka's Other Trial," in *The Conscience of Words*, pp. 60–139.
77. *Die Provinz des Menschen*, p. 81.
78. Ibid., p. 12.
79. Ibid., p. 163.
80. Ibid., p. 240.
81. Ibid., p. 8.
82. Ibid.
83. Ibid.
84. Ibid., pp. 14 ff.
85. Ibid., p. 38.
86. Ibid., p. 216 ff.
87. Ibid., p. 224.
88. Ibid., p. 29. Cf. Claude Lévi-Strauss, *Mythologica I–IV*, Frankfurt, 1973, where he compares the structure of myths with the architecture of symphonies.
89. *Die Provinz des Menschen*, p 185.

90. Ibid., p. 186.
91. Ibid., p. 199.
92. Ibid., p. 201.
93. "We cannot tell what harm the interpretation of dreams will cause. Their destruction remains hidden, but how sensitive a dream is! There is no blood on the butchers' axes when they go poking among the webs, but what have they destroyed!—and the same thing can never be spun again. Only a very few suspect the uniqueness of each dream; how else could they strip it down to some commonplace or other.

    "Perhaps of all people Klee was the only one to treat dreams with the reverence they deserve, as the most inviolable thing that happens within Man." (*Die Provinz des Menschen*, p. 245.)

94. Ibid., p. 72.
95. Ibid., p. 320.
96. Ibid., p. 343.
97. Bacon, the "systematic lover of power" (ibid., p. 54), and Hobbes, the most important thinker on power (ibid., p. 151)—Canetti's "thought-Bible"—are repeatedly appealed to in this connection.
98. "I like reading Hsun-Tse; he is undeceived in his view of mankind, and nonetheless he hopes. But I cannot deny that I like reading Mencius too, because he is deceived concerning Man.

    "I do not ever want to move on from the Chinese 'teachers.' Only the Pre-Socratics have been occupying me as long—my whole life long. I can never tire of either. Together, but only together, they contain everything the thinking man needs as a spur—or not quite everything, something of major consequence remains to be added, concerning Death, and I shall add it." (*Die Provinz des Menschen*, p. 312.)

99. Ibid., p. 306.
100. Ibid., p. 304.
101. Ibid., pp. 253 ff.
102. Ibid., p. 127.
103. Ibid., p. 43.
104. Ibid., p. 45.
105. Ibid., p. 108.
106. Ibid., p. 44.
107. Ibid., p. 310.
108. Ibid., pp. 221 ff.
109. The relationship between myth and technology repeatedly occupied Kafka as a problem of the human power of invention—in two ways, as the explanation of origins and the regulation of social communication. "The Cares of a Family Man," "Blumfeld, an Elderly Bachelor," and "A Crossbreed" are examples of the invention of origins; "The Great Wall of China," the Nature Theater of Oklahoma, and the telephone room in the Hotel Occidental exemplify the invention of communication rituals. It is true that Kafka was increasingly skeptical

concerning the emancipatory possibilities of human inventions—but he at the same time robbed myths of their shaping power ("Prometheus"); a note in octavo book H (the "fourth," dating from the beginning of 1918) still tries to establish an analogy between "creation" and "invention," to sustain hope of a possible reenactment of myth by technology. "Inventions are racing ahead of us, just as the coast is forever receding before the steamship forever pulsing to the engine's beat. Inventions do everything that can be done. It would be injust to say: Aeroplanes do not fly as a bird flies, or: We will never be in a position to create a living bird. No, of course not, but the error lies in the objection, as if the steamer were being requested to call in at its first landing time after time, in spite of its straight course. A bird cannot be created by some originating act because it has already been created, and the first Act of Creation constantly produces more birds; and it is impossible to force a way into this living, continuing series created by an original, unceasing will—just as the story goes that the first woman was admittedly created from the man's rib but that this was never repeated, but instead men subsequently took other men's daughters for their wives. The method and implication of the creation of the bird (this is the point) and of the aeroplane need not be different, and primitive tribes' confusion of gunfire and thunder may contain a certain truth, to a point." (Franz Kafka, *Hochzeitsvorbereitungen*, pp. 119 ff.) A later observation in a letter to Milena limits the questions of the origin of Man and the possibility of communicative realization to the question of writing as an identifying act, and, in a spirit of Enlightenment dialectic, notes the step-by-step mutual undermining of both the mythical and the technological organization of Man's realization of himself: "But to write letters amounts to stripping naked in front of ghosts, which they are greedily waiting for. Written kisses do not arrive at their destinations but are drunk up by ghosts on the way. It is this ample nourishment that enables them to multiply so staggeringly. Mankind senses this and combats it; to eliminate ghostliness between human beings so far as possible, and to achieve natural communication and the peace of the soul, they have invented the railway, the car, and the aeroplane, but nothing is any help anymore, they are all plainly inventions thought up as mankind is going down—the other side is so much more composed, so much stronger—after the postal service they invented the telegraph, the telephone, radiotelegraphy. The ghosts won't go hungry, but we will be ruined." (Franz Kafka, *Briefe an Milena*, Frankfurt, 1965, pp. 259 ff.; Max Brod's *Gesammelte Werke*.) The naturalness and communicability of the body as created has been replaced by the invention of writing and the technology by which signals are exchanged. Inventions intended to promote the possibility of physical verification are paralyzed by those that put distance between bodies, by the ghostly draining-empty of signs, by the canceling of their identifying power.

110. *Die Provinz des Menschen*, p. 342.
111. Ibid., p. 342.
112. Ibid., p. 40.

113. Ibid., p. 32.
114. Ibid., p. 203.
115. Ibid., p. 37.
116. Ibid., p. 51.
117. Ibid., p. 29.

Stefan H. Kaszyński

Dialogue and Poetics: On the Dialogic Character of Canetti's Notebooks [1]

The special issue of Elias Canetti's notebook *Die Provinz des Menschen (The Human Province)* published by Hanser in 1982 was provided by the publisher with a jacket band quoting from an essay on the notebook which appeared in *Die Zeit,* according to which the notes were "the center of Canetti's work." This statement, which for reasons of promotional psychology is presented as an authoritative decree, is essentially a value judgment of ideological and poetological significance. True, all it seems to offer is an indication of the position of the notes in the author's oeuvre, but as the center is thought to be the most important point on a literary landscape the notes are being recommended to the potential reader as *the* work by Canetti. The authority of a newspaper, and not, say, the name of the critic, underpins this evaluation for the general public. That it comes from a different context is of no consequence, at least for one of the parties to the purchasing transaction.

If this *Zeit* quotation could thus lead to misunderstandings, for the Canetti connoisseur it is not misleading, since the notes have today become essential reading for an understanding of his major works. They are also more frequently quoted by critics and literary scholars than any other statements by the author of *Crowds and Power*.

What is it that makes the notes so attractive? Their form, at once incomplete yet perfect? The broad spectrum of problems broached, or the explicatory dialogic manner of their formulation? No doubt all of this together, though of course the last of these is the unmistakable distinguishing feature or novelty that clearly marks out Canetti from other contemporary aphorists. His notes consist first and foremost of aphorisms, or of comments likewise molded by "aphoristic thinking."[2]

Aphorisms traditionally tend to have the character of monologue: not infrequently they aspire to a kind of totality by compassing in one concentrated statement a wide range of opposites. Canetti's models, the aphorists Georg Christoph Lichtenberg and Karl Kraus, are good examples of this. With Elias Canetti, however, things stand differently: for him, aphorisms are a means of taking up the "dialogue with the cruel partner,"[3] as he himself puts it in an essay on the subject.

Let us for the moment put the "cruel partner" out of our minds and attempt to describe the dialogic character of the notes. In his essay "Why I Do Not Write Like Karl Kraus," Canetti gives theoretical consideration to his relationship to the editor of *Die Fackel*.[4] He avows his intellectual support for Kraus, and at the same time dissociates himself from him as writer and thinker. Kraus's aphorisms express authoritarian, uncompromising verdicts on his times and fellow men. In his own notes, Canetti prefers to attempt a dialogue with the times—with the Nazi period and the Second World War behind him and in this way richer in experience than Karl Kraus, who died in 1936, Canetti is no longer as profoundly convinced of the moral impact and influence of literature. Granted, he never doubts its mission,[5] but he does see it rather as a dialogue, and not (as Kraus does) as a commandment.

It is no accident that the notes so far published begin in

1942, during the war. They are spontaneous reactions to the quotidian, the unbearable tensions of which are caught in pithy sentences which, like Canetti's (admittedly unpublished) diaries, are a soliloquy on the times conducted in dialogue form. In brief notes one speaks, as in a diary, with oneself, about things one does not even want to discuss with one's neighbor. "But what does that mean?" demands Canetti. "Does one, de facto, become two figures properly conversing with one another? And who are the two? Why are there only two? Couldn't there, shouldn't there be many of them?"[6]

At another point in the essay just quoted, Canetti tries to offer a poetological answer to the question too. "The sentence is always something different from the man writing it. It stands before him as something alien, a sudden solid wall which cannot be leaped over."[7] This is no doubt not the only answer to our (highly general) question concerning the dialogic character of the notes, but it demonstrates unambiguously that what we are dealing with here is also the poetics and structure of statement.[8] Canetti himself feels this, when he says, "It seems to me that there are certain contents in a life that can be best captured in diary form."[9] And since the notes must be seen in Canetti as an extension or indeed as a condensation of the diary form, this claim may be read in connection with them too.

In contrast to other authors of his time, such as Brecht, Canetti refrains on principle from conducting a direct dialogue with his reader; he does not mean either to educate him or to preach at him. His dialogue with the world starts on a quite different level and is primarily a dialogue with himself, and at the same time a debate of mythology, religion, history, and language. In his foreword to *The Human Province* Canetti stresses that the notes are to be seen in the first instance as an utterance running parallel to his major work, *Crowds and Power*, which he was then working on. At that time they were a safety valve to relieve the "pressure" (which he himself created) "of concentration on a single work."[10] In this way the notes made possible means of expression which Canetti denied himself in *Crowds and Power*. If the notes have meanwhile long lost their character as a safety valve and have acquired "their own inviolable right,"[11] they are still not meant to be in any fashion predetermined, not, that is to say, fixed according to some thoery, and certainly not burdened with any system or systematized thought. These indications, reconstructed from the foreword, are themselves sufficient to show clearly how close Canetti stands to modern aphorism theories. Harald Fricke, who writes on the theory of the aphorism and takes a highly critical stance with regard to his predecessors, has constructed on the basis of research a definition which seamlessly fits Canetti's notes. "An aphorism," Fricke writes, "is a contextually isolated element in a chain of written non-fictional prose texts, consisting of one self-contained sentence or a concise formulation, with a punch line either of a linguistic or of a content nature."[12] No exception need be taken to Fricke's definition in relation to Canetti; the individual character of Canetti's notes shows, however, that these non-fictional prose texts, as Fricke calls them, assuredly have a distinctive aesthetic function, which has an effect not least on their communicative aspect.

From a point of view of communication aesthetics, the communicative content of an aphoristic statement can certainly be heightened by aesthetic means; Yury Lotman, writing on communication aesthetics, even speaks of a "plurality of artistic codes,"[13] which, put plainly, means that communicative qualities attach to the aesthetic structure of the text. The question of the poetics of the notes is thus also a question of the world view of the writer. Peter Krupka, who has written well-received work on the aphorisms of the Pole Stanislav Jerzy Lec, lists among his theoretical considerations a number of aesthetic strategies which can equally well be found in Canetti's aphoristic technique, such as etymologizing, demetaphorication, distortion, innovation, etc.[14] Canetti, it is true, prefers to see his aphorisms as texts for everyday use, but their structure, which is organized along wholly literary lines, lends the notes the character of independent literary works of art.

What most of the analysts of these art forms (such as Luciano Zagari, Uwe Schweikert, Harald Fricke, Peter Laemmle, Manfred Durzak, Dagmar Barnouw) lose sight of is the dialogic character of the notes, which, by shaping them, in fact creates meaning in the total structure. Granted, Canetti himself repeatedly points out the dialogicity of his diaries and notebooks, as I have already indicated; but he does not go on to develop this thought into any original, systematized theory, for the simple reason that he rejects thinking in systems—in this respect, incidentally, he resembles his predecessors Lichtenberg and Bacon in being emphatically an aphorist. [15] If we consider Canetti's scattered comments on the dialogic character of his texts alongside the equally precise reflections of the Russian aesthetician Mikhail Bakhtin, a hitherto neglected interpretative option is opened up to us on the aphorisms of the author of *The Human Province*—which Gerhard Neumann, an expert in aphorism studies, once called the most important aphorisms of our time.[16]

In the essay I have quoted above, Canetti gathers together his notes, diaries, and notebooks under the heading "Dialogue with the Cruel Partner." From the explanations he adds we see clearly that the partner in these soliloquies is first and foremost the author himself. But if the author conducts a cruel debate with himself, the problems of the dialogue are at the same time problems of the inner structure of the texts: that is to say, to an extent poetological matters. In Canetti, some words develop into key words or determinata that allow us to perceive his whole world view, his response to the world. In all of his texts, Canetti is constantly debating concepts such as death, metamorphosis, language, war, religion, mankind, animals: he forever senses the challenge to conduct a head-on dialogue with them. In *Crowds and Power* he tries to outline them with sober objectivity, while in the notes he starts up a spontaneous dialogue with them which has an effect not least upon the structure of the aphorisms.

Mikhail Bakhtin, in his reflections on the theory of prose texts, evolves the concept of textually integrated inner dialogicity in artistic and in scholarly prose. "The life of language, in every area of use (everyday use, business life, scholarly work, artistic creativity), is interwoven with dialogical relationships," writes Bakhtin in his essay "Linguistics and Metalinguistics."[17] Speaking of creative prose, Bakhtin adds the term "physiognomy of discourse,"[18] which would be quite acceptable to Canetti.

The Russian scholar, writing of dialogic relationships in the creative prose text (e.g., the novel), particularly emphasizes the dialogic nexus between the speaker and his own word. Canetti too broaches similar considerations in connection with his metaliterary texts in "Dialogue with the Cruel Partner."

In all the numerous classical definitions of the aphorism, among them the scholarly theory of Franz H. Mautner, we find relatively clearly that the inner tension of the thought is susceptible to expression primarily through stylistic rather than other means, such as antitheses of content or of words.[19] This inner tension typifies Canetti's notes too; in his case, it first develops (as in the classical aphorism) between the "idea" and the "resolution," to use two of Mautner's terms;[20] but, beyond this, we must trace the dynamics back to the head-on dialogic confrontation between the ideologizing (a description Canetti would reject) determinatum and the elucidatory context. For example:

God was a mistake. But it is difficult to tell whether it was too soon or too late.[21]

The "unbearable tension" (Canetti's phrase) in this thought can only be put across by a dialogic procedure. As Bakhtin puts it, in general theoretical terms: "The word faces two ways: toward the object of discourse, as an ordinary word, and toward the other word, the alien discourse."[22]

In the process of constructing this aphorism, the determinatum "God" is semantically split by the elucidatory context: here, the dialogue is carried out between the original and the alienated meanings of the word. The dialogic effect in this case is thus attained by means of a doubting and division of the determinatum—with confrontation as the aim; viewed in terms of Peter Krupka's theory, a process is happening here that leads on from the denotation to the connotation of the concept of God.[23] That this is not an isolated instance in Canetti but in fact becomes a method can be proved by further examples from *The Human Province:*

To conceive a man so good that God would needs envy him.[24]
Language, pinned down as a system, falls silent.[25]
Hitler ought really to live on now as a Jew.[26]
Only when it lacks applause is nakedness truly nakedness.[27]

The method of unmasking by means of dialogic questioning of a familiar meaning demands, as Bakhtin says in another context, "a wholly new attitude toward the phenomenon of discourse, beyond the methodology, of traditional stylistic analysis and linguistic scrutiny"[28] which usually, according to Bakhtin, "examines the word solely in the frame of a monologic context."[29] In Canetti's notes, as the examples show, determinata are in a dialogue position between denotation and connotation, or, as Bakhtin has it: "The word is transformed into the arena for a struggle between two voices."[30]

Bearing in mind Bakhtin's theory, we can, moreover, formulate a further typical characteristic of the dialogic nature of Canetti's notes, and that is the equal matching in the dialogue of the basic idea (seen as a split in the meaning of the word) and the remaining context of the note. The mere emphasis of one word in the context leads to tension and to a dialogue, as

Bakhtin repeatedly stresses in his reflections.[31] In Canetti, this method seems well-nigh to be a "principle." The idea, which for him is so important, appears in the first instance in an opposition of word and text. The word becomes capable of dialogue only through its context: what Canetti thinks of as an idea originates not in the determinatum, since that is after all a fixed category for him, but rather in the context. This method is the result in Canetti, at least in part, of his general distrust of the communicative function of language. Death, for example, is always a firm basic category for Canetti, but it is one which he is forever attempting to question through various contexts, linguistic contexts among them.

I want death to be serious, and I want death to be terrible, most terrible of all when there is nothing left to fear but the void.[32]

This example enables us to propose a quite definite interpretation of that phrase Canetti uses as a synthesizing hold-all concept, "dialogue with the cruel partner." Without doubt, dialogue for this writer is a desperate game played with Death, whom Canetti aims to vanquish by linguistic creativity (as well as by other means). We see how very much this thought concerns him from a note dated 1943:

To portray death as if there were no such thing. A community where everything happens in such a way that no one knows of death. The language of these people contains no word for death, nor is there any conscious way of referring obliquely to it. Even if one of them planned to break their laws, particularly this first unwritten and unspoken law, and to speak of death, he could not do so as he would lack a word that the others would understand. No one is buried and no one cremated. People disappear, no one knows where; a feeling of shame suddenly impels them to leave; as it is considered a sin to be alone, no one speaks of the one who is absent. Often they come back, and people are pleased at their return. The period when one was away and alone is thought of as a bad dram one is not obliged to report on. Pregnant women return from such journeys with children, they deliver their children alone, they might die at home while giving birth. Even very small children suddenly get up and leave.[33]

For Canetti, language has not only a communicative role but also, and perhaps more importantly for his dialogue with himself, an inspiring function which not infrequently becomes apparent to him only later. "There are sentences that yield up their poison only years later."[34] The central category of metamorphosis, which dominates Canetti's world view and which, incidentally, is seen by him as the sole alternative to death, has to be understood dynamically rather than statically. In the notes the inner dynamics of this concept are constantly being imaged forth through pointers to its dialogic component:

I think I have found a key to transformation, and I have inserted it into the lock, but I haven't turned it. The door is shut and we can't get in. It will still give a good deal of trouble.[35]

It is characteristic of Canetti's aphorisms that he conducts his dialogue with metamorphosis with the door shut, as he puts it himself. As far as possible he avoids the word that lies closest to hand because he fears that daily use would leave it worn and trivialized; but it is present in the semantic background of almost every aphoristic note. Canetti, as his Munich speech makes plain, sees himself as the "keeper of metamorphosis," and it is these transformations that make the writer's inner dialogue possible in the first place, and significant. Don Quixote, an important key figure for Canetti, is in a sense a personification of the keeper of metamorphosis: his inner dialogue is heard by the world about him, true, but without the necessary decoding it remains mostly misunderstood. And surely this is also the fate of the central character in Canetti's *Auto-da-Fé*: Peter Kien, totally programmed to his own inner dialogue, cannot decode larger perspectives into questions of detail, and is destroyed by the context—that is, by his natural environment.

Harald Fricke remarks in his monograph on the aphorism that aphorists avoid making their material concrete on principle: they always aim at generalization, they expose (as Musil says)[36] the paradoxes of the wider context. Canetti is one of those contemporary writers who concentrate their entire effort on this very issue of rendering comprehensible this crux of modern epistemology. In his notes we see this especially persuasively. Here we find very clearly what Mikhail Bakhtin too considers an important concern of modern literature: that is, distrust of words and concepts that have gone rigid. Only a dialogic presentation of the inner debates of a writer attempting to catch hold of wider perspectives offers an effective method of combating ideologies, for ideologies—and in this Canetti agrees with Adorno—are, as it were, a "false awareness"[37] which on principle refuses to change. "The word is not a thing," states Bakhtin, "but the eternally moving, eternally changing medium of the dialogic function. One single consciousness or voice is never enough for it: the life of the word consists in its passage from mouth to mouth, from context to context, from collective to collective, from generation to generation. In this, the word remains aware of its passage: it cannot totally break loose of the power of those contexts it was once swallowed up in."[38] If, bearing Bakhtin's definition in mind, we take a look at Canetti's notes, which are fundamentally informed by the striving after metamorphoses, their dialogic character appears almost a matter of course. Naturally their effectiveness on the reader is another question, but that is no longer the concern of the poetologist but of reception studies.

To sum up these somewhat abstract thoughts on the dialogic nature of Canetti's notes, then:

1. Thought operating in patterns of dialogic confrontation is without doubt a shaping structure determining meaning in Canetti's notes, and can be of considerable significance in other literary and nonliterary texts by this author.

2. The dialogic thinking that constitutes the inner dynamics of content and structure in the aphorisms is apparent on three distinct levels in the notes—poetics, semantics, and individual perception of the world. That is to say, dialogic thinking is made an instrument for reading the world.

3. The dialogic function of the word and, in an extended sense, of language as a whole is used by Canetti as a challenge to rethink, and this principle of constant rethinking is closely allied to Canetti's own category of metamorphosis.

4. It is the dialogic character of the notes that most clearly shows us how Canetti puts his thought and writing to work against established systems.

5. The novelty of the dialogic thinking in the notes consists in the fact that it offers an alternative to the customary mon-ologic thinking of aphoristic prose texts—or at all events the notes, as Canetti's commentaries show, are programmed in this direction. This method is one of challenge and confrontation, with the final goal of verifying his own thought processes.

If we take the theses here drawn up from analysis of the notebooks and apply them to Canetti's whole oeuvre—which, for poetological reasons, it is only partly possible to do—we again see quite clearly that the claim raised by Hanser's jacket band for seeing the notes as central to Canetti's works is wholly justified—at any rate from the point of view of a future inter-preter of the complete works.

NOTES

1. This essay was written during a stay in the Federal Republic of Germany made possible by the Alexander von Humboldt Foundation.

2. The concept of "aphoristic thinking" was evolved by Paul Requadt through work on the genre of the aphorism as seen in Lichtenberg; cf. Paul Requadt, *Lichten-berg*, Stuttgart, 1964, pp. 133–65. The rules Requadt draws up through consid-eration of Lichtenberg can be applied to a number of modern aphorists, Canetti among them. This has been indirectly demonstrated by Uwe Schweikert too, in his paper "Elias Canetti und die aphoristische Tradition"; cf. U. Schweikert, "Schöne Nester ausgeflogener Wahrheiten," in H.G. Göpfert (ed.), *Canetti lesen*, pp. 77–86. Harald Fricke, however, in his monograph *Aphorismus*, Stuttgart, 1984, dis-putes the poetological validity of this concept and rejects it on the grounds of its "psychological approach." But as Requadt's concept of "aphoristic thinking," quite

apart from its theoretical validity, is among the shaping components in Canetti's aphorisms, it also ultimately has an influence on the poetics of the notes.

3. See the essay "Dialogue with the Cruel Partner," in Elias Canetti, *The Conscience of Words* (translated by Joachim Neugroschel), New York, 1979, pp. 40–54.

4. Cf. Elias Canetti, "Warum ich nicht wie Karl Kraus schreibe," in *Wort in der Zeit*, 1, 1966, pp. 41–47.

5. This firm conviction is behind "The Writer's Profession," in *The Conscience of Words*, pp. 236–46.

6. *The Conscience of Words*, p. 46.

7. Ibid., p. 40.

8. In his otherwise very useful paper, Luciano Zagari disputes the structural significance of the notes, writing: "Canetti's starting point seems to be of a morphological rather than a structural nature. This makes immediate sense if we pause to consider that both the earlier and the later notes are inconceivable without constant reference to the decades of work on *Crowds and Power*. . . ." Luciano Zagari, "Epik und Utopie," in *Literatur und Kritik*, 136–37, 1979, p. 430. But cf. the foreword to Canetti's *Die Provinz des Menschen*, which seems to rule out so close an association of the notes as a whole with *Crowds and Power*. As the notes have furthermore appeared as a book in their own right and are being received as an independent form of artistic expression, it seems legitimate to interpret them not only morphologically but also structurally, which I have here set out to do.

9. *The Conscience of Words*, p. 52.

10. Foreword to *Die Provinz des Menschen*.

11. Ibid.

12. Harald Fricke, *Aphorismus*, Stuttgart, 1984, p. 18.

13. Cf. Yury Lotman, *Die Struktur literarischer Texte* (translated by Rolf-Dietrich Keil), Munich, 1981, p. 43.

14. Cf. Peter Krupka, *Der polnische Aphorismus. Die "Unfrisierten Gedanken" von Stanislaw Jerzy Lec und ihr Platz in der polnischen Aphoristik*, Munich, 1976. Of particular interest is the chapter "Ansätze zu einer Theorie des Aphorismus," pp. 46–71.

15. According to Requadt, aphoristic thinking is a form of open thought which aphorists (Lichtenberg, Bacon) oppose to systematized thinking.

16. Cf. Gerhard Neumann (ed.), *Der Aphorismus. Zur Geschichte, zu den Formen und Möglichkeiten einer literarischen Gattung*, Darmstadt, 1976, p. 1.

17. Mikhail Bakhtin, "Linguistik und Metalinguistik," in M. Bakhtin, *Literatur und Karneval. Zur Romantheorie und Lachkultur* (translated by Alexander Kaempfe), Munich, 1969, p. 103.

18. Bakhtin's concept of "physiognomy of discourse" could be seen as a parallel to Canetti's "acoustic masks."

19. Cf. Franz H. Mautner, "Der Aphorismus als literarische Gattung," in Neumann, *Der Aphorismus*, p. 55.

20. Ibid., p. 46.

21. *Die Provinz des Menschen.*
22. Mikkail Bakhtin, "Typen des Prosaworts," in *Literatur und Karneval,* p. 107.
23. Krupka, *Der polnische Aphorismus,* p. 72.
24. *Die Provinz des Menschen.*
25. Ibid.
26. Ibid.
27. Ibid.
28. Bakhtin, "Linguistik und Metalinguistik," p. 107.
29. Ibid., p. 108.
30. Ibid., p. 119.
31. Cf. Mikhail Bakhtin, *Woprosy litieratury i estietiki,* Moscow, 1975.
32. *Die Provinz des Menschen.*
33. Ibid.
34. Ibid.
35. Ibid.
36. Robert Musil, *Tagebücher, Aphorismen, Essays und Reden,* edited by Adolf Frisé, Hamburg, 1955, p. 261.
37. Cf. Theodor W. Adorno, "Rede über Lyrik und Gesellschaft," in T. Adorno, *Noten zur Literatur I,* Frankfurt, 1958, pp. 73–104.
38. Bakhtin, "Linguistik und Metalinguistik," pp. 129–30.

Iring Fetscher

Elias Canetti as a Satirist

The daily news, from the Hamburger Fremdenblatt: *In Berlin over the Christmas period twenty attempts were made at suicide*, ten of which were crowned with success.

—*Karl Kraus*

Elias Canetti's three published plays, *The Wedding, Comedy of Vanity*, and *The Numbered*, are satirical experiments rather than comedies. Not that they lack humor, but their basic intention is satirical criticism. In his autobiography of the years 1931–37, Canetti speaks of the exciting and profound influence Georg Büchner's *Woyzeck* had on him when he read it in 1931, and how Büchner moved him to turn away from his earlier model, Karl Kraus. Kraus, whom he described in 1965 as one of his "idols," nonetheless continues in my opinion to leave his mark on Canetti's later work too. He was and probably still is rated by Canetti as the greatest satirist in the German language, indeed as the only one "whom one has the right to name next to Aristophanes, Juvenal, Quevedo, Swift, and Gogol."[1] If the radical severity and relentlessness of the criticism is to be our criterion, then surely there is indeed no other German-speaking writer to compare with Karl Kraus. For some years Elias Canetti, like many of his intellectual contemporaries, was under the spell of Kraus. He heard him read perhaps as many as a hundred times, and read just about everything he had written, above all, no doubt, the writings of his Vienna years. In 1965 Canetti explained his immense influence as deriving from "two main devices: *literalness* and *horror*."[2] Kraus was known for his sovereign mastery of the art of quotation. His quotations were the evidence in his unremitting case against stupidity, brutality, insensitivity, and lack of imagination. "The quotation, as he employed it, testified against the quoted man," and, as it were, served to convict the accused author. In order to quote in this way, though, Kraus needed an attentive and discriminating ear. He read everything that came into his hands, and within him the texts became spoken and audible—and often this was enough to make apparent the inappropriateness and stupidity of the images used. The standard he used was the German language of Matthias Claudius, Goethe, or Nestroy, a touchstone he had in his own ear. Before him, Nestroy had put on stage the speech habits and platitudes of the various Viennese social levels, in a less aggressive but equally satirical manner. Kraus, by contrast, "attacked and whiplashed" mercilessly, and against his verdicts there was no appeal. The subjects of his criticism were both lofty and trivial literary products: newspaper articles, advertising slogans, and small ads no less than critical or literary works. He could devote as much attention and analytic precision to a convoluted, confused editorial in the *Neue Freie Presse* as to a significant literary work. Canetti praises Kraus for having been filled with a "sense of absolute responsibility" which meant far more than that *engagement* (commitment) which "is now rampant everywhere like some weed." In the manner of his onetime master, Canetti instantly adds a reflection on the everyday senses of "engaging" and "engagement" which cuts the inflated value of the concept down to normal size. An employee is engaged to do a job, and is pleased at this new engagement. But one cannot well be "an employee of the most important things."[3]

Canetti doubtless learned from Kraus the ability to listen to the language, above all the everyday language of people—or at least his own ability was helped along by Kraus's precision in listening. Canetti's turn from his idol of the early years comes vividly alive in the 1965 essay. It was related to his realization that Kraus exercised a kind of dictatorship over his adherents and listeners, so that they adopted all his evaluations and assessments involuntarily, and those he disapproved of became outcasts. "Still and all, it was not a totally fruitless dictatorship, and since I had surrendered to it myself and ultimately also managed to liberate myself, I have no right to accuse it. Besides, through my experience of that dictatorship I forever lost all taste for the deplorable custom of accusing others."[4]

His reading of Büchner's *Woyzeck,* which as chance would have it happened at a decisive moment in his life, enabled Canetti to make the transition from a scourging, condemning, accusing way of writing to another which was no less critical but which availed itself of a quite different method. This, at least, is how it appears to the author in retrospect. After completing his novel, *Auto-da-Fé,* the twenty-six-year-old took up a yellow-bound volume of Büchner "and opened it at random: it was a scene in *Wozzeck* (the name was still spelled that way then), the scene with Wozzeck and the doctor. I was thunderstruck—I read the scene and all the other scenes in the fragment, I read the entire fragment over and over, I don't know how often, it seems it must have been countless times because I read the whole night long, nothing else in that yellow book but *Wozzeck* time and again, from the beginning, and I was so excited that before six next morning I left the house and ran down to the tram. . . ." In his excitement, Canetti visits his girlfriend Veza and wakes her. She had faithfully stood at his side as literary adviser and had already introduced him to so many writers, but she had never spoken to him of Büchner. To his blunt question whether she was familiar with *Wozzeck* she answers that of course she was, and, in reply to further questioning, calls it "the greatest play in German literature." It soon turns out that Veza is not only familiar with Büchner but has quite deliberately kept him from Canetti since she was afraid that reading Büchner would prevent him from completing his novel. But now Canetti, exhausted by his work on *Auto-da-Fé,* is led by his reading of Büchner to drama. "Although since the completion of the novel everything urged me on to drama," writes Canetti in his autobiography, "I do not think it impossible that, after a spell of exhaustion, I should have embarked on a new novel, no less lengthy, with madness once again as its subject." "But now that night when I picked up *Wozzeck* and the morning after when, in my state of excitement, I was beset by *Lenz,* decided everything. . . . Pride and defiance [in his debate with Veza, who had been against his fascination with the insane] were immediately things of the past. I did not write a new novel, and months passed before I recovered my confidence in *Kant Catches Fire* [later retitled *Die Blendung,* i.e., *Auto-da-Fé*]. By that time I was already obsessed by *The Wedding.*"

What follows gives us insight into the importance of Büchner for this young writer molded by Karl Kraus; possibly it was the most significant turning point in Canetti's development. Today, looking back, he views it in this way:

If I now say that I owed *The Wedding* to that night-time reading of *Wozzeck,* it will seem at first glance presumptuous. But there is no way around the truth simply to avoid this appearance of presumptuousness—indeed, I *must* not avoid it. The catastrophic visions I had been stringing together till then were still influenced by Karl Kraus. Everything that happened (and it was always the worst that could happen) happened without reason, and the actions were simply parallel. It was all caused by somebody writing, and *it was accused.* It was *accused from the outside,* by that very man who was writing and who wielded *his* whip over all the scenes of destruction. That whip gave him no peace and spurred him on, and he paused only when there was something to lash—and hardly was the punishment meted out but he was off again. Basically what happened was always the same: people going about their everyday business, uttering the most banal of words, were standing unsuspectingly at the edge of the abyss. Along came the whip and drove them in—they all fell into the selfsame abyss. There was nothing that might have saved them. For their words were never different, they were exactly fitted to them, and the one who had done the fitting was always one and the same, the *writer with the whip*. [Italics partly mine—I.F.]

In contrast to this method, taken from Kraus, of accusing, whipping, and punishing, Canetti discovers in Büchner something he terms *"self-accusation."*

The characters who make the greatest impression, apart from the protagonist, introduce themselves. The doctor and the major strike out: they attack, though in such different ways that one hesitates a little to use the same word for both of them. But it remains an attack, because it has the effect of an attack on Wozzeck. Their words, which are wholly distinctive, are aimed against him and have the most serious consequences. But they only have these consequences by portraying the speaker, who deals a wicked blow, a blow one will never forget and which would enable one to recognize him anytime and anywhere.

It is this that constitutes the total newness of this method as opposed to that of Kraus: that here the characters, each in his own way, "accuse themselves."

Whatever they are like, they are there, they exist prior to any moral verdict being passed on them. Of course *one thinks of them with abhorrence, but it is mixed with pleasure, because they present themselves without suspecting the abhorrence they excite.* There is a kind of *innocence in this self-accusation;* no legal net has yet been cast for them—it may be thrown across them some time later, if ever; but no accusation, not even that of the most powerful satirist, could mean as much as this self-accusation, for this contains the novel, too, where a man exists, his rhythm, his fear, his breathing.

As I write this essay a "real-life drama" is being enacted before the eyes and ears of the West German public, indeed before the world, which is not unlike the Büchner type of drama here described by Canetti. Those in high, in fact well-nigh the highest, public offices have been clearly found guilty of dishonorable and possibly even criminal conduct, yet they are not ashamed of accusing their critics of malicious slander and rabble-rousing, and attempt to preserve the image of the decent citizen—which no one any longer sees them as. They accuse themselves far more effectively than even a Karl Kraus could have done. There is even plenty of humor, when, for example, a man who draws a five-figure monthly salary is apostrophized as a case of hardship and it is suggested he try earning a little extra on the side.

Truly, the writing of satires is becoming ever more difficult, the more the real world is itself transformed into some third-rate satire, such as—even a few years ago—would have met with all-round rejection if seen on the stage, for its simplistic exaggeration.

The captain, the doctor, the booming major appear as if of their own accord. No one has lent them their voices—they speak for themselves and they strike out, at one and the same man, Wozzeck, and they come into existence through the act of striking him. He serves them all, he is their center. They would not exist without him, but he is as little aware of this as they are—it is tempting to go so far as to say he infects his tormentors with his innocence. *They cannot be other than the way they are:* the essence of self-accusation is that it gives this impression. The power of these characters, of all the characters, is their innocence.

By contrast, the satirist Kraus accuses, he

whips people as if they were schoolboys. He prepares them for those moral authorities they will one day stand before. He even knows what would make them better. Where does he get this absolute certainty? If he did not have it, he could not start writing at all. It begins with his being as unintimidated as God. Without saying as much he stands in for Him, and feels good in the part. He does not waste a moment on the thought that perhaps he isn't God at all. For as this authority exists—the highest—it follows that He must want deputies: one need only seize the moment, and the power.

Georg Büchner, on the other hand, quite ignores God and deals only with His creatures. He sees them in their "immutability, though he would [also] like to see them changed."

He knows that "hatred and punishment . . . are no way to deal with mankind." Canetti aims to adopt in his own plays the method of "self-accusation" he discovered in Büchner:

The justice of the writer cannot [then] consist in damning them. He can invent the man who is their victim, and he can show all their traces left on him like fingerprints. The world is full of such victims, but it seems to be the most difficult thing imaginable to define one as a character who speaks in such a way as to leave the traces recognizable, and not blurred into accusations. Wozzeck is that character, and we experience the things committed against him as they happen, and not a word of accusation remains to be added. The traces of self-accusation are perceptible through him.

Canetti's play *The Wedding* follows the Büchner model. In the prologue in particular, the characters all, without exception, accuse themselves. The only equivalent for Wozzeck among them remains the caretaker's dying wife, who is trying in vain to say something to her husband: but he only goes on reading aloud from the Bible. The five scenes of the prologue present five psuedo-conversations in which the participants do not so much speak to each other as reveal themselves. The granddaughter of landlady Gilz tries through frequent visits to work her way into her grandmother's good books, so that she, rather than her sister, is the preferred inheritor. However, her actual attitude is made plain by her aggressive utterances to her grandmother's cat and parrot, and also by her insistence that yesterday her grandmother was so ill and she herself said she "didn't have long to go." The old woman's robust will to live is revived by her granddaughter's legacy-hunting, though, and even confounds her ability to work out the difference between 75 and 73. The granddaughter's repeated question "I'll get the house, won't I, Granny?" goes unheard not only because of the parrot's noise: old woman Gilz simply does not want to hear, though previously she has understood her granddaughter well enough. "I can't tell what you're saying because of Lore's squawking." "I'm still alive," she says contentedly to her parrot when her granddaughter has gone. The talk of the young Thut couple is no less revealing. Here too the object of discussion is possession of the house. In order the better to listen in on the debates between the grandmother and granddaughter, the married couple have moved to another bedroom, and are now constantly being disturbed by the parrot's screeching. Their baby is especially bothered by the interruptions of its nocturnal slumbers and, as we later learn, is unlikely to survive the damage to its health. Professor Thut, however, intends to buy the house off old Mrs. Gilz in exchange for a life annuity and also for the assurance that he will care for the parrot after her death. This, admittedly, is no more than an intention, as his wife mockingly points out.

In the dialogue the man comes across as a conceited oaf and his wife as a companion who only appears to agree but in reality hates her "shabby civil servant." The child, on account of whose future they are trying to gain possession of the house, plays an inconsequential part as a mere pretext. It is no wonder that, in the main part of the play, it dies during an earthquake through the negligence of its parents.

The next scene seems harmless enough. A youth called Peter, who worships his girl Anita, arrives with a big bouquet to tell her of his love, and speaks of the girl's intact chastity. Anita is just getting ready for the wedding festivities upstairs; all she can think of is the fun she is going to have, and she merely tolerates in a spirit of boredom the attentions of the youth, who reveals himself in his words as a little bourgeois boy: "You've given me faith in a family, children, descendants. In the times we live in. My children will inherit—my life's been given its meaning. What would I do without you? I can't live without you. Tell me if you love me . . ."

A "purely" business world is shown in the scene with Gretchen and Max. They plan to buy the house jointly, and Gretchen offers Max a loan, against huge interest payments. Gretchen points out the "risk" she is taking; Max (like Professor Thut) turns out to be a man of small courage. The couple's erotic relations turn the power tables at the end: the lady, financially so proud, becomes an obedient sex object. The offer of a cheap interest rate may also have been the price of a sexual partner.

In the final scene of the prologue, caretaker Kokosch reads passages from the Old Testament to his wife, to keep her from dying. Later we discover that he finds this "method" cheaper than fetching a doctor and that, afraid of the funeral expenses, he wants to postpone her death as long as possible. What looks at first glance like devoted dedication to his wife proves to be the expression of a squalid miserliness. His imbecilic daughter Leni is also a victim of this meanness: her father would have needed to pay a contribution toward the fees of a school for the handicapped, where she would at least have been taught the ability to speak, but he declared she should marry—that would cost him less.

The main part of *The Wedding* presents the hypocrisy, lechery, and self-deception of a number of petit bourgeois figures. Here too our revulsion and abhorrence are unintentionally triggered by the characters themselves. First we encounter the pitiful Segenreich, a planning officer, whose pride in his wife and family is (to use the language of his building line) "built on sand": he has no notion that his wife is having an affair with their family friend Schön, and mistakenly supposes their children his own. His wife, Johanna, has fallen in love with young Michel, her daughter's husband; she "could just eat the delicious man up. He's so terribly refined, he looks so cuddly, with his teddy-bear eyes and his trusting hair. I like him, oh, ever so much. . . . He's just so cute, so sweet and cute." She cheats on her lover with her son-in-law. The near-octogenarian Dr. Bock does not bear his randy name without reason, but in fact has sex with his female patients and then, if the occasion arises, aborts their children. The "young idealist" Horch is somewhat ambiguous: toward the end of the play he takes charge and announces the earthquake catastrophe in which the egoistic attitudes of this entire society obsessed with money and sex are revealed.

The satirical self-accusation peaks in the talk between the two potential house purchasers, Gretchen and Max, who are already calculating how much the plot of land will be worth once the house has been demolished and a lodging house can be built on the site. For them, it seems, this first-rate earthquake is a sheer stroke of luck. They are even busy envisaging a cheap way of disposing of the rubble. Their conversation ends in a total harmony:

> *Gretchen:* What luck! What luck!
> *Max:* You know, it's so lovely . . .
> *Gretchen:* that we get on so well . . .
> *Max:* heart . . .
> *Gretchen:* and soul.
> (*A tremendous crash. The wall on the right collapses.*)[5]

We can laugh at these two. They attain harmony when both of them are thinking of the same thing: maximum profit. For a property speculator whose gaze is fixed far ahead, the terrible earthquake becomes a piece of sheer good fortune. But their harmony is of course deceptive because behind it there lies the attempt (by each of them) to outwit the other and cash in the profits alone. Their clichéd expressions, "heart and soul," "what luck," here accuse the speakers, since they are spoken against the background of a catastrophic earthquake. Nonetheless, this dialogue is the least hypocritical, because it is quite openly about what the rest seek to conceal: possession.

The other two plays, *Comedy of Vanity* and *The Numbered*, are more obviously than *The Wedding* illustrations of a thesis. They might be called philosophical plays. While the *Comedy of Vanity* presents a totalitarian state which is out to make people conform to its conception of virtue by banning mirrors and flattery, the rulers of society in *The Numbered* have hung around the neck of each citizen a locket with a date of death, and his name lays down the age he will live to. In this way everyone finally has "certainty." The time when no one knew the hour of his death seems in retrospect barbaric. It is the duty of the Keeper, a high-ranking official, to open the locket on death and to check not *whether* but *that* the person in question has passed away at the correct moment. In both cases unexpected and unwelcome consequences ensue. Human vanity turns out to be tenaciously resistant, and the ban on mirrors results in black-market abuses and strange behavior on the part of people done out of their mirror images. At the end of a rainy day thousands can be seen on the streets at night, trying by torchlight to see their reflections in puddles. For a price, well-to-do citizens can contemplate their beloved mirror images in a kind of mirror-brothel, sitting next to each other as at the hairdresser's. Flatterers offer their eulogies just as in former times prostitutes offered their bodies. Clearly severe penalties are no use, so that the government is in fact contemplating having the entire population blinded. The play is a well-aimed satire on totalitarianism and its real consequences: this is as true of those scenes where mass enthusiasm is shown toward the irrepressible ways and means, however devious, by which the people come by vanity's forbidden pleasures.

The Numbered goes beyond the thematic content of the *Comedy of Vanity* since it also shows resistance to state-decreed bamboozlement successful in the end. At the outset, true, Canetti gives us here too a highly realistic portrayal of the consequences of a society so structured: as everyone indicates his life expectancy simply through his name, the date of birth becomes an embarrassing secret to be kept to oneself at all costs. Social hierarchy now corresponds to the life expectancy shown in the name. Men with an expectancy of eighty or ninety are ranked "high," those with forty or fifty "low." An old rank likes to consort with "low women" because those who are soon to die open up for him the chances of ever new affairs and marriages. Of course, a man can be deceived if he is told an earlier date of birth, so that he has to hang on a few years longer, waiting for his beloved to pass away.

A man called Fifty finally finds deliverance. He opens up the locket of an old woman he has been threatening and cajoling and discovers that it is empty. His own locket is empty as well. All the lockets are empty. The state has been keeping the population in a state of mystification decreed from above. The people were being educated to accept the life expectancy officially allotted them, but that meant that really they were already dead from the start: they could not turn their lives to great use, nor could they even kill themselves—or at least that is what they believed. Only the Keeper knew—and kept—the secret. Fifty reveals the strictly guarded secret, thus incurring the highest penalty of the law, and frees his fellow men:

Listen, you people, you fine dead, the years that you carry around your necks are false. You think you have them. You are so certain. But nothing is certain. It is all false. You have empty lockets hanging round your necks. The lockets are empty. You have not even the years that you think you have. You have nothing. Nothing is certain. The lockets are empty. Everything is as uncertain as it ever was. He who desires to die, can die today. He who does not desire it, dies nonetheless. The lockets are empty. The lockets are empty.[6]

Fifty is acclaimed as the liberator of the people and they all throw away their lockets. Disaster, as both the Keeper and Fifty the rebel see it, can no longer be averted. Hitherto the Keeper has lived "among contented people," "people who had no more fear." But those who have no fear can teach one nothing.

The play concludes with a scene involving Fifty and his friend. After the secret of the lockets has been revealed, the friend decides to search for his sister, who disappeared shortly before her twelfth birthday. "People told her she had to die when she was twelve," but she did not want to accept this verdict. Now her brother intends to seek her out. But Fifty believes that after so many years he will scarcely recognize her again, and in any case she might not want to be reminded of her earlier life:

But why do you want to disturb her? Let her lead her new life. It will be better for her if she is not disturbed. Her fear must have been very great or she would not have hidden herself for so long. If I am not mistaken, it's more than thirty years ago now.[7]

In other words, her appearance will be that of a forty-two-year-old, not of a child of twelve. But the friend will not be put off; he wants to find the sister he loves

and toss her and swing her and hold her out of the window till she screams for mercy. Twelve, Twelve, I shall say, don't you see that it's all nonsense? All names are nonsense. It doesn't matter what one's name is. Twelve or Eighty-eight, or the devil knows what, if we are here together and see each other and speak to each other. Twelve, do you hear me? Twelve, do you see me? Twelve, it's me. Twelve, it will always be me.[8]

Fifty has his doubts about the quest and doubts too whether the sister who has been lost will be pleased to be found again: "You don't really love her. If you did, you would feel bound to let her live as *she* wants to. Unless you're just talking, you must renounce her." But his friend insists: "I'm not just talking. That's why I'm looking for her. That's why I shall find her." In this way the play ends. Perhaps this final duologue is meant to show that Fifty, the "savior," has not yet understood the implications of his act of liberation. This newly discovered truth, the friend is convinced, will finally set his sister free as well and take from her the fear she may still have of having done wrong.

With Fifty's act of liberation and his friend's plan, the satirical presentation of the characters is resolved. The most powerful scenes, however, are those in which the consequences of the state-decreed life expectancy are illustrated. A boy called Ten does not see why he should go to school and obey moral precepts. He throws stones at passersby and unashamedly denies having done so. Asked what he will do when he grows up, the boy is silent. He will never grow up, so why learn reading and writing, arithmetic and drawing? Perhaps his attitude is also connected with the fact that all these abilities are taught only with regard to their future usefulness and not because ability in itself is a pleasure and satisfaction. Most painful of all is the loneliness of the numbered, who cannot tell anyone when they were born, so that no one can have any fellow feeling with them. A loving couple has to renounce all hope because the woman's "moment" will be next day—the hour of her decreed death. Plainly most of those who live in this society of the numbered have so completely accepted their decreed life expectancy that, with the exception of a few who rebel or escape, they lie down at the "appointed hour" and die. Most of them seem quietly to have come to terms with this absurd and wicked rule, rather as inhabitants of actual totalitarian states have come to terms with other absurd rulings: the transportation and extermination of Jews and gypsies, the killing of those "elements unfit to live," the compulsory *Gleichschaltung* of the entire population, listening to nonsensical speeches by leaders and shouting out with loud enthusiasm, doing away with traditional forms of greeting and replacing them with heathen rituals, and so on. Satires have to exaggerate in order to alienate the familiar. The extreme forms of totalitarian rule scarcely admit of any further exaggeration, as they are already so exaggerated. A ban on vanity by destroying mirrors and imposing a death penalty in cases of possession of mirrors was one satirical option; state-decreed limits on life expectancy was another.

When he turned from his idol Kraus, Elias Canetti did not really bid farewell to satire. However, what he did was to replace the satire of denunciation with the satire of self-accusation. In his three plays a petit bourgeois run wild accuse themselves, unwillingly and unwittingly. The wickedness of their instincts becomes clearly apparent. But under the conditions of totalitarian rule, which aim at suppressing by force all human characteristics, something indestructible in Man comes to light against all expectation. In the *Comedy of Vanity* it is the inextinguishable love of oneself, without which there can be no love of one's neighbor either—self-love attaining its object in spite of everything along a thousand paths and detours; in *The Numbered* it is the will freely to shape one's own life, and death as well—resistance to a total elimination of independent self-determination which in the end would reduce humankind to mere puppets.

The humorist loves mankind, with their weaknesses too, or even on account of those weaknesses. The satirist hates mankind as they are because he would prefer them closer to the ideal, and he would like to improve them through his satirical criticism. Elias Canetti aims only to show them as they are, though he also shows the ways they behave in the extreme conditions of social and power structures they themselves have created. He makes us think about and criticize ourselves. When his stage characters accuse themselves, the audience or reader wonders what effect his own sayings and deeds have on others. I knew an old lady who used to say of her sturdy husband,

"You just can't put him down." Admittedly she meant it as an admiring recognition of his good health, yet unintentionally she nonetheless expressed her wish, understandable enough, to be rid of a man she did not love. She could not have put it better on Canetti's stage.

NOTES

1. Elias Canetti, *The Conscience of Words* (translated by Joachim Neugroschel), New York, 1979, p. 216.
2. Ibid., p. 31.
3. Ibid., p. 34.
4. Ibid., p. 38.
5. Elias Canetti, *Dramen,* p. 70.
6. Elias Canetti, *The Numbered* (translated by Carol Stewart), London, 1984, p. 86.
7. Ibid., p. 94.
8. Ibid., p. 96.

Hans Hollmann

Working on Canetti's Plays

In the second half of the 1960s the plays of Ödön von Horváth were at the heart of my work, first with rehearsed readings and then full-scale productions; and then in 1974 in Basle, and in 1980 in Vienna, I tried to put on Karl Kraus's great play *The Last Days of Mankind*. Both writers logically pointed the way to Elias Canetti's dramatic work—in 1978 at the Basle Komödie and in 1979 at the Vienna Burgtheater, I directed the *Comedy of Vanity*, and in 1983 at the Württembergisches Staatstheater in Stuttgart *The Numbered*, and when these lines appear rehearsals for a production of *The Wedding*, with which the Burgtheater is marking the writer's eightieth birthday, will be nearly concluded.* Prepared by directing his own plays and by conversations with Elias Canetti on Aristophanes and Nestroy, I shall in the next few years be placing the emphasis in my work on the plays of these two critical realists, who had so great an influence on Canetti's approach to drama and his views on it.

What major experiences did I have in producing Elias Canetti's plays? No doubt the most important in terms of practical theater work was getting to know Canetti's concept of the acoustic mask and deliberately applying this stylistic tech-

*The Austrian and German first publication of this festschrift was in July 1985. — *Trans.*

nique during production. As early as 1937, in an interview given to the Vienna newspaper *Sonntag,* Canetti formulated the concept of the acoustic mask: an ordinary human being does not simply speak German or some dialect, but develops his own way of speaking. To do this he needs some five hundred words, which are made into his almost unchangeable mask by their unique combination of pitch, rhythm, tempo, and slurring. Every single human being can be as easily recognized by this mask as by his physiognomy. In his plays, as a stylistic device, Canetti applies with total consistency this perception of what seems to me a truth. Naturally it is not only "ordinary" people who have acoustic masks, but all the characters in his plays. The intellectual Heinrich Föhn in the *Comedy of Vanity* speaks as much through a mask as Professor Thut in *The Wedding* does. The acoustic mask has nothing to do with use of dialect—Peter Hell in *The Wedding* and young Fant in the *Comedy of Vanity* speak a clear High German, but it is masked, while by contrast Anzengruber's plays are often written in dialect without any acoustic masks existing in them or being intended. What Canetti means by an acoustic mask can be heard as early as Nestroy, is taken by Karl Kraus to caricaturist extremes (an acoustic grimace), and is applied with some frequency by Horváth, though without any consistency and not in all of his plays; only Canetti creates his characters exclusively in these terms. The objection that in *The Numbered* there are no acoustic masks but simply one language spoken equally by all the characters is in fact not true. Granted, acoustic masks are absent in the sense of characters leaving a speech spoor of their own syntax, pet words, and so forth; but their way of speaking, and hence the way of acting the parts, is nevertheless laid down in mask form by the writer through his use of numbers to indicate life expectancy, numbers which are used as names. In this play, the name is the mask. A very young man called Eighty will count himself one of the elite, and his manner and way of speaking will reflect this.

Through his use of the accoustic mask, Canetti presents us

with more distinctive, finished characters than any other dramatist. Their external mold, their speech and behavioral patterns, are given from the start, but so too is their fear, a precondition of their existence. A character without fear would be a character without a mask, a hero. And there are no heroes in Canetti. From out of *The Last Days of Mankinds'* inferno of masks and mummery there towers—without fear and thus without a mask—the figure of the nitpicking hero, Karl Kraus himself, full of words and in possession of the truth. But every character in Canetti lives in fear; the greater the fear, the more extreme the mask must be—the caretaker Franz Josef Kokosch in *The Wedding* has the best because he no longer says anything of his own but keeps the bare text of the Bible between himself and the world, everything else seems dangerous to him. But the acoustic mask conceals not only the character's fear; these opaque curtains of words also hide their true intentions. The tension between these and the masks gives Canetti's characters their curious attraction, and to express it is the none too straightforward task the writer sets his performers.

But on the basis of my work on Canetti's plays I am now of the fundamental opinion that there must be an acoustic mask at the start of every dramatic project. As in the case of Canetti or sometimes Horváth, it may already be present; alternatively, though, it can be created through the actor's art. To support actors in this, and to invent masks through a mutual act of imagination, increasingly seems to me the most important part of my work; and it was from Canetti's plays that I learned how it could be done.

Before all of my productions I had talks with the writer, and with each new production these became richer and more precise. Both in Vienna and in Stuttgart Canetti attended the final rehearsals, and in the Stuttgart production of *The Numbered* two scenes were redone at his wish. In this way performances were produced that had the writer's approval. This is by no means to suggest that they were model productions of the plays;

there are too many things that I would do differently today, and in any case I reject the notion of a model production since I feel it is contrary both to living theater and to the interests of the author. But naturally in the course of work some experiences came to seem worth bearing in mind when Canetti's plays are put on: for example, Canetti's plays of the Word should be performed only on artificial sets—naturalistic scenery, any kind of caricaturing, denouncing, or ironizing space, even any non-functional object on the stage, would weaken the text and distort the impact of the outpourings. The sets Wolfgang Mai (in Vienna and Stuttgart) and Hannes Meyer (in Basle) created showed a limited emptiness, spaces and obstacles. On the other hand, the costumes done by Anuschka Meyer-Riehl (Basle), Alice-Maria Schlesinger (Vienna), and Franziska Loring (Stuttgart) were strictly realistic and historically exact. I often use music and sound effects for stylistic purposes, particularly when producing the classics; with Canetti's plays I tried the same, but it turned out to be untenable and indeed tautological—the texts themselves have so strong a rhythmical, musical quality that they brook nothing else of the kind. Similarly, even the slightest change, addition, or linguistic relaxation damages not only the line but indeed the whole play, with its precision working with acoustic masks. Of course, the plays should if possible be performed uncut, a requirement which usually can be met in practice only in the case of *The Numbered*; I had to cut the *Comedy of Vanity* a little, and *The Wedding* will also have to be trimmed a bit if the evening is not to be too long. All cuts must be carefully made and only the removal of single sentences is feasible. In the *Comedy of Vanity*, so precisely constructed as a mirror image, the cutting of an entire scene would do irreparable damage to the play.

Canetti, as is well known, wrote his plays according to rules he imposed on himself. He has no interest in taking a subject that has been wrung dry three hundred times and giving it a three hundred and first wringing; rather, he demands a surprising uniqueness in the dramatic idea, an idea which ought not to be of a private nature but one that is central and concerns everyone, and involves crowds. In Canetti's plays, the ideas create new worlds of their own, different from our own in nearly every detail but still comparable. What takes place in a world of this kind is not an action with a beginning and end: the dramatic content is the idea itself, and the world that has come into being through it, and for those who can grasp them these new thoughts have a remarkable, infective effect. When we were rehearsing *The Numbered* in Stuttgart—the play in which Canetti's dramaturgy is most consistently applied—the rehearsals were accompanied by lengthy discussions by the participants, in the course of which the thought content of the play (which I consider the most important of Canetti's three) was constantly being extended and the world the writer created being made more perfect. His idea had infected us. I think this is precisely what Canetti is after. And so, after the three productions of Canetti, the most amazing fact is that of the many plays I have directed in the last twenty years, none has stuck in my mind as much as the *Comedy of Vanity* and *The Numbered*. But it is not the play as such that I think about, its dialogue or scenes, but the world created in it—it continues to occupy me and the thought goes on growing. The infection of the idea remains—for those who are open to new ideas.

Before every production, and from time to time on other occasions too, I have been able to talk to Elias Canetti. He has told me about the plays, about the years when they were written, about the mistakes to be avoided in producing them, and also quite generally about people and things. I am grateful for these hours spent together, when we laughed a lot too; of all the aspects of work on the plays, it was these talks that made me happiest.

It's a strange thing—in *Crowds and Power* Elias Canetti showed us the way we are and instilled in us the fear and terror of recognition, *The Wedding* ends in global catastrophe, the *Comedy of Vanity* with something similar, and anyone who has read Canetti's work is perhaps more clearly aware of the disaster that threatens us all in the year of the writer's eightieth birthday than other people are—but whenever I go down the steps from his Zurich flat I go full of hopeful confidence in Man's sense and reason, in spite of everything. Canetti may well have spoken not a single reassuring word—we were talking about the people and things of the world. But the one who was talking was Elias Canetti, who is seriously out to vanquish Death.

Beda Allemann

Elias Canetti, Earwitness

In the same year, 1974, the Munich publishing house of Hei-
meran reissued in its series "Dialog mit der Antike" Horst Rüdiger's translation of the *Characters* of Theophrastus, originally dating from the 1930s, complete with the old Isaac Taylor
illustrations dating from 1824, and another Munich house,
Hanser, published Elias Canetti's slim volume *Earwitness*, which
is subtitled *Fifty Characters*. The former will have given new
delight to lovers of late classical Greek and early Hellenistic
literature; the latter has hitherto attracted no particular attention from critics or scholars, yet, given an adequately educated
readership attuned to nuances, would have deserved a better
reception.

Earwitness is a collection of miniatures which is at once both
a revival of an ancient genre and far more besides. If the term
"surrealism" still means anything, it should be used here, for
the realism of description is pushed beyond its utmost limits
into the realm of the fantastic—in, for example, the portrayal
of the greedy, grasping Lady Chattels, who quite literally and
painstakingly eats all the bank notes she had hoarded. This is
a rhetorical means of intensifying an effect, yet it is also more
than only that—the pure realism of portrayal, such as was familiar to late classical times, is transformed into something beyond realism, and the vision becomes the more penetrating as
realism is left behind.

The brevity of the individual pieces has been a stylistic feature of the "character" genre since Theophrastus, and in Canetti we in fact find it taken further: in these texts there is a brevity that draws attention to itself and is almost abrupt. Sentence for sentence we realize clearly enough that a good deal more might be said, and the image of the character considerably elaborated on—yet the texts demonstratively relinquish anything further and press on ahead to their conclusion. They leave behind them a regret in us that they are already finished, a regret that whets our curiosity for the next character.

Canetti's labels for his character types often enough turn out to be in themselves enigmatic and cryptic. A graphic example of this is the Namelicker, whose name conceals an association with a less polite epithet* but also, in his eagerness to seek out in person contemporaries who are famous or often mentioned in the newspapers, recalls coinages in other languages: the English "name-dropping" or French connotations of *lécher* (e.g., *les vitrines*). Nearly all Canetti's characters bear eloquent names.

We should be tempted to call the exactness of observation which has always been Canetti's hallmark as a narrator merciless, if it were not at all times able, notably so in these miniatures, to preserve its brightness, which is both sheer fun and a genuine serenity.

What gives the characters their harmless appearance is the fact that they indeed read like miniatures, precisely and effectively shaped as we would expect of such precious creations, though for that very reason we might the more readily expect to come upon them tucked away as gems in feuilleton pages rather than assembled between the covers of a book. But this impression too, though it may not be deceptive, is at all events superficial.

La Bruyère had already, with results significant for literary history, imitated the *Characters* of Theophrastus (where the

---

*The German *Namenlecker* suggests the vulgar *Arschlecker* (ass-licker), slang for a toady or sycophant. —*Trans.*

word "imitation" is used in the older, meaningful sense of the poetological term). In this he was responding to the challenge to write in that form, which comes not least from the tension between its seeming smallness and its venerable tradition.

The form's requirements of brief reports on the writer's findings and a cool, objective syntax are scrupulously observed by Canetti. But he is adept too at subverting the requirement with relativizing interpolations along the lines of "but it has to be said that he also . . . ."

Some of the punch lines could hardly be bettered: often they are given their impact by some unexpected contradiction, a kind of turnabout or argumentative volte-face that exposes the true meaning behind a character description that seemed so objective. Particularly clear examples of this are the Woman Who Gives to Herself and the Funeral Hunter.

Even the headings of the individual pieces have a function beyond mere labeling: their very life often derives from the essentials of language. The old man bearing invitations to a funeral *(Leichenbitter)* and the legacy hunter *(Erbschleicher)* become the Funeral Hunter *(Leichenschleicher)*: the neologism creates an additional onomatopoeic effect produced by the matching sounds of *Leiche* and *Schleiche(r)*. The unusual qualities of the names Canetti provides his characters with are matched by their exotic natures. These are not the characters of Theophrastus, everyday figures with which we are all familiar and which are simply exaggerated into a hyper-clarity bordering on caricature, but instead very special, unusual, choice, and rare phenomena in the characterological firmament which the telescope of descriptive artistry is studying. One prefers to think of them, albeit they certainly have their "characteristic features," as subspecies numbering few examples, or in extreme instances as single specimens. This by no means (as we know from the laws of poetic models) robs them of the basic representativeness each character has: this is true even of an eccentric as unbelievable as the Water Hoarder. And we see it even in labels as wholy ordinary as the Tired Woman or the Blind Man—for they, as we soon learn, are tired or blind in a quite specific sense.

And of course this genre itself, to which Canetti's texts *From the New Theophrastus* (as they were originally called on first publication in *Akzente* and other literary magazines) belong, is a singular one, as we ought not to forget. It is no accident that philologists have to this day failed to agree on the genre that the Theophrastian *Characters* belong to. They have as little place in the rhetorical-poetological scheme of classical times as they do (even if we force them) in the more relaxed categories of the modern age. Translator Horst Rüdiger renders Theophrastus' title as *Character Sketches,* which no doubt gives our modern sensibility something akin to the original meaning; an absolutely identical translation of this matter of classification, a matter which is in fact crucial, does not seem possible. Thus it is a unique instance—a single example constituting an entire genre: in our consideration both of Theophrastus' and of Canetti's "characters" we shall have to live with this paradox, and in this sense we may even think it consistent if the later writer extends the singularity of the form into a singularity of the content of the individual pieces too, and thus leaves behind, once and for all, the merely "typical" qualities of his classical model.

No doubt it may be taken as understood that the new Theophrastus differs from the old in his more "psychological" nature: true, he abides by the old rule, which Goethe underlined, that says a character is not to be described as such but should always be shown in the mirror of the acts and behavior of individual examples of that character—still, he renders these deeds and modes of conduct in a far more varied and multilayered manner than would have been conceivable in Hellenistic times. To insist on this would be to preach the obvious.

In the nature of things, the milieu of Canetti's characters is no longer the Theophrastian Greek agora and household full of slaves, either. It is the intellectual-literary average milieu of our times, high or at any rate better society, complete with its restaurants and private parties. If we for the moment stay with the first character sketch in the series of fifty, the Kingmaker, we find it even begins in the haute bourgeoisie, and with courtly-cum-clerical reminiscences of feudal society across the spectrum from royalty to beggars. But the "kings," or, to be more exact, those who for the time being are king, are no more than young, promising talents whose discovery and presentation is celebrated by the ambitious hostess before her assembled guests, with all the pomp appropriate to the moment: the old, abdicated kings have parts as extras, as beggars. As we can see, this immediately goes beyond a personal character study of the kingmaking hostess and touches the roots of what literary journalism likes to call social criticism.

Are not all of Canetti's characters, aside from their distant derivation from Theophrastus, descendants and variants of Dr. Kien in *Auto-da-Fé*, who at first, in the early stages of work on the novel, was called Kant? With this question in mind we may well find it significant that the project of the novel itself originally envisaged a number of central characters, and indeed eight novels, complete in themselves, which were to have eight "extreme individuals" as their heroes and, taken together, were to comprise a *"Comédie Humaine* of the insane."[1]

Theophrastus did not give to his *Characters* the names of the bearers of those characters but, more basically and abstractly, the names of the qualities that determined each one of them. For him, character is not yet primarily a particular personality distinguished by its idiosyncrasy, but is in fact the idiosyncrasy itself: the individual merely has the function of a means of demonstrating this, as clearly as possible. Theophrastus speaks (and he chooses his titles accordingly) of *eironeia*, not of the ironist: the ironist is not of interest as a person and individual human being but as an illustration of the quality of irony—and we should note that the Greek concept is not exactly identical to the mode of behavior which we today understand by the word. (Horst Rüdiger draws attention to this too, and also to the fact that Theophrastus indeed took the quality as such as the title of his sketch, in this and all other cases, rather than the *nomen agentis*—differing in this way from modern translations of the text.)

Canetti, on the other hand, proceeds, as we have said, from the individual case, which may be untypical and often enough baffling, and in doing so he just as often creates the "aha!" effect: I know him (or her)—or his descriptions at least leave us with the impression that they are probable, and even more true than the mere probability of daily life, and that this very type, who is also atypical and thus never existed, had to be created, right up to and including his name. All of them appear not as representatives of the everyday but as outsiders, in the precise sense of being outside existing society and thus being specifically related to it. Now, of course, today's society (if we take the term in a literary rather than a sociological sense) is known to be difficult to define or delimit. It is hard to go beyond the generality we have spoken of—that Canetti's characters move in a milieu which we are tempted to see as literary and intellectual, whatever that may mean. As outsiders within a societal subset that likes to see itself as consisting of outsiders, they are both that set's exaggerated exemplars and its antithesis. They are also subject to the suspicion of being basically petit bourgeois and philistine, like their progenitor Dr. Kien. Where he isolates himself behind his walls of books, a typical scholar, they appear to move more freely, yet they are quite as confined to their particular natures as the eccentric sinologist. The diametrical distinction between the Blind Man in Canetti's *Characters* and the hero of *Auto-da-Fé* is that the former seems on the surface to be a representative of modern travel-agent tourism, subsection *study tours*. His blindness comes from his ability to perceive the world exclusively through his single-lens reflex camera. But the common denominator that deeply links him and all the other characters to Dr. Kien is that they themselves cultivate their own eccentricities. This is not always as striking as in the case of the Poser, who poses in front of a mirror like a model. But on closer inspection we see it in all of them, even in the Funeral Hunter, who is constantly traveling about and thus only occasionally (but then with all the more insistency) approaches one of his acquaintances and reports on the latest death in their circle of friends, to oblige him to go to the funeral. The comic elements in Canetti's characters result from the determination with which they have withdrawn into their own idiosyncratic manner and isolated themselves there—one leaves a trail of lost objects behind him (the Loser), another always repays with interest, figuratively too (the Overbidder), yet another simply takes back all the presents she has given (the Woman Who Gives to Herself). This sort of character description may owe its origins to clear observation of human behavior and weaknesses, and nothing more; there may be something playful in labeling fellow human beings with their conspicuous idiosyncrasies in this way, and categorizing them once and for all; there may be no more behind it than *Médisance* and small talk. Yet at the same time it becomes apparent, and not only, I feel, to the Canetti connoisseur, that a human crisis and a desperate reaction to it is being shown in behavioral patterns like this. Canetti's characters are innocent (innocent?) victims of some menace that has driven them into the comical straits of their "characters." Is this connected to the fact that the Earwitness, who gives his name to the whole collection, appears as a listener and agent, indeed literally as the hangman, in the piece where he makes his solo appearance and where, incidentally, literary convention suggests we perhaps find the author and his own self-portrait? Such clues to the actual background of the matter are rare here, as they are in the novel *Auto-da-Fé*. Nowhere are we explicitly told what the whole enterprise is meant to add up to, and undoubtedly this constitutes a good deal of the poetic quality of Canetti's texts: the artist's task is to create, not to talk about creation! Nonetheless, we can hardly miss the fact that here too, in these very characters, the individual is fighting for survival. What makes the Funeral Hunter's invitation and challenge to attend the funeral so irresistible is the fear (this is the point of this particular miniature) that the one he is asking this time might be the one whose funeral he's inviting others to next time. And the Kingmaker, beyond all social satire, is enthroned as an emissary of the power of Fate over the talented people she crowns; through the unceasing cycle of her pronouncements she represents the wheel of fortune too, and warns *sic transit gloria mundi*.

But we are given another warning against eye- and ear-witnesses of this kind too—to use the words with which Celan's poem "Aschenglorie" (in the collection *Atemwende*) ends: "No one / bears witness for the / witness." Let me in closing venture something that literary critics and scholars ought not to do, as they are not quite good enough at it: a little paraphrase.

The Witness's Witness

He begets* witnesses. So, whether he wants to or not, he has to bear witness for them. There are some among his friends and acquaintances, and he watches them closely. Sometimes that is enough, but mostly he even has to invent his witnesses.

When he does this he is quite right to think them his spiritual progeny. Not only to think them that, but to demand their filial service. He has them go through the trickiest turnabouts and takes a paternal pleasure in it.

He puts a tight bridle on his free-ranging imagination, and even, if need be, a bit. Fifty times he performs a cavalry charge

---

* Allemann is punning on the two meanings of the German verb *zeugen*, to beget and to testify. —*Trans.*

in a (voluntarily) confined space, and each time he concludes laconically by vaulting from the saddle with an elegance you would scarcely have expected of one so short in the leg. (Similarly, he hardly lets you see the fun he is having.) It would be unjust to call him a sly dog, because in spite of everything that would be to underestimate him greatly. But he is a world champion at laughing up his sleeve. No doubt it was for this that he was awarded (wasn't it dynamite?*) the Nobel Prize. He accepted it as he accepted everything life put his way, starting with his study of chemistry—and even that was useful for his literary work, in a methodological way, of course, not thematically.

There are no explosions in his *Characters,* but no doubt we are right to infer hidden currents and reactions.

If he were to write another novel he would perhaps have some major, put out to grass, turning up with his box of experiments and starting up a conversation about elective affinities.†

As this is not the case, we had best content ourselves with the *Earwitness*—there is more to it than we might think from briefly listening in.

NOTES

1. Cf. Elias Canetti, "The First Book: *Auto-da-Fé,*" in *The Conscience of Words* (translated by Joachim Neugroschel), New York, 1979, pp. 203–13, especially pp. 210 ff.

*English in Allemann's original. —*Trans.*
†The allusion is to Goethe's novel *Elective Affinities.* —*Trans.*

Martin Bollacher

"I Bow to Memory":
Elias Canetti's
Autobiographical Writings

𝓀𝓮

Autobiography, which has a long tradition as a literary form
of self-portrait and description of one's own life, owes its specifically modern cast to the eighteenth century and, in German-
speaking areas, to the age of Goethe. In Goethe's autobiographical writings, above all in *Dichtung und Wahrheit,* we
see the culmination and unification of the evolutionary lines of
a genre which now takes its place alongside poetry, drama,
and the novel ("the epopee of a God-forsaken world"—Georg
Lukács) as one of the great artistic forms of modern times.
Thus in Goethe's autobiography, though we perceive the after-
effects of the literature of religious confession and self-search-
ing that reached from St. Augustine's *Confessions* via medieval
mysticism to pietistic revivalist and devotional literature of a
providentia Dei kind, nevertheless *Dichtung und Wahrheit* is
not a religious book, a "book of God and the soul" (Erich
Trunz), in spite of its numerous religious motifs. And just as
in *Wilhelm Meister* the entirety of the "confessions of a beautiful soul," according to Goethe's own judgment (in a letter to
Schiller of March 18 1795), "rests on the noblest of delusions

and the most delicate of confusions of subjective and objective," so too, in the conception of *Dichtung und Wahrheit,* Goethe must surely find religious inward-looking and unworldly analysis of the soul a particularly one-sided and therefore false bias for a life history fitted to its times. What is characteristic in this context is his aversion to the old pedagogic dictum "Know thyself," which he expressed most succinctly in his 1823 essay "Bedeutendes Fördernis durch ein einziges geistreiches Wort": "I herewith confess that that task *'know thyself,'* which sounds so great and important, always seemed suspect to me, a trick by priests secretly in league, out to confound mankind by demanding the unattainable and to divert Man's activity in the world at large into an inner and false contemplativeness. Man knows himself only insofar as he knows the world; and he perceives the world only through himself, and himself only through the world." In casting doubt on that gnomic "Know thyself," originally inscribed on the temple of Apollo at Delphi, and suspecting it of being a priestly deceit, and in indicating the interplay of knowledge of the self and knowledge of the world, Goethe not only is formulating for himself the worldly credo of the great pagan but at the same time is giving expression to that modern, autonomous conception of reality which he encountered in the Renaissance autobiographies of Cellini and Cardano: for this reason, the main task of the autobiographer is not the description and analysis of "psychological torments" *(Maximen und Reflexionen)* but the presentation of actuality and of an individual life history seen through the reality that determined it. It is through Herder's influence in particular that Goethe interprets the conditions of reality primarily as the conditions of Time: Time, which he understands as shape-shifting according to the dictates of Chance (Tyche) and as the configurative distinctness of the historically unique era, is fateful for the individual, so that "one can assuredly say that anyone, born a mere ten years earlier or later, might well, as far as his self and his influence on the world around him are concerned, have become a quite different person" (foreword to *Dichtung und Wahrheit*).

But the autobiographer ought not therefore to turn historian: after all, it is his task to be certain of the "truth" of the story of his own life, and the interplay of the individual self and the era that gave it its stamp, through memory—in other words, through the imagination, which is as much as to say by poetic means (cf. Goethe's letter to Ludwig I of Bavaria of January 12, 1830). The organic essence of autobiography as an art form consists in its conveying both an authorial present and the author's past, and the truth presented in autobiography is the truth of the one remembering, who is using the past for his own ends. A poetic autobiography (and this is true not only in Goethe's case) thus takes on the character of a confession, as it is intended to "fill in the gaps in a writer's life, complete this or that fragment, and preserve the memory of enterprises which were dared and which are lost or cannot be found" (*Dichtung und Wahrheit*). It both presents and comments on the writer's own existence and life story, but at the same time it is more—an art form in its own right.

In spite of the structural rules that the modern genre of autobiography is based on, it may nonetheless be disconcerting if we associate Elias Canetti's autobiographical writings, three parts of which have appeared (*The Tongue Set Free,* 1977; *The Torch in My Ear,* 1980; *The Play of The Eyes,* 1986*), with Goethe's autobiography and the tradition it founded. The classical concept of a harmoniously matured personality true to its own entelechy now seems too remote for us to concede that one of our contemporaries might see his life in terms of fortunate success, fulfillment, and the favor of Fate. The rich satisfaction of a privileged, fulfilled life can be heard—at a playful, fairy-tale distance, true—in Goethe's self-portrait, when in his *Märchen* of the New Paris he sees himself elevated as the darling of the

---

* Dates are those of original German publication. —*Trans.*

gods! By contrast, the fundamental experience of Canetti, the contemporary and witness of a reality falling blindly apart, a writer in exile and scarred by war, mass hysteria, and the experience of death, who sees himself as a victim, slave, and "the dog of his time" ("Hermann Broch"), is one of "the slaughterhouse horror which underlies everything" *(The Human Province)*, and fear. The fear which the ogres of oriental and Grimm fairy tales instilled in the boy when he was barely seven, that fear which also confronted him in the mocking lack of understanding of a "cannibal" adult world, is still vividly present to the seventy-year-old autobiographer:

Fear thrives strongest; there is no telling how little we would be without having suffered fear. An intrinsic characteristic of humanity is the tendency to give in to fear. No fear is lost, but its hiding places are a riddle. Perhaps, of all things, fear is the one that changes least. When I think back to my early years, the very first things I recognize are the fears, of which there was an inexhaustible wealth. I find many of them only now; others, which I will never find, must be the mystery that makes me want an unending life.[1]

Fear appears as an abiding and unchanging companion of childhood and adulthood, yet also, surprisingly and paradoxically, as the mysterious fundamental force in a life open to infinity: indeed, it is an elixir of life. By reinterpreting fear in this way, as a positive element in life and survival, Canetti sets himself essentially apart from the presentation and understanding of this central human emotion in contemporary literature, as seen, for example, in the fear-haunted dirges and laments which Christa Wolf's dying Cassandra wrests from her "memory of fear" *(Cassandra)*, sitting in apocalyptic judgment on the gods, mankind, and the world. Canetti too shows us, in *Auto-da-Fé*, the early plays, and parts of his autobiographical works, a Brueghel-like world of the infernal and the insane, the inhabitants of which are in the sway of a "self-preservation gone wild" (Adorno), and of the religion of power and commands. The ethos of Canetti's art, as his friend Hermann Broch early recognized, is "to show the origins of events in fear," but it is a "fear which to an extent has been rendered positive" ("Introduction to a Reading by Elias Canetti in January 1933"), a fear which, in the face of experiences of inhumanity, never loses hold on the image of Man in possession of himself, of the individual redeemed and transformed into humanity. This kind of obstinate belief in the dignity of the individual human being, in the midst of a chaotic world bent on self-destruction, seems to us out of step with the times, since it recalls, in an Enlightenment spirit, those goals which were set by hope and never attained, in an era long gone. Yet it is in this non-contemporary resistance to times enamored of death that the conscience of the writer's words originates, and the responsibility of the writer's life. In a moving note dating from the final years of the war—which for exiles, Jews, and authors writing in German created the most powerful distress and identity crisis—Canetti links the question of his own survival to an unconditional declaration of allegiance to Goethe and the assertion of life that sounds through Goethe's own existence:

If in spite of everything I should remain alive, I owe it to Goethe, as one can only owe it to a god. It is not any one work but the mood and attentiveness of a fulfilled life that have suddenly overwhelmed me. I can open Goethe where I please and read poems and letters here or a few pages of some account there, and after a few sentences it grips me and I am filled with hope in a way no religion can fill me. . . . Since I have been reading Goethe, everything I take on seems legitimate and natural; they are not the things *he* took on, but others, and it is very doubtful whether they can lead to any conclusions. But he asserts my right: Do what you have to do—he says—even if it is nothing earth-shattering: breathe, observe, consider! (*The Human Province*, notebook entry from 1943.)

Canetti's autobiographical writings, which cover the period from his Ruschuk childhood (1905–11) to the turmoil of the 1920s and 1930s, which he spent mostly in Vienna, put into practice this Goethean law of breathing, observing, and considering, and it is this that gives the writer's life unfolded in the auto-biography its own, immutable rights. The chaos of an era that worshiped the idol power, that chaos which multifariously and menacingly dominated the early works, and which her-alded the universal conflagration of the war, lost its aesthetic attraction for Canetti the survivor. In his later works, we see the chaotic reality of the twentieth century reflected in an art form which orders and organizes a disparity of elements, an art form which owes its existence to the unifying perspective of a contemporary first person which, without haste and with-out shrill self-exposure, tells its own story and the story of the times. If Canetti speaks of the necessity of breathing it is more than a metaphoric turn of phrase: breathing, as he stresses in his birthday address for his friend Hermann Broch, is one of the indispensable "vices" and passions of the writer, who as a breathing being has access, thanks to his "breath-memory," to the "diversity in the world" and its "individual splintering," and thus too keeps his respect for life. The retrospective gaze of the autobiographer, mediating between the present of the narrator and the past he narrates, is governed by this respect too. Ever since St. Augustine's exploration of the "vast halls of memory" in the tenth book of the *Confessions,* memory, the prime sine qua non of autobiographical writing as a conflation of the documentary and the fictive, has been among the fun-damental constants and problems of autobiographical litera-ture, which in modern times has increasingly availed itself of analytic psychology and its methods, of this "experiential sci-ence of the soul" (Moritz). Canetti the autobiographer, in this once again comparable with Goethe, takes a different path: that truth which is shaped by recollection of one's own life story is stubbornly defended against any psychology (or indeed psychoanalysis) that would dismember and explain, dispel and diminish the diversity of the individual phenomenon. In the chapter of *The Torch in My Ear* headed "Escape," Canetti expresses, with all the force of a confession of faith, his high regard for integral memory:

Contrary to many people, particularly those who have surrendered to a loquacious psychology, I am not convinced that one should plague, pester, and pressure memory or expose it to the effects of well-calculated lures; I bow to memory, every person's memory. I want to leave memory intact, for it belongs to Man, who exists for his freedom. And I will not conceal my abhorrence of those who perform surgery on a memory until it resembles anyone else's memory. Let them operate on noses, lips, ears, skin, hair as much as they like; let them—if they must—implant eyes of different colors, even transplant hearts that manage to beat along for another year; let them touch, trim, smooth, level everything—but let them leave memory alone.[2]

Canetti's reverence for the value of individual memory left intact, the faithlike quality of which is if anything underlined by the appropriated Luther quotation ("Let them leave the Word alone," from the Protestant hymn "Ein feste Burg ist unser Gott"), plays a part in his autobiographical writings as an important shaping principle. Those who expect the autobiographer to provide first and foremost psychological analysis, a vivisection of the unconscious, or the description of an *éducation sexuelle*, must thus be disappointed by Canetti. His narrative takes its bearings from things, from "external" facts, both because of his aversion to a psychology which categorizes and classifies everything and because of his conception of an individuality that is unique and exists in order to be free. Canetti is very well aware that memory may interpret things past differently from the way they were when the past was the terrible present—"different, but no less cruel, no more bearable, no less meaningless, cutting, bitter, and not content that it is all over and done, for nothing is ever over and done" (*The Human Province,* notebook entry from 1971).

Memory keeps in our consciousness what is terrible, but also what is comforting and gives hope, without prettifying and without false reconciliation; time and history remain open-ended toward the present and future. Memory gives autobiographical narrative its beginning and its end (for the time being). At the outset of the first volume we find a blood-red image of fear and distress in early childhood, which illustrates the basic theme of this part (saving the tongue, and thus language and the ability to speak) and which, in its archetypal horror, casts a spell on both the retrospective narrator and the reader: a young man approaches the child, who is being held by a girl, orders him to stick his tongue out, pulls out a penknife, and says, "Now we'll cut off his tongue." Only later does the child, with his mother's help, discover the meaning of this scene: the red color suggests a Carlsbad guest house where the Canettis spent the summer of 1907, and the young man was the lover of the girl who was two-year-old Elias's nanny, afraid that their liaison would be discovered. The child saves his own tongue, but, the command vividly present before him, remains silent about the traumatic experience for ten whole years. Fear of the loss of language and of the human self expressed in language is constant: at the close of the second volume, which, after the school of speaking, is now dedicated to the school of hearing under *Fackel* editor Karl Kraus, we read of the scholar Peter Kien, protagonist of the novel *Auto-da-Fé,* meeting his death in the fire—a terrible image of fire and flames in which the red of that earliest childhood memory has become emblematic of the world's inflammability. The trauma of loss of speech, seemingly personal and wholly bound up with a unique situation, has expanded into a fearful image of an era that first robs men of the peculiar characteristics of their own free speech and silences them, in order then to lead them all the more easily to their destruction. To this extent, the final chapter of *The Torch in My Ear* recapitulates an early horror of the power of commands, which threaten not only the ruled but also the ruler.

Canetti's path to reality takes him via images, and reality for him is transformed into images, in a way that inseparably mingles what has happened and been experienced with what has been seen or read. Certainly the autobiographer points out the decisive influence of paintings (Michelangelo's frescoes for the Sistine Chapel ceiling, Brueghel's "The Parable of the Blind" and "The Triumph of Death," Rembrandt's "The Blinding of Samson") and of a series of literary ancestors and models from the Gilgamesh epic to figures of his own time (Karl Kraus, Franz Kafka, Robert Musil, Hermann Broch). But these images are awoken into reality only through individual experience—only through direct personal experience do they give the observer new perceptions of experiences which were lived earlier and are now acquiring contours in memory. Thus Canetti writes of his encounter with Rembrandt's painting "The Blinding of Samson" in Frankfurt's Städel Gallery:

I often stood in front of this painting, and from it I learned what hatred is. I had felt hatred when very young, much too young, at five, when I had tried to kill Laurica with an ax. But you don't know what you have felt: you have to see it in front of you, in others, in order to recognize it and know it. Something you recognize and know becomes *real* only if you have experienced it previously. It lies dormant in you, and you can't name it; then all at once, it is there, as a painting; and something happening to others creates itself in you as a memory: now, it is real.[3]

The observer's past—in this case his childhood wish to murder his cousin, who refused to let the five-year-old boy look at her schoolbooks and thus excluded him from the magic realm of writing and literature[4]—is made real through the imaged recognition, just as, conversely, the autobiographer's childhood turns out to be a present which exists latently and arises anew in memory. The basic themes of Canetti's work and of his very being as a writer all derive from his early years, and all of these fundamental themes—hatred of death, the dichotomy of crowds and individual isolation, power and powerlessness, the obsessive drives and metamorphic adaptability of Man, but equally, too, Canetti's fascination with language, writing, and literature—originate in early experience: "Anything I subsequently experienced had already happened in Ruschuk,"[5] we read in his description of his childhood.

Separation from the scene of his early childhood provides a continuing drama which to a large extent gives the autobiographical narrator his motivation. His parents' plan to emigrate from cramped, oriental Ruschuk to England met with his tyrannical, patriarchal grandfather's fierce opposition, an opposition which, on the day before they departed, even extended to a ceremonial cursing of his disobedient son. This grandfatherly curse seemed to have been fulfilled in a terrible way when Jacques Canetti suddenly died soon after his arrival in Manchester, and similarly the curse of an age that paid homage to power and death-dealing orders also seemed fulfilled—for the child sensed a link between the death of his beloved father, only thirty years old, who not long before his heart attack had read in his morning paper of Montenegro's declaration of war on Turkey, and the outbreak of the First World War and that rule of death, commands, and power he had at that time also encountered in an English biography of Napoleon. "There has been warfare in the world since then," we read in the chapter headed "Father's Death; The Final Version," "and each war, wherever it was, and perhaps scarcely present in the consciousness of the people around me, has hit me with the force of that early loss, absorbing me as the most *personal* thing that could happen to me."[6] In relation to his mother, the seven-year-old is forced by his father's death into a dual role, that of son and that of father and husband, which lays the foundation for a lasting climate of mutual dependence and domineering, of love, and of ultimate rebellion by a son grown independent. His "early horror at the death penalty and at the order to carry it out" never relaxed its grip on Canetti and became a central theme in his oeuvre, as his first work, dedicated to his mother, shows—the dramatized tale of Junius Brutus, who had his own sons executed, finishes with the sentence: "The father's curs'd who murders his own sons!"[7]

As this one example may indicate, all of Canetti's texts are "autobiographical in a way at once distanced and intimate" (D. Barnouw); here too we might say, as Goethe does in Mann's *Lotte in Weimar*, "It remains a life story." Even when it grotesquely and satirically exaggerates "reality," the story of an individual life is still of the present, though in its seemingly unrepresentative uniqueness (this is a significant difference from Goethe) it may well be characteristic of a time that is out of joint! Canetti's approach to autobiography does not aim at an artificial isolation of an unchanging self from its time and the people around it, but rather subscribes to the insight that the self is only constituted through contact with others. The intensive reading evenings with his mother, who introduced the ten-year-old to Shakespeare and the literature of German classicism, produced (as we are told in *The Tongue Set Free*) a kind of statement of belief: "that I consist of many people whom I am not at all aware of. I believe that they determine what attracts or repels me in the people I meet."[8] The same relationship is repeated at the level of literary invention: the author *lives* in his characters, who are themselves reflected in him.[9]

Both *The Tongue Set Free* and *The Torch in My Ear* attest this intimate and emotional nexus of the writer and the people portrayed there. Both books contain an inexhaustible wealth of evocative thumbnail portraits and character sketches which try to convey the unique individuality of a man, not from within, from the psychological, but from without, from the particular appearance of that person and his "habitus." What seems of secondary importance (facial expressions, gestures, physical characteristics) takes on in the incorruptible observer's telling an enlightening, revelatory significance which extends the reality of the concrete to include another, concealed reality. The chapter "The Skull; Dispute with an Officer" in *The Tongue Set Free* affords a typical example. On one of her walks through Zurich, in 1917, Elias's mother suddenly stopped dead in front of a coffeehouse and pointed out to her twelve-year-old son "the enormous skull of a man sitting near the window, a huge pile of newspapers lay next to him; he had seized one paper and held it close to his eyes. Suddenly, he threw back his head, turned to a man sitting at his side and fiercely spoke away at him. Mother said: 'Take a good look at him. That's Lenin. You'll be hearing about him.' " [10] The fascination and, indeed, magical power of the scene, its forceful effect, is seen by the autobiographer less in his awareness of having seen Lenin, at that time already famous, with his own eyes, than in the instantaneous elucidation of this *tableau vivant:* the monstrous head of a man reading a newspaper, as if frozen behind the glass pane, his sudden turn to his companion, the transmission of his energetic gesture to the mother, and her immobility when confronted with a man she hoped would put an end to the war. His mother's abhorrence of killing, which had early been instilled into her son, lends to this scene from memory an emotional power that extends into the present, into the autobiographer's own distress, and thus connects his own story to the history of his century.

In addition to the taboo on killing, which was kept up unassailed, Canetti's mother imposed on her son a second taboo directed against anything of a sexual or erotic nature, a taboo which even in his Frankfurt school days encouraged him in the belief that love had merely been invented by writers. Yet it was a writer, Strindberg, in his autobiographical *A Fool's Confession* (which provided a chapter title in *The Torch in My Ear*), who confronted the young Canetti with the "reality" of love, with an alarming reality which the seventeen-year-old tried to avoid and which he was nonetheless experiencing at the same time in a manner hardly less off-putting. In the Pension Charlotte in Frankfurt, next door to the Canettis, there lived a young model, Fräulein Rahm, and every evening the adolescent lad was the unintending earwitness of a puzzling struggle between the woman and her visiting friend. It began with the man's requests, which his beloved answered with a harsh no; the requests became pleas, whining, and heartbreaking sobbing, at times whimpering, which lasted till the hours when receiving guests was permitted were at an end—and sometimes the woman threw her admirer out sooner. One evening Canetti was using opera glasses to look at the stars from the balcony. As if by accident he lowered the glasses and looked in at his neighbor's brightly lit window, and there she stood in the reddish light, naked, took a few steps, upright and erect, behaving as if she neither saw nor heard her whimpering friend, "as if she were alone. I didn't see him either; it was as if he hadn't been there."[11] Love as a fight between the sexes, as a tough and merciless confrontation of power and powerlessness, exaltation and debasement, conquest and defeat: in images such as these there was revealed to the distraught eye- and earwitness the demon of an age which seems to know Man only in his perversions and humiliations, his madness and obsessions.

The writer's responsibility originates in his opposition to such an age, and Canetti sets living memory against forgetting and death: "Keeping people alive by means of words—is that not very nearly the same thing as creating them through words?" (*The Human Province*, notebook entry from 1945). It is not only the autobiographer's individual life, which took him from Ruschuk via Manchester to Vienna, Zurich, and Frankfurt, and from there once more to Vienna, Canetti's "true home town" (*The Human Province*, 1945), that is governed by the remembering and preserving qualities of the Word, but also his roots in that peculiar, now forever lost world of exiled Hispanic Jewry.

Just as Canetti's personal biography, which unites the Latin, Oriental, Greek, Slavic, English, and German heritage, bears all the signs of a European life story, so too his life perpetuates what for centuries has characterized the Jewish diaspora: the experience of exile, of homelessness, and at the same time the preservation of a sense of *Heimat* by holding tight to a tradition almost exclusively determined by language and written records. Early in life Canetti makes his break with the religious content of the Jewish-Sephardic heritage, but in his approach to language, in his religion of the Word, and in his writer's sense of responsibility, he remains committed to the *conditio judaica*. He had grown up speaking the old-fashioned Spanish of the Jews driven into exile from Spain, but the German language became his true *Heimat* and, under the influence of his mother, who had been shaped by Viennese culture, "a belated mother tongue, implanted in true pain." [12] Even in the times of the most fearful distress, Canetti remained faithful to the German language, which he bore with him as the language of exile just as his forefathers had taken Spanish with them centuries before. "The true language of my soul will remain German, *because* I am a Jew," he states in a 1944 note.

The transition from Spanish via English and French to German—that is to say, the process of finding and keeping a language—is traced in the first autobiographical volume in vivid, sharply delineated scenes as a path followed unwaveringly and consistently, with Canetti's vocation as a writer as its objective. The tale of the saved tongue is followed in the second volume by description of the school of hearing, where we see the Viennese student under the spell of the raging magus Karl Kraus and his magazine *Die Fackel*: at the end of *The Torch in My Ear*, after *speaking* and *hearing* have been learned, comes *writing*. The life history turns out to be the genesis of a writer, a genesis which was filled with a sense of vocation and also with the "dignity of learning." [13]

In the final part of *The Tongue Set Free*, which concentrates on happy postwar years in Zurich and ends with Canetti's banishment from the paradise of his youth, there is a chapter where both motifs (the writer's vocation and the dignity of learning) are woven together into a declaration of belief in the fate that has governed his life, a declaration as sensitive and uninsistent as it is enduring in its persuasive power. The chapter called "The Marked Man," which marks the center of the final section in formal respects too, contains two scenes which follow one upon the other without apparent link and which are nevertheless to be understood as representing mutually complementary episodes. The first presents us with the schoolboy, living in the Yalta Villa in the Tiefenbrunn part of Zurich, who one evening stole away into the house's peaceful and secluded orchard and saw, out on the lake, a brightly lit ship gliding silently by: "Its soundlessness spread out as expectation. It shone for a long time, without flickering, and took possession of me, as though I had come to the orchard for the sake of that ship. I had never seen it before, but I recognized it."[14] In the second episode, Canetti recollects a French teacher, Jules Vodoz, who survived an avalanche—in which nine pupils and another teacher died—with a serious head injury, and because of this wore a hat as protection against inquisitive eyes. It is only the creative power of memory that links the appearance of the lit-up ship to the man branded with the mark of Cain: for the autobiographer, they are linked as images of branding, of marking, and serve to manifest an unrepeatable initiation into the writer's profession, initiation which, as an "innocent wonder,"[15] underlies responsibility for life and the life-giving Word. In Canetti's autobiography, this respect for "the conscience of words" has become reality.

NOTES

1. Elias Canetti, *The Tongue Set Free* (translated by Joachim Neugroschel), New York, 1979 and 1983, p. 53. Chapter headed "Napoleon; Cannibal Guests; Sunday Fun."

2. Elias Canetti, *The Torch in My Ear* (translated by Joachim Neugroschel), New York, 1982, pp. 308–9.

3. Ibid., pp. 117–18.

4. Cf. *The Tongue Set Free*, pp. 28 ff. Chapter headed "The Murder Attempt."

5. Ibid., p. 4. Chapter headed "Family Pride."

6. Ibid., p. 86.

7. Ibid., p. 194. Chapter headed "Phylogeny of Spinach; Junius Brutus."

8. Ibid., p. 89, and cf. chapter headed "The Asylum" in *The Torch in My Ear*, pp. 155 ff.

9. Cf. Canetti's commentary on the sleeve of the record *Elias Canetti liest Canetti: Der Ohrenzeuge*.

10. *The Tongue Set Free*, p. 151.

11. *The Torch in My Ear*, pp. 38-39.

12. *The Tongue Set Free*, p. 70. Chapter headed "German on Lake Geneva."

13. *The Torch in My Ear*, p. 312. Chapter headed "Escape."

14. *The Tongue Set Free*, p. 222.

15. Ibid., p. 222.

Claudio Magris

The Many People That Make Up a Writer: Canetti and Cacania

In the Café Central in Vienna, at a little table immediately to the left as one comes in, there sits a life-size model of Peter Altenberg, one hand on his knee and, above his walrus mustache, his deep melancholy eyes gazing who knows where. A few meters further on, among the patrons of the café, sits another Altenberg model, in hat and spectacles, reading a paper. Near it, one forgets time and again that this mustachioed, motionless gentleman in the old-fashioned suit and with the vaguely familiar face is not real. How often in that coffeehouse does one steal a glance at the newspaper in his hand; imagination casts adrift, and we can suppose the newspaper is today's and the same as the one we're reading, and every morning a waiter slips it between his fingers.

It was at these tables that, at the beginning of the century, Peter Altenberg—the writer without a home, who loved anonymous hotel rooms and postcards—wrote his lightning-fast and wafer-thin parables, his sketches devoted to brief, tiny details (the shadow on a face, the lightness of a stride, the brutality or desolation of a gesture), details which reveal the grace or emptiness of life and which point up the as yet imperceptible cracks in the fabric of the world's history, hints of a coming catastrophe. Our make-believe neighbor remained concealed in the half-shadow of that catastrophe, hid away in anonymity and silence, and, condemned to starve after the First World War, refused one job offer on the grounds that all he could now occupy himself with was leading his own life.

No, it isn't that this model starts one thinking about the "real" Altenberg, because he of all people knew, when he wrote his apologues at these tables, as if on the deck of a sinking ship, how hard it was to tell real life from the unreal—and he would have considered himself not much more authentic than these models. One's own existence was a theater one watched, and Altenberg warned that it should not be taken seriously— though no *less* seriously either—than a Shakespearean play: he felt one should feel both inside and outside it, now and then one should take a few steps in the open, at night, to snatch a breath of fresh air and to mix lived experience with the un-lived.

The great culture of Vienna had unmasked the increasing abstraction and unreality of life, which was being absorbed to a high degree into the mechanisms of collective information and was being performed in their productions. Altenberg, Musil, and their great contemporaries had understood at a pro-found level how difficult it was becoming to distinguish exis-tence, one's own included, from that image of it which was reproduced and disseminated in countless copies: to distin-guish, say, an unfounded report of a banking crisis from the genuine crisis itself, which prompts the report by causing clients to withdraw their investments; or to distinguish the Mayerling affair from the clichéd gothic tale it became.

At any rate, our discreet wooden neighbor at the Café Cen-tral urges us not to take too seriously the things that happen, and to bear in mind that Chance also plays a part, perhaps the most important part, in determining the way things go—and that they might very well go quite differently.

What makes the identity of this model dubious is not only the uncertain boundaries of the genuine and the false, which are given to exchanging roles, but also its own plurality. The supranational diversity of Central Europe, with all its potential for conflict and for harmony, is one of the great birthplaces of the contemporary individual, himself diverse and centrifugal, yet longing for unity.

"Since I was ten," writes Canetti in his autobiographical book *The Tongue Set Free,* "it has been something of a dogma for me that I consist of many people whom I am not at all aware of." As one of the great voices of the culture which was brought forth by the Danube monarchy, Canetti personifies that diversity which made it so difficult to define the Habsburg identity, and which, in fact, made that identity a model of the lost or fractured identity of the modern individual. In imperial Austria-Hungary, whose anthem was sung in so many languages, one could define oneself only by subtraction or negation: the Austrian, wrote Musil, was an Austro-Hungarian minus the Hungarian, and doubtless he was not the same as the inhabitant of the territory which is today the republic of Austria. Nor did he identify with the individual nationalities grouped together under the Dual Monarchy: rather, he was the ribbon that tied the bundle together, the invisible element that was common to them all and identical with none. The Austrian existed in the abstract idea of unity, in a non-material or "internotional" * dimension, as the Prague writer Johannes Urzidil put it.

The colorful diversity of the Empire, which was threatened by centrifugal forces (which in turn were mitigated by a circumspect wisdom and a skeptical yearning for unity), had sharpened awareness that any apparent, unified reality in fact represents a plurality of heterogeneous components and irreconcilable contradictions. It was no accident that, in the old

---

* Urzidil's German word is *hinternational,* which punningly combines *international* with *hinter,* or "beyond." The word suggests that the notion of "the Austrian" did not correspond to any actual nationality, and this I have tried to convey in rendering Urzidil's word as "internotional." —*Trans.*

Austria, there was a particular élan in the development of scientific disciplines such as mathematics, which laid bare the deficiencies in its own basic fundaments, or psychoanalysis, which explored the multifarious structure of individual personality. There was no one so prone to the experience of consisting of many people as that "man without qualities" who was Franz Josef's subject: a sum of qualities lacking a man (said Musil), or, rather, devoid of a unifying center and thus the most modern of men, suspended between attachment to the past and availability for future changes.

The true Austria was the whole world, as Musil ironically wrote, for in it one could see the epochal crisis of the West with particular clarity. When in Musil's novel the Coordinating Committee for the Collateral Campaign (for the celebration of the Emperor's jubilee) is searching for the central idea, the first principle on which Austria (and thus European culture) is based, it cannot find it. The Empire unmasks the whole of given reality.

It is a global experiment which, with the clarity of a laboratory test, brings to light the essential emptiness of this reality. The Collateral Campaign, which is looking for the basic principle of the Austrian culture it wishes to celebrate but fails to find it, is an ironic parable of an absence throughout modern Western culture, an absence which is evident in paradigmatic fashion in Austria.

The whole of Austrian literature in the twentieth century consists of an unmasking of this crisis: from Hofmannsthal to Musil, from Andrian to Rilke, from Altenberg to Broch and Canetti, Austrian writers diagnose the insufficiency of the word, which can no longer express experience and give order to the uncertain flux of life—and they announce the foundering of the subjective self, which is no longer capable of placing the net of language between itself and the chaos of life but instead is lost in a whirlwind of sensations and images. "The ego," Musil writes in *The Man Without Qualities*, "has lost that significance it hitherto has, as a sovereign decreeing acts of government."

Reality becomes an endless chain of individual centers, and art, to remain true to it, imitates and reproduces in its own isolation the anarchic plurality of reality, a multiplicity of styles that cannot be traced to any single unity—just as Ulrich's flat is characterized by the eclectic overlapping of incompatible styles. That non-style of Vienna's Ringstrasse which Broch attacked, that inorganic coexistence of heterogeneous and fake elements, is the true expression of the falseness of modern life. "Our whole being," Musil claims, "is nothing but a collective delirium," and "man's profoundest attachment to this fellow man consists in his rejection."

Canetti's Vienna, almost always unnamed, or grotesquely symbolized, which so often constitutes the backdrop for his magnificent and distorted representation of reality, is first and foremost the place where the true and the false are mixed—a mirror of the world, misted over by ambiguity and thus appropriate to that falseness that the world is made of.

But the Cacania* Canetti grows up in is also that of a Kafka, a Broch, and a Karl Kraus (to whom Canetti tellingly paid tribute in his Nobel Prize acceptance speech)—that is to say, of the grim trackers of truth. This world, which was obscured by the flood of reproductions of life, like a tree with a poster pinned to it, educated writers to an extremely acute perception of inevitable existential falseness, of what is bogus in historical destiny; but it also educated them to rebel against this contamination, and forced them to expose the falseness that was all around them and which penetrated into their inmost beings. It is no coincidence that Canetti admires Musil, for whom truth is a sack whose shape changes according to what is put in it;

---

* Cacania (in the German, *Kakanien*) was Musil's coinage in *The Man Without Qualities* for the Austro-Hungarian Empire. The coinage had twin sources in *k.u.k* (i.e., *kaiserlich und königlich*—the imperial and royal Duel Monarchy) and Greek *kakos* (bad). —*Trans.*

but Canetti also views Kafka with the trust one places in a witness—Kafka, for whom art meant being blinded by truth; and he looks to Broch, the faithful watchdog of his age; but above all, at least at a certain period, he looks to Karl Kraus.

From Kraus, Canetti learned impetuousness, absolute values, and passionate pitilessness in the struggle for truth. Every morning Karl Kraus found the world buried in newspapers, lying scraps of paper that threatened to smother Nature. Kraus did not underestimate the power and inevitability of this process, but he did not believe that the individual's powers of resistance had wholly ebbed away, that they had been absorbed totally by the anonymous fabric of society. Like some heroic and tireless street cleaner, he went wrathfully about the business of making a clean sweep, gathering up and removing the litter lying about, somehow confident that he would once again touch upon a true fundament of life and would be able to regenerate and restore Nature. "In the beginning was the Press / and then came the world," he says in one of his poems, which sees the world as the product of the information industry, set up by the latter for purposes of profit. Karl Kraus's fight is that of a man who still believes it is possible to set the world free, to re-create it and give it back its original creativity.

As a satirist or, in Schiller's definition, as Nature's avenger, Kraus is opposed to Hegel, who rejected satire because it presumed to view the history of the world from an absolute perspective, some Archimedean point beyond the course of world events.

Our age has refuted this view of Hegel's; in the course of world history, a process which ought to be identical with that of Reason yet which goes round and round in circles in the void, the satirist returns to passing judgment on the world—crouching on some meteoric rock that the gyroscopic dialectic has torn out of history and flung out into the void.

Canetti has given us impressive reports of the formative influence of Karl Kraus on him, and his own subsequent turning from his impassioned teacher. At that school Canetti learned the greatness but also the intolerant and unbearable sides of a total, monomaniac devotion to truth, which in the end withers and suffocates life. Kraus was a great Don Quixote but without a Sancho Panza: and so Canetti compares him, in an image of genius, to a Chinese Wall built against the barbarians, a wall which is the more solidly reinforced as fear of an enemy attack grows stronger and stronger, till in the end the wall smothers between its stone confines the empire it was to protect—the empire is absorbed into the wall, buried beneath it, reduced to nothing but the wall.

The great task Canetti has set himself is the cancellation of the mortal antithesis of Life and Truth, the antithesis between the ambiguity of the Altenberg models—an agonizing toleration of the false—and the unremitting absoluteness of Karl Kraus, who burns Life in the name of Truth. Canetti's poetic challenge consists in this last-ditch attempt at a total rescue of existence.

Canetti is the great poet of a dilemma which, as unresolved as ever, has our century by the throat: the interchangeability and lethal symbiosis of self-defense and self-destruction. Excessive defense is the same thing as death—just as, in Kafka's famous story, the underground passages dug by the creature to escape the unknown enemy that is following it in the end lead into that very tunnel the archenemy has prepared for it. This abnormal threat, which obliges life to concentrate on defense and then, in this reduced state, to destroy itself, has swollen to terrible proportions in our century, and Canetti, mindful in this of Kafka's lesson, sets out as writer to defy this delirium of Reason which is being perverted into a self-destructive irrationality. As Kafka's characters well know, the summons of life is deceptive—but those who do not hear or follow it are courting disaster.

The heterogeneous culture of the universal Danubian Babel

taught Canetti with particular power the great modern truth of the negative: it taught him the solar eclipse of real life, the awareness that it had vanished or was in hiding; that one should not imagine it can be seized hold of; that, rather, it is manifested only in the knowledge of its absence, in the reflection that registers its lack, and in the longing this calls forth. Those who have lost this sense are often not able to cope with the loss, cannot manage to endure it, and so they smother and repress awareness of it. They suppress life and the longing for life, for they could neither do justice to the vital obligation of its diversity nor stand the pain of its absence.

Canetti is the poet of a humanity that is killing itself for fear of being killed, a humanity that puts up barricades against life, like Dr. Kien. *Auto-da-Fé* is the mighty parable for this twentieth-century delirium. Canetti published the novel in 1935, at the age of thirty; the book appeared and was not given the attention that was due a work of its caliber; it was given a handful of intelligent reviews and then disappeared from the literary scene for almost thirty years. In 1963, true, it was rediscovered and welcomed as the work of a new, unknown author, but only in the mid-1970s was Canetti to make his real impact.

As the author of *Auto-da-Fé,* a masterpiece of the century which for nearly three decades was almost totally forgotten, Canetti doubtless suffered in his long banishment, but he bore it with a calm certainty, and behind his friendly modesty there was concealed an unwavering, well-nigh arrogant knowledge of his own genius. The shadows he remained in were nonetheless indicative of his radical consistency, indeed of his truth: in *Auto-da-Fé,* the preeminent modern parable of the intellect which does not feel up to the chaos of life and destroys itself in a delirious defensive reflex, Canetti had expressed the endless unbearability of existence, the grotesque and paranoid shipwreck of the individual, crowded by the multiplying masses which inundate him from all sides and which he fears, but also secretly dreams of, being engulfed by.

The novel is the tragic, and tragicomic, history of the individual who clads himself in armor until he is nothing but armor and goes down. This individual kills off the hubbub of the world in the funeral-parlor order of his library, and stifles every wish and temptation because he is afraid the fascination of love might draw him forth from his armor, drag him out of his trench of bookshelves and cultural classifications and into the chaotic flux of reality. Dr. Kien, the novel's protagonist, perfects his own blindness in order not to have to perceive the myriad aggressions of things; and he is pleased that the weighty spines of the books conceal behind their apparent immobility the billions of high-speed electrons they are made up of. He is an amusing and painful portrait of every one of us, the mirror of the phobias and rites with which, in our endeavor to keep our fear in check, we waste our lives.

Auto-da-Fé describes with absolute logical consistency a total lack of love, a world insanely shriveled up and sterilized against each and every desire. Paranoia prevents the characters from projecting their emotions into the reality around them, from seeing things, bodies, and faces with that passion that invests them with magic. Fear of death, and the obsession with power that results from this fear, have extinguished all their capacity for feeling. In showing the frosty coldness of the lack of love—and in fashioning from this, by a stroke of genius, the very point of view of the narrative, that awry and blinded way of seeing that does not *see*—Canetti makes plain, as few other writers do, what a life without love would mean, and thus what love itself means. This drastic radicality, which constitutes the human and the stylistic greatness of the novel, throws many readers.

Auto-da-Fé is a book that admits no half-judgments. There are readers who recognize themselves in it totally as in the distorting mirrors in fairground halls, and accept the novel as an everyday Bible, and there are other readers who turn away from it, confused and repelled. It is an impossible and contrary book that makes no concessions and resists assimilation by cultural institutions: its rejection by that ideal happy medium which the well-considered historiography of the literary republic portrays is quite clear. Canetti's novel was a truly heterogeneous, indigestible, and—measured against other literary products and intellectual consumer habits—"different" book, which did not fit into that preprogrammed outsiderdom to which the avant-garde gave its a priori sanction either.

This one massive work, which makes no concessions and cannot be assimilated by the literary histories, would not alone have won the Nobel Prize for the author, though. Not even Canetti's other major works would have forced the literary world to clear his rightful space for him. Even when *Crowds and Power* appeared in 1960 it fascinated but above all irritated many critics and readers, who did not know what label to stick on the work, whose daring and unusual method penetrates to the roots of existence. Perhaps "Kafka's Other Trial" or the further essays and notebooks would not have brought Canetti his due recognition either.

The Nobel Prize which was awarded to Canetti honored two writers: one who remains hidden, the mysterious genius who wrote *Auto-da-Fé*, an author who has perhaps disappeared and can no longer be found—and one making a new appearance; one who withdraws and one who enters the debate. Maybe another writer was needed so that Canetti and *Auto-da-Fé* might be understood and accepted—that writer who, thirty years later, stepped into the limelight and gave a commentary on the fate of his books, as if that fate were posthumous. This is the Canetti of a series of essays and above all of the autobiography, interviews, and conversations—a Canetti who tells us of his multinational and polyglot upbringing, starting with his birth in 1905 in the Bulgarian town of Ruschuk, in a Jewish family.

This development has made it possible for Canetti openly to express what *Auto-da-Fé* shrouded in jealous silence and only indirectly, negatively expressed: love of every pulse beat of life and of his freedom, the defense of metamorphosis and of evolutionary becoming against any power that would prevent it, the utopian struggle against Death. Canetti's whole existence is a refusal to accept Death, a struggle to tear from his clutches every living being, a dream of defeating him. At times it seems he feels he is there to defend Man in a duel with Death, as if he were trying to take hold of the faces of all the people he meets, preserve them in his head (which is capable of containing the world), and thus save them from the great enemy. Tirelessly he combats Death, without giving in to the constant and terrible reversals history inflicts on his program of resistance— as if secretly he were indeed convinced he is able to eliminate Death, actually to subdue him, and were keeping this scandalous certainty to himself only for the time being, out of consideration for convention and good manners. Those who know Canetti feel supported by him, feel they are preserved inside his head, which (like a library, but with human passion) keeps every detail of every life.

In Canetti's imaginative work, individual existence is the anguished, scandalous, absurd experience of a truth that is radically opposed to all communication. In his essays and his aphorisms too he as repeatedly emphasized the threat to the individual which integration and laying himself open represent—by this means the individual is seized and drained by the power machine. Like his favorite writers Kafka and Robert Walser, Canetti prefers the minor and insignificant, the anonymous and the dark—the defensive tactics of one who eludes power by submitting to it, then wresting himself from its grasp like a Chinese wrestler, disappearing into the crowd and hiding away in the impersonal masses . . . or who lies flat on the ground like a little hunted animal shamming death.

One who is identified as an individual is offering the hunter his body and person as a target; he is distinct and thus exposed to aggression; he allows his name to be confiscated by the world and registered. He no longer has the freedom of the wanderer with no fixed abode, who cannot be registered because he has no name, a nobody who can undergo metamorphoses and take on new identities, like beings in fairy tales who change their physical form to escape pursuers.

Canetti is now in the limelight. Now he has to organize his own defense by means of a tricky ritual as alien and unfamiliar as Kafka's and invent tactics that enable him to disappear at will and then to reappear, to make himself generously available for personal talk with friends or strangers but to keep his distance from the lethal and alienating machinery of the culture industry. He is one of the few men famous worldwide who refuse to be crushed by that industry and know how to say no to its pressure. He knows that this pressure takes away one's breath, that airy and absolutely vital creative liberty to which he has devoted important passages in his work. In order to remain himself, he must go into hiding, wear masks, undergo metamorphoses, or disapppear. The writer who hides in order to be able to breathe is fighting his great fight not only in his own defense but in defense of life, which is continually under threat of being dispossessed or rendered impotent. And anyway, the real poets of the Empire always lived at the edge of life, like Joseph Roth's characters at the eastern periphery of the monarchy; they lived on the run, in the shadows or in silence.

Within the wish to flee, which is now legitimately besetting Canetti, there is perhaps another, more disquieting sting. In his works, Canetti has marvelously shown the paranoid fear of the individual who feels menaced from all sides and in the end is afraid of any contact or touch, and longs to be alone in the world, like God before the Creation or like the insane *Senatspräsident* Schreber, on whom Canetti has written masterfully.

A little of that fear of contact is perhaps now infecting the writer too, who at times, just for a moment, resembles the powerful in his books, in their desire to have life under their control—a desire he has so skillfully analyzed and laid bare.

As in the days when he lacked success and was unknown,

Canetti is now, in the days of his fame and familiarity, a magnificent example of individual resistance to the world. Naturally the price of this resistance, which so few are capable of, is very high. As Kafka very well knew, the individual has to pay dearly for escaping the world's tentacles. Resistance demands constant vigilance and keen scrutiny to the point of mania, incessant assessment and calculation of risks and ruses, a watchfulness that uses up energies and prevents a full living of life, a detailed estimate of debit and credit.

Every autobiography is a return to one's own past in quest of one's own identity, an exploration of the fluid and uncertain meanderings of one's own personal continuity. He who writes about himself reveals and conceals himself at the same time; he is transformed into the mask of his faithful and yet distinct alter ego, who gradually takes on fuller form page by page. The diverse whole that constitutes the self is split into colors and figures, falls apart and multiplies, takes camouflage among numerous faces and hides between the pages. He who writes his autobiography seems to be delivering himself up to the others totally and without defense, and they already have their claws outstretched to snatch possession of his image. This self-portrait seems to be saying that its author has become incapable of metamorphosis and can no longer flee. In reality, however, the proffered self-portrait is a face borrowed for the time being by the secret, manifold self to deceive its pursuers, like the hunted animal in the fairy tale that changes physical shape very time it is about to be caught.

Canetti remains the great poet of metamorphosis in his autobiography too, which conceals him even as it appears to reveal him. He visits his past, but we will never learn what happened on this journey, whether or where he rediscovered his identity.

The author of the autobiography sets out in quest of the author of *Auto-da-Fé*, but he strays from his path and misdirects his companions on the journey. The writing first person presents itself as "compact"—like the first person Canetti sees in Tolstoy—but in this way it conceals the rifts within itself, and its own centrifugal diversity. The interplay of bottomless depths and a readable surface covers up the astounding uniqueness of the writer and presents him in a less disturbing shape, such as the pacified literary scene can now recognize and celebrate.

In his autobiography, written in his customary crystal-clear style, which masks some undefined secret, we sense European culture veritably exploding, a centuries-old order collapsing; love of life and the rejection of death permit Canetti to convey the indelible intensity of experience, the one and unrepeatable meaning of each face, every gesture, which fix memory and word forever, to save them from time, history, and death. But this autobiography, which seems to be saying everything, hides an absence, a kind of black hole that seems to be swallowing up the essential truth of this life. Canetti means to tell how the idea for *Auto-da-Fé* came to him and how the novel was written, but basically he tells us nothing about this grotesque and magnificent book, and in fact he says just as little about its unexpected author, that thirty-year-old who was Canetti and whom one cannot quite imagine, who must have found himself at the edge of catastrophes and a drastic void—a man who has perhaps disappeared, but perhaps, like fire, is still smoldering behind the amiable affability of the now eighty-year-old writer— a man whom Canetti is veiling from our sight and who assuredly will not make his appearance in the pages of the autobiography.

Like any real book, Canetti's autobiography has to be read with passion and distrust, of what is said and of what is kept back. In one fine chapter Canetti remarks that everyone confronted with reality resembles Samson when he was blinded, torn away from his last view of the world, which went dark for him and was lost. Maybe Canetti shares this fear, and in his autobiography is mastering it.

Behind the accessible smoothness of this autobiography, which is in such contrast to the contrariness of *Auto-da-Fé* and gives the deceptive appearance of telling all, there is a reserve which, twisting and taking on disguises, conceals an unsuspected otherness, an ungraspable and inconceivable identity. Behind the friendly gentleman evolving his extremely polite form in order to protect his own reserve, there is another, the abnormal and impossible other. Both of them are teaching us day in and day out to unmask the mad delusion of power and of death, and both remind us of a statement in *The Human Province:* "Everyone is the center of the world. Everyone."

Three

The Reception History of *Auto-da-Fé:* A Documentation

*A prefatory note
on the publication history of the novel
by Herbert G. Göpfert*

Quite probably few other books have had so curious a publication history as Canetti's *Auto-da-Fé*—a history determined by the idiosyncrasy of the work and its author, by the headlong rush to catastrophe of the times in which it was written (or, indeed, which produced it), and last by what we call chance. Normally we do not need to pay particular attention to the publication of a literary work: after the author has completed it, the work is published, and then its reception and influence can begin. Admittedly, publication is a sine qua non for a work's reception, but it is generally taken for granted—still, what if publication is a problem? The facts which follow are intended to serve as first notes on this, and as a preamble to a selected number of representative reviews from various stages in the book's publication.[1]

The manuscript of the novel was finished in October 1931. At this point, the author's name was as good as unknown to the public, and his only efforts then available to readers were two translations of Upton Sinclair, *Leidweg der Liebe* and *Das*

Geld (both Berlin, 1930; *Alkohol* followed in 1932). No publisher could be found for the novel. True, the Berlin publishing house of S. Fischer had managed the sale and distribution of the play *The Wedding*, written immediately after the novel, duplicating the typescript for theater use, as was usual; but clearly the house did not want to risk the hefty novel. To an extent this may also have been because of the political tensions which filled 1932 and were starting to cripple cultural life. Then, from the beginning of 1933, there was no longer any chance with German publishers; but Austrian and Swiss houses too, quite apart from their limited sales potential, were hardly feasible for this first work, for a variety of reasons.

Nonetheless, in the next few years in Vienna, Canetti no longer remained unknown. He was not only familiar to those in the know in various literary circles and groups in Vienna; he also repeatedly read from the novel, and presently from the play *The Wedding* too, in private and in public—one of these readings, in January 1933, was introduced by Hermann Broch.[2] So there were people who not only knew of the book but to whom Canetti the author already meant something. In his third autobiographical volume, Canetti tells of some of these readings, and about the various responses of the listeners. In this volume he also describes how publication of the novel then came about in 1935, by the newly founded Viennese house of Herbert Reichner. The Strassburg newspaper publisher Jean Hoepffner, whom Canetti had got to know, had taken the risk, but what is more remarkable than this fact, unusual enough in itself, is the way he came to take it. Books meant a good deal to Hoepffner, and he believed in the good in Man. Experience told him that there was no such thing as "bad" people, you just had to avoid attributing the wrong motives to them and instead had to see them as they were. That, he felt, was the writer's task. At most, in a well-written book, and in order to provide a "deterrent," one might show, just once, "by way of make-believe," "how the world would look if there were bad people in it." When he had heard Canetti speak of it, he supposed *Auto-da-Fé* to be a book of this kind. He did not, he said, want to read it, and indeed he didn't—but he wanted to make possible its publication. It was not the book that moved or persuaded him but its author, the man Elias Canetti. It is this human effect of Canetti's, then, that marks the start of the publication history of his work.

The novel's appearance without doubt amounted to a literary success. The critical notices prove it, and among them special mention must be made of Peter von Haselberg's firm and understanding review in the *Frankfurter Zeitung,* a courageous and laudable piece of work. Of the Austrian reviews, Ernst Waldinger's in *das silberboot* was later to have a further effect. That reviews also appeared in important places in Budapest, Prague, Holland, and Switzerland shows that the publishers made efforts to get the book and its newcomer author known. Alfred Kubin had agreed to design the dust jacket, and was so fascinated by the work that he would have liked most of all to illustrate the entire book. His first design, though, was rejected by the publisher: it showed a toad on a pile of books. This was how Therese presented herself to the artist. (This drawing was not found among the papers left on Kubin's death, though.) If we consider the events of the time and the severely restricted sales area, it is understandable that the novel did not sell well; but, over and above the reviews, it had brought Canetti the recognition of, among others, Alban Berg, Thomas Mann, and Robert Musil. From this point the book could have been influential. This, however, was no longer possible after the German annexation of Austria in the spring of 1938. In the autumn of 1938 Canetti emigrated.

And yet the novel had very soon started to have an effect abroad, and not only through reviews. Hitherto it has been noted in bibliographies, but scarcely registered as a fact, that as early as 1936, in other words one year after the Viennese first edition (which was postdated 1936), a Czech translation by Zdenka Münzrová was published in Prague by L. Mazáč. This publisher was beginning a series of "contemporary novels of world literature": each country to be included was to be represented by one novel, and *Auto-da-Fé* was suggested to the Czech publishers as the Austrian novel. Canetti traveled to Prague for a reading, which met with not inconsiderable interest, and got acquainted with literary circles there. It seems the Czech translation sold well too. Unfortunately we do not yet have any knowledge of reviews that may have appeared: it would be worth hunting them out. Here too it was political events once again, first in 1938 and then in the spring of 1939, that brought literary life to a standstill and thus cut off any wider effect the book might have had in Czechoslovakia.

If the next edition of the novel listed in the bibliographies is that of Jonathan Cape in London, the English translation which appeared ten years later in 1946, it is tempting to suppose that during the war no publisher cared to issue a book of such difficulty by a writer who was still barely known. Not so. Urged on by émigré readers of the novel, Jonathan Cape—and this must be stressed—had decided while the war was still on to put out an English edition. Its translator was the historian C.V. Wedgwood, who did her work in close collaboration with the author.

The publisher's contract was signed in 1943, but Elias Canetti made the condition that the novel should appear only after the war was over, as he felt it was "not tenable" to publish an émigré book of this kind while the war was still in progress. For this reason the translation did not appear until 1946. Again we might suppose that a book of this sort would be unable to attract many readers so soon after the war, but again the response was different. Doubtless it was attributable to the literary climate and high literary standards in England (and it would be worth analyzing this), but *Auto-da-Fé* was immediately acclaimed and before 1946 was out a second printing had to be run, and in the next year, 1947, a third.

The wide press response[3] in a broad spectrum of newspapers and periodicals gives a good idea of the recognition the book received. Walter Allen, for example, made comparisons with Ben Jonson. It is no exaggeration to say that it was the English edition and English criticism that first made the novel visible for a longer period—during the 1950s reference was repeatedly made to it in books. Most important of all, and fundamental to subsequent examination of *Auto-da-Fé*, was the BBC critique by Jacob Isaacs. The BBC Third Programme had commissioned from Isaacs a retrospective of the literature of the first half of the century and a description of the works which in his opinion would endure. These six one-hour talks, which met with a great response but in which only a handful of German-language authors were mentioned, were published in book form in 1951. By contrast, the critical reaction to the American publication of Wedgwood's translation, by Alfred A. Knopf in New York in 1947, was scant.

Strange to say, it was not this success which then prompted the French edition of the book. Perhaps international contact among publishers in the immediate postwar years was not yet very intensive. The novel appeared in French in 1949, in a translation by Paul Artex, as *La Tour de Babel,* from B. Arthaud of Grenoble and Paris; but in this case it was Canetti's brother Georges, who practiced as a doctor in Paris, who had struck up an acquaintanceship with Arthaud's director, Jean Contou, and had brought the book to his attention. Through Contou, who was instantly convinced of the significance of the novel and of its author, others were made aware of *La Tour de Babel,* among them Raymond Queneau, who was instrumental in the book's winning its first literary award, France's coveted Prix International for the best foreign novel (in 1949). The critic Marcel Brion, it should be noted, knew the work from its first German publication and expressed astonishment that it should appear "so late" in France.

And what of the book's further fortunes in Germany? Its

fate there was quite different from that in England and France. It demonstrated the extent to which the noticing and reception of artistic works are dependent on the given historical situation. At first glance the external circumstances did seem favorable, it is true. A reprint of Ernst Waldinger's review (of June 1936) in the autumn 1946 *Silberboot-Almanach,* edited by Ernst Schönwiese in Vienna, brought the book to the attention of Rudolf Hartung, literary adviser to the Munich publishing house of Willi Weismann, and he saw to it that it was issued by that house in 1948. Hartung, who has devoted intensive journalistic labors to Canetti's work ever since, also wrote the first extensive, in-depth German-language essay on the novel. Otherwise, though, there was but little response: with few exceptions, the reviews reflect the helplessness of criticism isolated from the European transition when faced with a work of this kind, and also, no doubt, an inability to confront the book in that period of rubble and ruin. Max von Brück of the old *Frankfurter Zeitung* was admittedly able to see what was what; but the book did not make its mark, and furthermore the publishers ran into financial difficulties, as many did after the currency reform of 1948; and about the same time that the novel was awarded a literary prize in France, it was remaindered in Germany. Thus the second German edition too remained largely without results in the short term.

A number of attempts were made to get the novel published by well-known German houses, but without success. It is a measure of the alienation then felt in Germany vis-à-vis the novel, a feeling which from today's perspective seems incomprehensible, that even Claassen of Hamburg, the house which in 1960 issued Canetti's second major work, *Crowds and Power,* completed after many years of work, did not want to take on *Auto-da-Fé.* In Germany, where so-called essayistic literature is usually received with reserve, *Crowds and Power* initially met with a decidedly limited response in the press. In England it was again a different matter. There, Carol Stewart's translation, which appeared as early as 1962 from Victor Gollancz, prompted a lively press debate with highly productive reviews, among them the penetrating one by Iris Murdoch. And in the spring of that year, the fourth printing of *Auto-da-Fé* appeared and, astonishingly, was greeted with extensive press coverage.

If we take our bearings only from bibliographical data, the new German edition of *Auto-da-Fé*, which finally appeared in 1963 from Carl Hanser of Munich, might seem a result both of *Crowds and Power* and of Canetti's renewed critical acclaim in England. At this point the present author must add his own testimony. At that time I was head of literary publishing with Hanser, and I must positively assure the reader that Claassen's *Crowds and Power* had remained unknown to me and that I also knew nothing of the English Canetti publications. Rather, it was Jean Contou of Arthaud who, when I was visiting in Paris, urged on me this novel (which I had never heard of) by the "most important German author" (with a name that did not sound at all German: Elias Canetti). I do not need to describe how, after one or two hitches, this publication then came about.[4] But it is not true in general terms that in 1963 "the situation was more auspicious" for the third German edition than it had been earlier.[5] In terms of the book trade it was in fact extraordinarily difficult to put on the market, after thirty years, a book that had already appeared twice without lasting success. In order to accomplish this, the house had to take considerable pains.[6] But the attempt was successful, thanks above all to the intensive collaboration of a number of influential reviewers—of those who were writing about the novel for the first time, Günther Busch should be particularly singled out. A further printing was called for before the year was out; after a few years the novel appeared in paperback too and was included in the lists of book clubs. Since then it has been constantly available on the German book market. Thus after a long time a novel written in German had finally found a secure place in the country of its mother tongue. Amazingly, this had been far from unproblematic, but it was no less astonishing that the novel's international influence now gained greater momentum. Certainly the powerful response called forth by the English translation, which was followed in 1964 by a new American edition, and also the attention given to *Crowds and Power* both in England and in the United States, played an important part in this, as did the efforts of the German publisher. And naturally, further books by Canetti, particularly his new ones, which followed—at first quite rapidly—from Hanser after 1964, served to make his intellectual world and his personality more widely familiar. Nevertheless, it remains an unusual phenomenon, to find a first book, so demanding, and written out of a 1930s situation, being newly translated into so many languages more than forty years after it was written: by 1981, that is to say before Canetti won the Nobel Prize, the novel had appeared in a total of eighteen countries. This cannot be explained by any kind of manipulaton or external circumstances: it can only be explained by the vitality that is in the book itself.

NOTES

1. Cf. Dieter Dissinger, "Erster Versuch einer Rezeptionsgeschichte Canettis am Beispiel seiner Werke *Die Blendung* und *Masse und Macht*" and "Bibliographie zu Elias Canetti," in Herbert G. Göpfert (ed.), *Canetti lesen*, pp. 90–101 and 152–56. Further information is contained in Canetti's own essay "The First Book: *Auto-da-Fé*, in the same collection and also in Canetti's *The Conscience of Words* (translated by Joachim Neugroschel), New York, 1979, pp. 203–13, as well as in the third volume of Canetti's autobiography. The present writer has also drawn upon a conversation with the writer himself in June 1984.
2. Cf. Göpfert (ed.), *Canetti lesen*, pp. 119–21.
3. Cf. Dissinger, pp. 95–97.
4. A detailed account is given in *Titel*, vol. 1, 1982, no. 1, pp. 77–79.
5. Cf. Dissinger, p. 101.
6. Cf. Florian Tielebier-Langenscheidt, "Werbung für deutsche Gegenwartsliteratur," in *Archiv für Geschichte des Buchwesens*, vol. 23, Frankfurt, 1983, columns 182–226. Weismann's efforts to make Canetti known in Germany, and Rudolf Hartung's part in them, are now described fully, with numerous quotations from letters, in *Broch, Canetti, Jahnn. Willi Weismanns Verlag 1946–1954. Mit einer Bib-*

liographie der Verlagsproduktion, edited by Jochen Meyer, in *Marbacher Magazin,* 33/1985, pp. 26–45. (This was published after the present essay was finished.)

Parts of the reviews that follow have been omitted, for two reasons. First, the plot summaries which most reviews naturally include would—for all their variation—be wearisome when repeated, and in any case familiarity with the novel can be presupposed in readers of the present book. Second, reviewers sometimes begin with lengthy literary-historical or poetological considerations of a general character in order to classify *Auto-da-Fé,* according to their own lights. These reflections are of marginal interest today and can be dispensed with—though care has been taken not to alter the overall argument of a review by such cuts, which are all indicated thus: [. . .].

Inconsistencies, or indeed points which from a present-day interpretative point of view are wrong, have of course been left to stand wherever they may occur in these earlier reviews, without any kind of commentary, for their documentary value.

Peter von Haselberg

Experimenting with the Novel

[. . .] Canetti's novel is the first step beyond Joyce's *Ulysses,* as it were. For this reason it is of greater importance than some novels whose perfection within a tried and tested framework may be higher. When Joyce concatenates a man's inner experiences, reflections, associations, images, the entire stream of what remains in the unconscious, then this subjectivity rendered unconscious embraces everything that happens and, starting as an impulse, becomes the sole reality. In *Auto-da-Fé* the boundary between real happenings and fantasies is, as it were, experimentally shifted; the novel's three sections are called "A Head without a World," "Headless World," and "The World in the Head." In the end what this means is that every character behaves according to his individual notions.

This bedlam has two striking features: a tremendous tension that comes across to the reader too, and the total absence of loving, "human" character traits. This latter reaches astonishing proportions and is itself proof of the difficulty of conceiving such a situation—consolation, thus, in the negative. But in this nasty world—there is no other word for it—things, and situations themselves, come alive all the more, not only books and the ghosts of Indian and Chinese writers but also memories, returning to life and intervening, and fantasy projections, free-ranging, asserting their force time and again beside the course of external events. As all of this surrounds Man and slowly but surely grows over his head, he himself loses impact, and the power of external circumstance competes successfully against his own activity. The realistic novel, confined within a positivist theory of milieu, was never able to describe the fluid boundary between what happens and what is experienced, a boundary which can be clearly defined only with hindsight, nor could it describe the supreme power of that environment Man constructs for himself and which then seems strange to him, hostile, and continually growing; these are what Canetti's novel, taking an extreme case and working with new means, tries to bring before us. In the course of the attempt the world of books curiously remains a mere backdrop. What seems at first glance a professional blunder is in fact dictated not by Chance but by a fundamental law: just as a stage set serves only to indicate the place of the action, so too the novel's environment of books is not permitted to reveal its own background of deceptive life but must instead offer its book spines to mark the scene's limit, almost didactically, like a puppet theater.

It could be objected that this way of writing, departing so

far from the psychological and so closely approaching a rhetoric of gesture, is a factor that would explode the nature of the novel. But it is less this and rather the absence of communicating human sensibilities that raises the tension to a point where it threatens to shatter the form. It is no longer clear whether the characters are living beings or only figures in the game. At this point it is debatable whether the novel has reached a frontier or is perhaps en route to new possibilities.

[*Frankfurter Zeitung*, April 12, 1936 (*Literaturblatt*, p. 18)]

Ernst Waldinger

Comédie Humaine *of the Insane*

The greater the superficial knowledge one has of them, the more one will inevitably misunderstand the intentions of Elias Canetti's important experimental novel *Auto-da-Fé*, first in a novel sequence of a Balzacian kind, which sets out to view the entire misery of the world through the insanity of the individual and, consistently enough, to cure human agonies from that perspective. In the work itself (and this is to Canetti's credit as an artist) this basic conception is never directly expressed except in a few sentences spoken by a psychiatrist (who symbolically represents—as we easily guess—the writer himself with his interpretations and solutions) and also in the discussion in the final chapter, which bears a distant formal similarity to passages in Thomas Mann's *The Magic Mountain*. In the novel, everything is condensed, and structured—structured into strange shapes, it is true, but what else is one to expect, given the task of breathing life into madmen's views of the world? But if one knows from hearsay that the author believes that the annihilation of the individual being, and the biological transition of conscious personality to a new unit of life, the crowd, is the goal of all human evolution, that everything subjective (not excepting creativity—indeed, perhaps creativity most of all) is a sickness that leads to death, indeed that all individuality is a "sickness unto death" (Kierkegaard's notion is the aptest here)—then the reader, already sufficiently disturbed by the horrors of our times, will be even more disturbed, which seems indeed to be Canetti's intention. But the reader who cannot follow Canetti in his relentless thoughts will be all the readier to misunderstand. "Is not psychosis in the masses just as much a sickness as madness in the extreme individual?" he will ask. "Aren't there enough examples, from the Flagellators through to present-day forms of mass hysteria? Can a future collective originate (not only organically) in the interplay of individual organisms, or societal responsibility in the harmony of individual responsibilities?" But for Canetti phenomena such as mass psychosis are merely the inevitable transitional stages on the road to the new form of some future mass unit. He is anti-humanist: responsibility, too, is a restriction that cannot help Man out of the vicious circle of greed he is caught in.

Canetti takes the much-discussed termite state of Man seriously, and if his views can be quite painfully off-putting, his daring consistency remains admirable. In insect states, the social awareness which in Man, even at best, is at odds with egoistic hampering factors, has become an all-powerful social instinct, a blind will to work and to sacrifice oneself for the community; the dull coexistence of the animal herd instinct becomes in them a spontaneous mutual benefiting in a higher kind of community. For Canetti, the crowd is not plurality harnessed into harmony, as a humanist collectivist might see it, but a perfect unit or entity, beyond the sense of the Other, occupying that very position which for mystics is occupied by the soul united with God.

Here, as in anything of a religious character, the thought of a conquest of death seems to play a part in Canetti's concept: Man as he will be in future, according to Canetti, has no ego-consciousness and thus a personal death is unknown to him—while the crowd, the true unit of humanity, is immortal, however much single individuals may come and go.

It is necessary to elucidate this ideology of Canetti's, at first glance shocking or at least startling, because otherwise the reader will be liable to misunderstand both his thought content and his form. Distortion in Canetti's characters, the characters that bear his plot (which at times is extraordinarily exciting in spite of the novel's psychological difficulty), is by no means ghostly or gruesome caricature; rather, the characters' own lunatic notions are personified *in* them. This stylistic strategy can even be heard in the use of speech patterns, where we hear an insane dialectic; and even in the book's local color we perceive reality only through the veil of madness, as it were—that madness which is its true home. The novel, then, is not some eerie or gruesome thing tricked out with psychological frills, but rather a work of the order of James Joyce's prose, though it restricts the Irishman's boundless associative technique to individual cases, working with precision and a kind of counterpoint. As *Auto-da-Fé* is the first volume in a novel sequence Canetti himself calls a *"Comédie Humaine* of the insane'' (alluding to Balzac), the broad stream of Joyce would not be in place and indeed hardly bearable. Still: if the author himself invokes Balzac's shade, it seems appropriate to point out that there are certain links. In Balzac's novels too, we find extreme individuals; there, though, the characters' will takes them in the opposite direction, as we would expect, given the difference between the century of emancipation and the century of bourgeois decline. If Canetti's figures, shy unto sickness, flinch away from contact with the world back into their own folly, Balzac's are obsessed with ambition and are impelled into the world at any price, even that of crime; if the tragedies of ambition, of the craving for recognition, are in Balzac of Shakespearean dimensions, Canetti's tragedies are intimate, as in Strindberg's chamber plays.

In Elias Canetti's *Auto-da-Fé* a creative start is made on a comprehensive social pathology of a different kind from that of the unhappy optimist Müller-Lier. The undeniable difficulties of the book should deter no one from following the experiment.

[*das silberboot, Zeitschrift für Literatur*, edited by Ernst Schönwiese, no. 3, June 1936, pp. 143 ff.]

Walter Allen

New Novels

[. . .] *Auto-da-Fé* is not easily described: it is partly satire, and one also suspects allegory. Put in the simplest terms, it creates the world of a paranoiac—all the characters, except one, are more or less mad. It is terrifying, and often very funny: a truly savage comedy. The nearest parallel I can think of are the plays of Ben Jonson, and Jonson's definition of a humour provides a clue to the book.

> [. . .] *when some one peculiar quality*
> *Doth so possess a man that it doth draw*
> *All his affects, his spirits and his power*
> *In their conflixions all to run one way;*
> *This may be truly said to be a humour.*

The "one peculiar quality" that possesses Mr. Canetti's hero, Dr. Peter Kien, "the greatest living authority on sinology," is love of books. Entirely devoid of personal relationships, he lives for books and his whole knowledge of life comes from books: "He took the roses from Fischerle's hand, remembered their sweet smell which he knew from Persian love poetry, and raised them to his eyes; it was true, they did smell. This soothed him completely." Kien, as much as Sir Epicure Mammon or Volpone, is the complete humour: for him, what exists does so solely in relation to his books. He marries his illiterate old housekeeper because it seems to him that she has a proper regard for at any rate the physical condition of books; and when she finally drives him out of his flat through her brutality and her continual screams for money, for his bankbook and his will, he falls in with a hunchback pickpocket—also a humour, living only for chess and dreaming of becoming world champion—and with him takes up his position at the state pawnshop in order to ransom the books their wretched owners are intent on pawning. Ironically—Mr. Canetti is a master of irony—it is the one sane character in the book, Kien's brother George, an eminent psychiatrist, who brings about the great scholar's end, the destruction by fire of his library and himself.

Auto-da-Fé demands close concentration on the part of the reader: skip a sentence and a vital link in the development may be lost. Mr. Canetti draws no distinction between his characters' actions and their fantasies; they are all, save the psychiatrist, who alone is aware of objective reality, obsessed, and to read the novel is to live through a series of obsessional states. The author's own point of view seems to be indicated in the following passage, spoken by the psychiatrist to his colleagues:

"You see, gentlemen [. . .] what miserable singletrack creatures, what pitiful and inarticulate bourgeois we are, compared with the genius of this paranoiac. We possess, but he is possessed; we take our experiences at second-hand, he makes his own. He moves in total solitude, like the earth itself, through his own space. He has a right to be afraid. He applies more acumen to the explanation and defence of his way of life, than all of us together do to ours. He believes in the images his senses conjure up for him. We mistrust our own healthy senses. Those few among us who have faith still cling to experiences which were lived for them by others thousands of years ago. [. . .] But look at him! He is Allah, prophet, and Moslem in one. Is a miracle any the less a miracle because we have labelled it *Paranoia chronica?"*

As I understand him, Mr. Canetti uses madness in order to expose and satirise the inadequacy and thinness of ordinary normal life. I have read nothing so disturbing or terrifying in its implications since Céline's *A Voyage to the End of the Night.* To most readers its vision of life will be no more acceptable than Céline's; but *Auto-da-Fé* can no more be ignored than any other great work of satire. For Mr. Canetti has created a world of his own, entirely self-contained and ferociously funny, rich in character, irony and that unflagging exuberance of invention which is a sign of the great comic writer. Miss C. V. Wedgwood's translation from the original German, made in collaboration with the author, is a remarkable *tour-de-force.*

[*New Statesman*, June 7, 1947, pp. 418 ff.]

Jacob Isaacs

An Assessment of Twentieth-Century Literature

[. . .]The finest book of this kind that I have ever read is Elias Canetti's masterpiece, *Auto-da-Fé,* published originally in Vienna in 1935 and magnificently translated by Miss Veronica Wedgwood in 1946. It has been hailed as one of the great novels of the century, and yet it is hardly known here. It is a book of giant stature, one of those books whose multitudinous intensity sweeps one along in a torrent like the first reading of *The Brothers Karamazov* or Joyce's *Ulysses,* leaving the richness of the detail to be savoured at leisure. Its theme is the disintegration of culture and the degradation of man. In the treatment of evil, compared with Canetti, François Mauriac is a mere amateur and Graham Greene as innocent as a babe unborn. And it is not theological evil. No God appears or is implied in this hell which boils up from the calmest beginning. The story, the surface story which carries the theme, is of a scholar who lives only for his studies and his library of twenty-five thousand volumes, who tricks himself into marrying his avaricious housekeeper, is thrown out by her, lives a phantasmagoric life in the underworld of the city, exploited by a monstrous hunchback dwarf, and in the madness which has been forced on him sets fire to his library and perishes in the flames. As narrative it has the crystal clarity and directness of all great allegory, of Dante, of Bunyan, and of Kafka. It is an allegory of the peace of the ivory tower shattered by the incursion of the beast and the bully, raw instinct and brute force. It is a morality tale in which the characters are the purest and most refined of abstractions. For his victim Canetti chooses the most rarefied abstraction of pure scholarship—the philologist—the textual scholar, the specialist in Chinese, the furthest removed from reality, whose world is in the head but whose head has no world, whose activity is pure reason—pure self-deceptive logic. In this *Everyman* of a crumbling culture Pure Knowledge is beset by the forces of Ignorance, Cupidity, Anger, Cunning, Hatred, and Envy, and is beaten to a pulp. Yet everything is sufficiently human for us to take an interest, sufficient for us to feel a guilty complicity and identification with parts of the victim—the victim, certainly, for no figure was ever less the hero of a book. It has wisdom and fairness, lunacy, and comic invention on a grand Satanic scale. I suggest, as an experiment, that you should read it alongside of Joyce Cary's *The Horse's Mouth*.

[*Six Lectures Delivered in the BBC Third Programme*, London, 1951, pp. 60–62]

Marcel Brion

Elias Canetti and Auto-da-Fé

When, in 1936, I read for the first time Mr. Elias Canetti's novel—which had just come out in Austria under a title which, in my view, is preferable to that of the French translation (*Die Blendung* means at once "blinding," "bedazzlement" . . .)—I was surprised to conclude that, outside the German-speaking countries, such a remarkable work had produced such a small impression. In France, it was all but ignored. Germany itself had not tarried before including the novel on the list of forbidden books, not so much for the political ideas that it might express as for its tone, for a form deriving in part from surrealism and in part as the heritage of Kafka. After several foreign translations, the book has now been reissued in its original language, and, simultaneously, in French. No doubt it will, thirteen years later, prove less surprising to a world which has grown accustomed to other acts of literary daring, and for which even the expressionist element will seem familiar, if not, indeed, dated.

Auto-da-Fé is an extremely strange book, one which is capable of disconcerting the reader but, at the same time, has a vigor and an originality which compels acquiescence. A certain infernal atmosphere may well satisfy an age which is taken with cruelty. As for the symbolism contained in the book, this is subtle and florid enough for each reader to interpret it according to his lights. The "city of books" in which the unfortunate Kien lives is in no sense an ivory tower, Sylvain Bonnard's gentle retreat. Kien becomes the laughingstock of everyone with whom he is in contact, but he is already the martyr of his library, a man overwhelmed by the din of all the languages that clamor in this "Tower of Babel."* Before banning the book, the German censors, on watch for "cultural misdeeds," might have reflected that a work like this one was capable, as interpreted by them, of denouncing the disasters engendered by the dangerous and inebriating profession of writing. But the book's irony, which in fact is devastating and which permeates the narrative, seemed itself suspect, and *Die Blendung* sank into the index of "degenerate literature."

After the publication of a book which announced the appearance of such a formidable storyteller's gift, I looked forward to new works by Mr. Canetti. I am well aware that for most writers in this century the ten years we have just lived through were in large measure taken up by other cares than those of literature, but nonetheless the silence of so writerly a writer as this one was inexplicable. It only became comprehensible if it signified, after such a dazzling beginning, a falling back upon oneself, a moment of recoil, of deepening and maturation. This was in fact what had taken place: the author of *Auto-da-Fé* had undertaken two other novels, which remained unfinished. Why? But then why are Kafka's novels, which in a number of ways we are justified in linking with the work of Mr. Canetti, also unfinished? Canetti consecrated himself to a vast work of sociology, of political theory, all concerning the "psychology of crowds and of power." He has written one or even a number of stage comedies, which are themselves neither performed nor even published.

If it seems odd to enumerate in this way works which an author has not published with the same scrupulous attention which one grants to those he has, this is because *Auto-da-Fé* in fact strikes us with its prodigious exceptionality. To be honest, even though the book's characters are described in a light which renders them both gigantesque and monstrous, the real hero of the novel are the books: that is to say, Professor Kien's library. It is the books, as they are worshipped by this old-

* Title of the French edition of *Auto-da-Fé. —Trans.*

fashioned humanist, as they are coveted by the greedy servant, abused by vulgar people, dragged to the pawnbrokers', until everything ends in a huge fire—the day when the "red rooster" awakens.

There are of course a number of ways to interpret Kien's adventures. He is trampled underfoot by the universe which surrounds him: by his concierge; by the servant he is weak-minded enough to marry; by Fischerle, the little chess champion, who exploits Kien's benevolence and confusion and who, each night in their small hotel room, makes packages of imaginary books which Kien then grabs from him. Must one infer from the story of this humanist trampled on by the people he lives with a larger society in which men of culture find themselves in a universe in which the problems of culture are all but irrelevant? Is one to perceive the dangers which a bookish cultivation where reality is all but nonexistent poses for an individual?

I do not think this book needs a gloss. It is a novel, and, as such, its narrative is self-sufficient. But it is of such richness that all sorts of commentaries come to mind uninvited and en masse. Above all, it seems to me that *Auto-da-Fé* is first and foremost a novel, one which suffices unto itself, which is captivating enough to retain our attention throughout its five hundred pages: one may discuss it afterward, one may look for the hidden meaning in this or that episode of the book, one may try to connect various portions of it, one may recognize a terrible similarity to actual life—all this is legitimate. And I should add that a superficial, amused reading would scarcely penetrate the surface of a book whose depths demand our attention.

I have already evoked Kafka in discussing *Auto-da-Fé*. The atmosphere of the book is, indeed, Kafkaesque. Not that there is any question of imitation, though, of course, Mr. Canetti, like the rest of us, has been affected by *The Castle* and *The Trial*. Moreover, Kafka and the author of *Auto-da-Fé* share a heritage which accounts for their similar conceptions of the world. They are both Jews—one a German-speaking Czech, the other a Viennese of Sephardic background—and both write in German; not surprisingly, they see things in much the same way and their methods of exposition are also similar. The anguish which dominates *Auto-da-Fé* is analogous to that which dominates Kafka's novels, even though Mr. Canetti's book is less burdened with the comic disquiet of *The Castle* or *The Trial*. It also shows a certain taste for virtuosity, a spirit of playfulness, which are both wholly absent from Kafka's *oeuvre*.

What strikes us in *Auto-da-Fé* is less its resemblances to other works of literature so much as the author's profound nature, his talent for transposing rather ordinary events into a narrative in which reality is presented both as fantastic and as hallucinatory. Professor Kien's adventures unfold both in the realm of fact and, at the same time, in a sort of wonderful distant place where, thanks to the way in which Mr. Canetti has lit his tale, colossal shadows dance and gesticulate. Until that moment when he summons fire into the "city of books." of liberation—the fire—Kien is nothing but a little fellow crushed by monsters. He himself does not become a giant shadow until that moment when he summons fire into "the city of books." Then the same reality (or, perhaps, the same unreality) takes all the characters in this tragic puppet theater and carries them away in the smoke and sparks of this quick, clear fire.

We are happy that a French editor has been willing to issue a translation of this book which, self-evidently, is addressed to those "best readers" Stendhal also sought. *Auto-da-Fé* is in fact a book of rare quality which, beneath its somewhat jesting aspects, is of a seriousness and gravity that will retain the sympathy of the attentive reader.

[*Translated by David Rieff*]

Rudolf Hartung

Fable and Character: Observations on a Novel by Elias Canetti

[. . .]It may reasonably be doubted whether we do justice to the meaning of this novel if we say that in it a schizophrenic process is portrayed with unique daring and persuasive clarity. First, of course, we must make clear that questions concerning the "meaning" of the work in no way relate to those ideas or interpretations which readers, in their ill-advised zeal, may bring with them to works of art, from without, in order to ignore the sole legitimacy which is in the nature of the work itself. What we mean by meaning is the inherent fertility, the wealth of meaning, of the characters, situations, and plot, which can be read out of the words on the page and interpreted; and we mean in the last analysis the figured-forth answer an artwork makes to questions of the possibility, and the possible representation, of a vision of being.

The specifically artistic quality of this first great novel by Canetti consists (first) in the suggestiveness of his characters, achieved through a kind of "screening": the world has again become portrayable in a convincing and penetrating way, since the author, with a radical courage, has done away with the received view of the world, now bereft of all eloquence, and has made his own daring choice of the "signs" at his disposal. Thus from the word go he avoided the profound inconsequentiality of those works which owe their gamut of emotions and their realistically perceived detail to an enthusiasm which has now had its day. And then (second) Canetti, in a highly personal adaptation of the Joycean internal monologue, has created his own stylistic means of conveying the inner physiognomy and unique world view of his characters.

If we consider the individual characters we are astonished to find that the world of the novel is populated almost exclusively by lunatics and half-insane scoundrels. And as the plot unfolds we find with still great consternation that this world has lost the touchstone to assess madness. Peter Kien's brother George, who was once a famous Parisian gynecologist, "became a psychiatrist out of admiration for the greatness of the insane [. . .] with the firm intention of learning from them and healing none. He had had enough of polite literature." He is horrified at the success he has with his new therapeutic method, and secretly hopes that those he as psychiatrist cures will reproach him: "His ex-patients looked plump, well and ordinary. Their speech was in no way different from that of any passer-by. They were in trade or served behind a counter. At best they minded machines. But when they had still been his friends and guests, they were troubled with some gigantic guilt, which they carried for all, or with their littleness which stood in such ridiculous contrast to the hugeness of ordinary men, or with the idea of conquering the world, or with death—a thing which they now felt to be quite ordinary. Their riddles had flickered out; earlier they lived for riddles; now for things long ago solved. George was ashamed of himself, without anyone having suggested that he should be."

"He had had enough of polite literature": are we perhaps to understand the conception of this world of the insane as a dubious escape from the dull daily monotony of our times and its representation in literature? If the world of *Auto-da-Fé* did indeed owe its existence to romantic longings of this order, its creator would needs be sorely disappointed in the objects of his love, for their madness is rarely "great." But is it permissible to take a character's opinion as that of the author? (Quite apart from the unbroached question of how far artist XY can generally be identified with the man XY.)

Once characters have been called into existence they go beyond their creators and are more than some documentation of the motives they owe that existence to. A creator's opinion on his creations is not the last word if it originates in the same perspective as his motive in creating—or, to put it differently, Elias Canetti's (or the psychiatrist's) view of the "greatness of the insane" and the ordinariness of normal people cannot so readily be taken as our guideline for interpretation of the whole work. Still, the tremendous urge we have to interpret takes us back to the work itself: to the unenlightened countenance of the life mercilessly contained in its pages: to the hopelessness of an existence which does not even include lamentation or the prospect of meaning; to the Babylonian confusion in the language of the characters, whose grotesque dialogues reflect the irreversible loneliness of the individual in an atomized world. (The American edition of the novel is entitled *The Tower of Babel*.) If Kafka's bureaucratic apparatuses could also be read as metaphysical structures, if that ultimate silence in his world (a message is on the way but will never reach us) allowed the mute presence of the message to be heard for a few moments, the world of *Auto-da-Fé* lacks clarity to a degree we can scarcely grasp. In it, life seems to have survived its meaning, and to be out to prove that there is still life even when the sinister logic of the mad has replaced truth and Eros has been transformed into obscenity.

Finally we must mention that the quixotic schizophrenia of the hero is not the last word of the author (or of one of the characters) on Man's life in this world without a sky, a horizon, or a trace of landscape. "We wage the so-called war of existence for the destruction of the mass-soul in ourselves, no less than for hunger and love. In certain circumstances it can become so strong as to force the individual to selfless acts or even acts contrary to their own interests." Mankind "existed as a mass long before it was conceived of and watered down into an idea. It foams, a huge, wild, full-blooded, warm animal in all of us, very deep, far deeper than the maternal. In spite of its age it is the youngest of the beasts, the essential creation of the earth, its goal and its future. We know nothing of it; we still live supposedly as individuals."

Here we see what has replaced that meaning we can no longer detect in the characters or events: an objective process the individual himself can hardly experience and which cannot be directed, and at the end of which comes the extinction of the individual man in one great crowd. Without examining the truth content of such a theory closely—it is in any case not given any detailed exposition—we should note what effect the highly transcendent sun of this theory has on the non-transcendent scenery of *Auto-da-Fé:* there may be a universal law, but this law cannot be discerned by the individual; perhaps it is possible to formulate this law, but it seems to be one of the inner facts of our time that it is impossible to express this law other than as a theory. Thus the gap which exists between the present shape of life and its meaning is an exact counterpart of that gap so accurately pointed up in *Auto-da-Fé:* the gap between the spirit, which betrays life and goes wandering off in the wild blue yonder, and life, which sticks in dull monotony for reasons of greed.

With this in mind we should also note the connection of the existential and the aesthetic in Canetti's novel. In a world cleft in this way, the dialogue and action involving the individual characters can take place only on an unreal plane! Any real encounter of the characters immediately reveals the (in a special sense) *unreal* position they occupy, and necessarily makes evident life's hidden insanity, which continues like a chain reaction in the novel. And now we see clearly why that massive explosion, in which the hero Peter Kien and his mummified cosmos come to grief, must follow upon these endless outbursts of insanity called forth by encounters in this world. And

at the same time we can also perceive the absolute necessity of
the artistic form of *Auto-da-Fé:* the grotesque, that unique union
of real and unreal which is the true fundamental "element" of
Canetti's world, is the sole form in which a life detached from
and ex-centric to its own meaning can possibly be manifested.

[*Literarische Revue,* III, 1948, pp. 341–47]

Max von Brück

The Unwilling Monad

The life of the author is as unusual as this book. Born of
Spanish-speaking Jewish parents in Bulgaria, Canetti spent his
early childhood in England, went to school in Zurich and
Frankfurt, studied in Vienna, and published his first novel there,
Auto-da-Fé, which was suppressed after the occupation. From
1938 he has again been in England, working on a comedy in
the style of Aristophanes, two new novels, and a scholarly work,
The Psychology of Crowds and Power.

A man who is at home in three languages, by origin and
career, is quite automatically a citizen of the world. The plurality of his mother tongues gives his art a European basis un-
confined to any one people, which defies all pigeonholing according to tribe or native landscape—Josef Nadler's *Literary
History of the German People* would probably be hard put to
find a place for Canetti. It is enough that he is an important
author writing in German: his linguistic range includes the id-
ioms of our tongue, and gives his characters firm contours almost tonal in quality. But these characters could just as well
live in Barcelona, Prague, or Marseilles as in Vienna, where
Auto-da-Fé is set. Their external appearance is merely a stage
set. The civilization they inhabit is the decaying *habitus* of people everywhere in our times, for whom traditional conventions
and ties have long become mere routine and cliché. Their ex-

istence is forever becoming more unreal and fantastic, and external events, even actual murder or physical torture, have the contingent quality of dreams.

Many see a similarity between Canetti and Kafka, Canetti and Joyce. But in this novel the world of things is not broken up, nor is its substance transformed; the hero, Peter Kien, "the greatest living authority on sinology," passes things by like a shadow, yet they are there and retain their full presence. Nor is the fable an internal monologue like Joyce's *Ulysses*, however monologic Kien is. He seals himself off and becomes a windowless monad against his will, and on its inner walls is reflected an imagined world which corresponds to the outside world only in part, and mostly is remote from it. With familiar instruments and in a not unusual environment, Canetti lays bare a hidden mental cell. The games played in Kien's brain are out to structure life as he conceives it: a pathological case close to schizophrenia. But this case is still a character in a novel, extremely vivid in his strangeness. Wholly bound up within himself, Kien almost literally dies off, and becomes skeletal, a bag of bones insensitive to pain, knocked about by everyone. And yet he is no ascetic but rather the opposite: he does not despise the body as some adversary, he completely overlooks it in his concentration on his hypertrophied brain. He is a paradigm of the extreme idealist, with no environment. In the absence of all personal relationships, his remoteness from the world becomes extreme: writing letters is mere idleness, his brother the psychiatrist does not "even" know any Chinese, university chairs are so much humbug as all students ought by rights to fail, he thinks his onetime housekeeper has inherited millions.

A great deal of artistry goes into showing this isolation leading to catastrophe. Significantly, Kien is afraid of going blind. He can see very well, but he is "blinded." His blindness is of a mental or spiritual kind, a total loss of the ability to perceive external human reality [. . .]

What Canetti shows us is the horrific, distorted mirror image of humanity fragmented at its opposite poles—Kien's head-world, Therese's headless world. Man has gone astray in a cul-de-sac with no exit. The mean point Canetti calls for lies where head and world meet.

After this testing ground of a novel, we can look forward to new and radical insights in the author's *Psychology*. He hints at those insights when he speaks of future mass humanity as one of supra-individuals, where the individual being and the species will be as one. What remains walking around on two legs, erect, will be no more than a number, not Man. The state for such mass beings is the totalitarian state; and this novel too could only be written through experience of a totalitarian state which denies humanity, or Man's mean point.

[*Die Gegenwart*, IV, no. 7, April 1, 1949, p. 20]

Günther Busch

A Novel of Shock: Auto-da-Fé

Written at a time when in Germany literature was being ruined by politics, *Auto-da-Fé* was one of the last works of literature published in the German-speaking area that diagnosed the sickness of the times. What may today look like the grotesque, fantastic portrait of a disorderly, ailing world is revealed, if we take a glance at its date, as a dismal anticipation of the course of history. In *Auto-da-Fé* Canetti wrote a novel of deep shock. It is a novel of horror—rage, shame, and grief are at work behind the prose, which is stripped of all pleasantry, and the various exaggerations of reality which the novel presents bear the signs of important caricature. The headings of two sections of the novel, "A Head without a World" and "Headless World," are the common denominators the writer reduces his literary aim and his decisive question to: the question of the humanity

of Man and the monstrosity of power. The connection between *Auto-da-Fé* and the sociological and cultural study
Crowds and Power, which appeared twenty-five years later, is
no coincidence. Both books, the novel and the study, are descriptions of catastrophes, and in the ashes left by those catastrophes Canetti reads the future of society.

Like any author whose writing is not dictated by Chance,
Canetti's imagination returns again and again to the same few
themes, obstinately, no matter what digressions or excursions
he has been off on, and he reorders them and makes them
speak. Whatever he reports or invents comes from a threatened world—outsize images of a deformed society and dam-
aged, exhausted consciousness. Crowds and power were and
remain the sources of his inspiration and the true subjects of
his texts. And he does not tire of presenting them. Hence the
monotonies in his prose, the oppressive quality of his fables,
and the sense of an interrogation we get from his dialogues.

His narrative mode has traits in common with forensic in-
vestigations: its instruments are distrust and doubt, and the
effect it aims at is the unmasking of a state of affairs. Corre-
spondingly *Auto-da-Fé* does not have a hero such as the traditional novel knows and needs: Peter Kien, the protagonist,
plays the part of principle witness, turned King's evidence, in
the case the book is hearing against reality. He betrays the fact
that the order he stands for is unbalanced, and in his gabbling
gives away its monstrosity.

Like the evil eye, a penchant for extreme situations is among
the idiosyncrasies of this author. He takes reality as his basic
material and then jinxes the everyday into a picture puzzle.
Canetti won't take anything for granted, his texts render familiar things strange and strange familiar; constantly perspectives are being altered, proportions blur, the trivial comes out
dominant and the important things dwindle to episodes. Even
the plot he has thought up for the novel makes apparent the
process of unceasing metamorphosis of the actual into the

probable, the banal into the perplexing, things into signs, and people into guinea pigs. The tale of Peter Kien, the famous solitary sinologist who stubbornly leads his cave life in a library of twenty-five thousand volumes, is the story of an all-consuming vice—a rigorous contempt for humanity. Kien hates people, the times, stupidity and ignorance, and he feeds this hatred, which devours anything that comes its way, with letters and illustrious philosophies. Kien's world is in his head, but his head lacks a world.

Kien's noble service of the spirit and the cultural heritage is not free of wicked interruption: when once his vigilance slackens he walks into his housekeeper's trap. He loses the fight for his property, is turned out of his own door, ends up under the thumb of dubious creatures and a degenerate caretaker, and finally, in despair and need, beaten and impotent, falls victim to the barbarians whose doings he had refused to believe in, and to those base demons whose fateful activities play so small a part in the thoughts of the wise yet which contain so much material.

The novel presents the tragedy of a blinded spirit and blinded society. *Auto-da-Fé* speaks of the human condition, of Man's willingness to be tempted, of Man's brutality; the dissolution of culture, civilized behavior, orderly and decent conduct, is the real theme of the book. In choosing this theme, Canetti aimed high. In parts the destruction he is painting in horrific, glistening colors attacks the structure of the work and, like rust, eats away at the characters and the syntax. The epic fabric tears. The material takes the upper hand, the plot falls apart—above all in the third section of the novel, which can only show the confusion in Kien's life, the collapse of his dreams, and the hopelessness of his struggle for freedom, in twitching, staggering anecdotes. And the language, instead of resisting the pull of the story, yields; panting, it runs races with the plot: "Animals forget—a dreadful memory has seized them—what they are, blind cells of a fanatical whole. Each one of them wants to be alone, and with a hundred or a thousand of them it starts, the madness spreads, *their* madness, a mass madness, the soldiers quit the entrances, the whole hive is burning with unhappy love . . . , the noise, far beyond anything that is usual, attracts a storm of ants, the mortal enemies pour in at the unguarded gates, not a warrior has a mind for defense, everyone is out for love. . . . A sudden reversal of the greatest sanity into the greatest insanity."

The reversal of sanity into insanity [. . .] The great passages in the novel proceed from a conscious interpretation and enactment of such a reversal. Experiments with the real. This is the basis of the book's fantastic and satirical character. Half an image of hell, half a Last Judgment, it shows things and ideas, illusions and faces, the household belongings of an era and the prevailing values of a culture, in a condition of gradual disintegration. Masquerading and unmasking are the same thing for this author. And so Elias Canetti created in *Auto-da-Fé* one of the rare and, in many respects, most unusual examples of so-called absurdist literature in Germany, on the eve of the outbreak of absurdism. Radical invention as radical criticism; the distorting mirror as a means of discovering the truth; the extreme exaggeration of facts as a way of veiling those facts— all of this is today counted part of creativity's basic resources. But we must remember that *Auto-da-Fé* was published in 1935. Reading it, the contemporary reader is starting a chapter in the history of European literature.

[*Südwestfunk Baden-Baden, Kulturelles Wort (Das Buch der Woche),*
November 3, 1963. Broadcast transcript, abridged]

The Contributors

Beda Allemann, Professor of German at the Friedrich Wilhelm University, Bonn.

John Bayley, Warton Professor of English Literature at the University of Oxford.

Martin Bollacher, Professor of German at the University of Tübingen.

Roberto Corcoll Calsat, Professor of German Language and Literature at the University of Barcelona.

Johannes Edfelt, poet, critic, translator, and member of the Swedish Academy; lives in Rönnige in central Sweden.

Iring Fetscher, Professor of Philosophy at the University of Frankfurt am Main.

Herbert G. Göpfert, Honorary Professor of Books and Publishing at the University of Munich.

Werner Hofmann, director of the Kunsthalle, Hamburg.

Hans Hollmann, Vienna/Basle, has directed productions at all the major German-language theaters, including productions of all Canetti's plays.

Alfred Hrdlicka, sculptor in Vienna, professor at the Art Academy in Karlsruhe.

Stefan H. Kaszyński, Professor of Austrian Literature and Culture at the Adam Mickiewicz University, Poznań.

Claudio Magris, Professor of German Language and Literature at the University of Trieste.

Serge Moscovici, Directeur d'Etudes at the Ecole des Hautes Etudes en Sciences Sociales, Paris.

Gerhard Neumann, Professor of German at the Albert Ludwig University, Freiburg im Bresgau.

Edgar Piel, social researcher and head of the press office at the Demoscopic Institute, Allensbach.

Salman Rushdie, author; lives in London.

Manfred Schneider, Professor of German at the University of Essen.

Franz Schuh, author and critic; lives in Vienna.

Susan Sontag, author and critic; lives in New York.

Barbara Surowska, lecturer in German at the University of Warsaw.